STO

POLITICAL ECONOMY

VOLUME 2

POLITICAL ECONOMY

VOLUME 2

by

OSKAR LANGE

Translated from the Polish by

S. A. KLAIN and J. STADLER

Translation edited by

P. F. KNIGHTSFIELD

PERGAMON PRESS

OXFORD · NEW YORK · TORONTO

SYDNEY · BRAUNSCHWEIG

PWN—POLISH SCIENTIFIC PUBLISHERS

WARSAW

Pergamon Press Ltd., Headington Hill Hall, Oxford
Pergamon Press Inc., Maxwell House, Fairview Park, Elmsford,
New York 10523
Pergamon of Canada Ltd., 207 Queen's Quay West, Toronto 1
Pergamon Press (Aust.) Pty. Ltd., 19a Boundary Street,
Rushcutters Bay, N.S.W. 2011, Australia
Vieweg & Sohn GmbH, Burgplatz 1, Braunschweig

First edition 1971
Library of Congress Catalog Card No. 65-367

The book is a translation of the original
Ekonomia polityczna, Vol. 2, second edition,
published by PWN—Polish Scientific Publishers,
Warsaw, 1968

Printed in Poland
08 016572 9

Contents

1674891

Contents

Foreword

The reader no doubt expects at least a sketch in broad outline of what Oskar Lange intended for this unfinished work, irrevocably interrupted by his death. Although this expectation is more than justified by the importance of *Political Economy*, which was treated by Professor Lange as a definitive summary of his creative activity, we are precluded from such an endeavour by the lack of the necessary materials.

Unfortunately, the scholarly inheritance left by Lange does not contain any other fragments of draft plans for any further chapters of *Political Economy* other than the four chapters of Volume 2 and the four versions of the draft outlines of the work as a whole and of Volume 2, all of which are appended to the present work. Besides the author's Forewords to the first and second editions of the first volume of *Political Economy*, and his short work, *Człowiek i technika produkcji* (*Man and Production Techniques*), brought out in Warsaw as part of the "Omega" science-popularization series, the following are the only pages written by the author which can be used as a basis for ascertaining to what extent the published text is near to the originally projected whole.

From these spare documents it is clear that Lange was consistently carrying out his original plan of tackling *Political Economy* by beginning with broad methodological problems, then analysing general economic laws, and finally discussing various socio-economic systems, especially capitalism and socialism. In the course of writing, important changes cropped up, but they tended towards a broadening of the general introductory part, and thus gave additional emphasis to the general character of this work, as opposed to other attempts at a Marxist presentation of the overall problems of political economy. For Lange, the

economic laws of various socio-economic systems were not just
a point of departure, preceded by a short introduction on the
subject and method of economics, but rather the goal of his
work, whose attainment required a scrupulous preparation of
methodological instruments and a multi-faceted analysis of the
general laws governing economic processes. It was his belief
that only on this basis can one properly understand the characteristics and regularities specific to particular systems, especially
to socialism, its development perspectives against the background
of contemporary capitalism, and the "third world" of underdeveloped countries.

The design for an exposition of all the more important problems of political economy was born in the years 1956 and early
1957. At first, Lange felt that he could realize his intentions,
as is shown in his original overall plan, in one volume, consisting
of three parts: I, General Assumptions; II, Political Economy
of Capitalism; III, Political Economy of Socialism. In the course
of writing, it became apparent that the problems covered in
Chapter I (Political Economy as a Science) were so broad as
to require a separate, extensive volume. The reaction both at
home in Poland and abroad is evidence that this decision was
both fruitful and met a definite need.

Volume 2 was to continue the analysis of general problems,
but rather than from the point of view of methodology, on the
level of two basic and essential problems of economics: the theory
of reproduction, primarily in terms of physical relationships,
and the theory of commodity production, which under given
conditions becomes an aid to making apparent the physical
laws of the process of reproduction. Lange considered it possible
to present the economic theory of social systems only by an analysis of these two important problems. This theory was to represent the final portion of Volume 2, in which the problems
of generation and distribution of the surplus product, and against
this background, the social structure, the role of the superstructure, and the kinds of economic incentives which are specific to
various social systems, were to occupy a central place.

The four chapters of Volume 2 cover essentially the first of the three basic problems which were to be dealt with in the second volume. They deal with the basic problems of the process of reproduction, with emphasis on a precise analysis of the inter-relations of the reproduction elements. A cybernetic conception of the problem was planned for a special annex, in which new methods for investigating these interrelationships were to be presented; in its place is given an excerpt from *Wstęp do cyber-netyki ekonomicznej* (*Introduction to Economic Cybernetics*). The final two groups of problems (commodity production and the law of value, and the theory of social systems) were not even developed in outline. We only know from the author's conver-sations and correspondence that he attached much weight to the theoretical point of view of Piero Straffa's *Production of Commodities by Means of Commodities.*

A formal answer to the question of how much of the planned complete contents of Volume 2 was actually finished would be more or less one-half. However, for Lange's *Political Economy*, the assessment of the "unfinished work" goes beyond mere quan-tity.

There are two reasons for this.

The first reason is connected with the concept of "exposition" as used by the author in the first edition of the work. "An expo-sition of the entirety of the more important problems of political economy" would suggest that a systematic presentation of current fully developed viewpoints and solutions was intended. This is not the case. Both the above-mentioned process of broadening the subject-matter, and the evolution of the various conceptions, are clear evidence for stating that the process of writing (lectures in written form) was a creative process in the full meaning of the word "creative". It was a process of stating and solving prob-lems, a search which, as it proceeded, changed its perspectives, and in the course of analysis earlier-discussed problems were often further refined.

A good example is the key problem of production relations as analysed by Lange in the first volume. He also discusses con-nected problems, such as the method of production, distribution relations, economic relations, and the economic base. However, in the course of repeated studies on the complex of problems, presented in Chapter I of Volume 2, Social Process of Production and Reproduction, Lange introduced the new concept of "co-operative relations", and thus separated production relations into "co-operative" and "ownership" relations. It is clear that this forces us to take a second look at all the above-mentioned concepts.

Another example: the problems of the connection of praxeology with economics has a central place in Lange's first volume. But it was only in the course of writing the second volume that Lange made use of praxeology to interpret certain laws of economics which had been treated as universal laws of technology by certain economists, and discarded by others precisely because they were not confirmed by the development of technology.

A praxeological interpretation of these laws not only permits us to explain an old misunderstanding, but it also encouraged the author to formulate several conceptions of his own. This took form in several supplements to subsequent editions of Volume 1, especially on the Lagrange Multiplier "as a measure of the acuteness of various balancing limits". This sheds new light on the problems of the technical and balancing laws of production.

Several other problems would have no doubt received the same treatment, and would have been explained differently as the other problems in the Table of Contents were articulated. The author himself realized this. As he stated, later volumes were to be presented in the light of a "second look at the first volume and its basic revision".

The second aspect of the unfinished character of Lange's work is even more important. It often happens that later parts of a scholarly work are merely more detailed, broadened, or develop supplemental aspects of concepts already presented. However, it often happens (in the social sciences too) that various parts of a work can be fully understood only in terms of the whole; their meaning is determined by the whole. This is certainly the case in Lange's work, a result of its intended character as a "systematic monograph of the subject". Of special importance

in this context is the statement by the author that the final crystalli-
zation of his design "was a result of the conviction that many
arguments, discussions and polemics in political economy can be
resolved only against the background of a systematic exposition of
this science. The various economic problems are connected within a certain whole, and it is difficult to conceive them separately."
It is true that Volume 1 "represents a certain closed whole which
deals with the general bases of the science of political economy",
but in terms of the intended whole it is only a foundation. It is
a systematic collection of general conceptions and an exposition
of research methods, whose sense, meaning and applicability
were to be finally verified in the course of analysing the realities
of capitalism and socialism. The systematization of conceptions
and methods, which is the main interest of Volume 1 and also
partly of Volume 2, was to be merely a means to the final goal
of analysing contemporary society. The author was unable to
finish this task. All this once again underlines the serious loss
to science by the death of Oskar Lange. It also emphasizes both
the difficulty and the necessity of continuing the work begun
by him.

Social Process of Production and Reproduction

I

Economic activity includes production and distribution of material objects which satisfy human needs. Production and distribution are two closely connected aspects of continually repeated economic activity, or, in other words, of the economic process. Production turns out goods, or products, which are then distributed among the members of society. At the same time, distribution also influences the conditions under which production takes place, and thus influences its character and pattern. In this manner both aspects of the economic process form an inseparable whole.

Both in production and in distribution, social inter-human relations are formed; these relations of production and of distribution taken together are called "economic relations". In production man both affects nature and is himself shaped by it in the course of his activity. According to the materialist conception of history, the process of mutual interaction of man with nature in production creates incentives which lead to continual changes in the productive forces of society, and, as a consequence, also to changes in economic relations and in other inter-human social relations. These incentives are the source of social development. For this reason, we begin our examination of the social laws governing the economic process with an analysis of the process of production.

Production is conscious and purposeful human activity which adapts the resources and forces of nature to human needs. This takes place by extracting and manufacturing the resources of nature, conveying their physical, chemical and biological prop-

1

erties, transferring objects in space, and preserving them in time. This activity has a social character, for it occurs under conditions of human social life, in which the actions of various individuals combine, supplement, cross, and even contradict each other. These actions are continually repeated, so that taking into consideration their social character, we speak of the production process as *the social process of production.*

In the social process of production there appear certain regularities and certain laws emerge. These laws are partially the result of the process of interaction of man with nature which occurs in production. They are also the result of economic relations, especially of production relations which form the framework of the production process. The first kind of laws are certain constantly repeated relationships which arise in the course of various operations and activities forming the process of production. These relationships are the result of the material features of this process, i.e. the features of the material technology applied in production, the material features of the means used and of the commodities produced, and, finally, the material features of human work, or labour, partaking in the production process. As production becomes rational activity, its laws are also the result of the praxeological principles of behaviour, that is, of a concretization of these principles adapted to the material features of the production process.

These laws, which we call the technical and balance laws of production,[1] are the creation of social development, as are other economic laws. The material features of the production process are dependent on the productive forces of society, which in turn are the result of social development. As we know, the development of production forces leads to a production process with ever new material features and their increasing diversification. It is for this reason that aside from universal laws occurring at every

---

[1] See Oskar Lange, *Political Economy*, Vol. I, Warsaw–London, 1963, pp. 58–59, 64–65. The technical and balance laws of production also include certain praxeological characteristics which are directly connected with the material features of the production process.

level of development of the productive forces—provided there is a permanent process of production—new laws are created along with the development of productive forces which are more detailed and more complex. As a rule, these laws do not cease to be operative with the transition from one social system to another; they are merely emerging in more complex and detailed variants which correspond to the development of the productive forces of the new social system. This is so because the laws are not only the direct result of economic relations, but are also connected with the material features of the production process determined by the interaction of man with nature, and are thus dependent on the state of the productive forces.

The character of the technical and balance laws of production presented here leads to the conclusion that an analysis of these laws can be best carried out by an examination of the productive forces[2] at their highest stage of development under which these laws emerge in their most complex and richest variants. In the light of such an analysis it will be possible to investigate next how these laws operate under conditions of less-developed productive forces. Here should be applied Marx's saying that "the anatomy of man is a key to the anatomy of ape"; this means that the beginnings of higher forms of development which occur at lower stages of development can only be understood when the higher forms of development are already known. Consequently, we shall examine the social process of production from the point of view of the present state of the productive forces, sometimes

---

[2] We refer here to the development of productive forces brought about within the framework of capitalist and socialist social systems. The socialist system, in eliminating obstacles to the development of productive forces which capitalist relations of production entail, makes possible a higher development of productive forces than is possible under capitalist conditions. Nevertheless, due to the special historical conditions which brought about the first socialist relations of production—namely, the fact that they arose in backward or economically underdeveloped countries—in the initial period of development of the socialist system, the level of development of the productive forces was lower than in the more highly developed capitalist countries. Hence the problem of "catching up" with the latter countries. At the present time, this period is drawing to a close.

turning back to history for an explanation of the origin of certain characteristics and regularities.

The second kind of laws observed in the production process concern the relations of production which are connected with this process. Production relations constitute a complicated system of inter-human relations; the various parts of this system are connected, to a greater or lesser degree, with the material features of the production process. We shall examine here those elements of production relations which are the direct result of the interdependences of various human activities determined by the material features of the production process. These elements are the result of inter-human co-operation in the production process.[3]

II

Human activity which makes up production entails various kinds of activities, all included under the general heading of "labour". Labour is a complex of activities, undertaken in the production process whose goal is the production of goods, that is, of objects which satisfy human needs. These activities are varied. This is why we speak of varied, concrete kinds of labour, or, more simply, of varied, concrete labour. Inasmuch as these activities are continually repeated in the production process, we also speak of *the labour process* and sometimes also of concrete labour processes. The production process is a system of such concrete labour processes which are consciously and purposefully interconnected for the production of a desired commodity or product.[4]

We distinguish between various kinds of production processes according to the character of the resources and forces of nature

---

[3] A description of broader aspects of production relations which are associated with various historical social systems is postponed to subsequent chapters.

[4] S. Strumilin defines production in the following manner: "Production may be defined as a system of labour processes necessary for the production of a given kind of product — for example, the production of footwear (shoes, boots, sandals, etc.)." (*Problemy ekonomiki truda* [*Problems of Labour Economics*], Moscow, 1957, p. 11.)

which are subject to transformation, and according to the character of human activities connected with each process, i.e. according to concrete labour processes. Production based on the use
of land for cultivation and breeding of stock to meet the needs
of man is called agricultural production, or agriculture. Production based on transforming the physical, chemical and biological
properties of objects is called industrial production, or industry.
Conveyance of objects and people in space is called transportation, while storing of objects over time is called warehousing.
Warehousing is often connected with distribution, and is sometimes inseparable from it.

The above-mentioned kinds of production processes, or *production departments* as they are sometimes called, may be further
subdivided into *production branches*. Thus, agriculture may be
subdivided into the cultivation of crops and the raising of livestock;
although included in the department of crop cultivation, forestry
is often distinguished as a separate branch. Industry is divided
into extractive industries, which extract the mineral resources
of nature (mining of all kinds, also fishing and hunting); the power
generating industry, which transforms the sources of energy found
in nature into a form useful to man (e.g. electric power generation); and manufacturing industries, which further process resources extracted from nature. Within the manufacturing industries we can, in turn, distinguish machine-building, electrotechnical,
chemical, textile, pharmaceutical, foodstuff, and other industries,
depending on the nature of the objects subject to processing and
the natural resources used. Often, the construction industry is
distinguished as a separate branch. Transportation is divided
according to the kind of traffic into land, ocean and air transportation. Warehousing may be simple warehousing based on the
ordinary storing of objects over time, or it can also involve several
additional services for the purpose of preserving the object in
a usable state (e.g. refrigeration).

In production man makes use of a given material technique
or a complex of material means leading to the realization of the
production goal—the manufacture of given products.[5] We call

[5] See O. Lange, *op. cit.*, Vol. I, pp. 148–50.

this technique *the production technique*. It consists in the skilful exploitation of causal relations which are found both in nature and in man—physical, chemical and biological laws and also physiological and psychological laws of the human organism (e.g. in connection with efficiency of labour and fatigue). We call the material means used in production techniques *the means of production*. The use of these means consists in the realization of those causes whose effect is the desired product. This occurs in the labour process. Human labour uses means of production and "sets them in operation"; the result is the product.

The labour process in which means of production are used consists in transforming the material resources of nature and in exploiting the forces of nature in this transformation. "In the process of production man can only work as nature does", says Marx, "that is, by *changing the form of matter*. Nay more, in this work of changing the form he is constantly helped by natural forces."[6] In this connection we distinguish two kinds of means of production. Firstly, material objects which are transformed in production. Since transformation is carried out by labour, we call these objects *objects of labour*. The second kind of material means are those which transform objects of labour, and we call them *means of labour*.[7]

The object of labour is the substance from which the product is made. It is often called the "material", especially in technology, or the science concerned with various kinds of production techniques.[8] The primary objects of labour are natural resources, such as land, water, air, coal, oil and mineral deposits, sea fish, forest animals, etc. Certain products, or objects shaped by earlier

[6] K. Marx, *Capital*, Vol. I, London, 1918, p. 10.

[7] *Ibid.*, pp. 157–8.

[8] Tadeusz Kotarbiński defines "material" as follows: "material ... is a certain object ... from which products are made ...". He states further that "all products are manufactures of their own material, or the manufactures of that out of which they were made; this pertains to an earlier phase of things which are changing". (*Traktat o dobrej robocie* [*Treatise on Good Work*], Łódź, 1958, p. 48.)

labour, are also objects of labour. We call them *raw materials.*[9]
A raw material may also be a product used otherwise than as an
object of labour. For example, coal may be used both as a fuel
in the home and as a raw material in the production of coke or
in the petro-chemical industry producing coal byproducts; grapes
may be consumed or used as a raw material in wine production.
We call products which may only be used as a raw material
semi-products.[10] Examples of semi-products are cotton, coke, iron
ore, raw rubber, mineral fertilizers and unassembled machine
parts or unfinished machines. We distinguish *finished products*
from semi-products. Finished products are not raw materials,
but they may be either means of production (e.g. machinery) or
consumption goods (e.g. bread or clothing).

Raw materials are further divided into *basic* and *secondary*
materials.[11] The former, upon transformation in the labour process, enter into the product as its primary material content or
the main source of its material content (e.g. pig iron and scrap
in steel production; hard and soft leather in the manufacture of
footwear; cotton, wool and flax in the manufacture of textile
goods; coal in the production of coke or lighting gas; and crude

---

[9] "If, on the other hand, the object of labour has, so to say, been filtered
through previous labour, we call it *raw material*; such is ore already extracted
and ready for washing. All raw material is the [object] of labour, but not
every object of labour is a raw material; it can only become so, after it has
undergone some alteration by means of labour." (K. Marx, *op. cit.*, Vol. I,
p. 158.)

[10] "A product, though ready for immediate consumption, may yet
serve as raw material for a further product, as grapes when they become the
raw material for wine. On the other hand, labour may give us its product
in such a form that we can use it *only* as a raw material, as is the case
with cotton, thread and yarn." (*Ibid.*, p. 162.)

[11] "Raw material may either form the principal substance of a product,
or it may enter into its formation *only* as an *accessory.* An accessory *may*
be consumed by the instruments of labour, as coal under a boiler, oil by a wheel,
hay by draught-horses, or it *may be mixed with the raw material* in order to
produce some modification thereof, as chlorine in unbleached linen, coal
with iron, dyestuff with wool, or again, it may help to carry on the work
itself, as in the case of the materials used for heating and lighting workshops."
(*Ibid.*, p. 161.)

oil in refining of gasoline). The latter are an addition to the basic material which gives the product certain characteristics (e.g. dyes in the production of textiles or varnish in the production of furniture). Sometimes the secondary material is an addition, not to the object of labour, but to the means of labour used in production (e.g. oil grease for machinery, fuel oil or electric power for the motor which operates the machinery, or coal for heating the workshop).

However, in many cases it is not possible to divide raw materials into primary and secondary materials. This is often the case in chemical and pharmaceutical production.[12] Here it is often not possible to determine which of the ingredients are primary and which are secondary. All of them are completely transformed in chemical synthesis, and the ingredient determining the medical usefulness of a medicine is by no means that which is quantitatively the most important (often this is water). Thus, the division of raw materials into primary and secondary materials cannot always be applied.

Means of labour are used to transform and process the object and give it the form of the desired product. They either do this directly, when used by man to give form to the object of labour, or indirectly, when they enable or make easier the use of means of labour which directly give form to the object of labour.

We call the means of labour which directly shape the object of labour *tools of labour*.[13] Except for the very primitive state of the productive forces at the dawn of the emergence of the human race from its animal existence, when the tools of labour were

---

[12] This was pointed out by Marx: "The distinction between principal substance and accessory vanishes in the true chemical industries, because there *none* of the raw material *reappears*, in its original composition, in the substance of the product." (K. Marx, *op. cit.*, Vol. I, p. 161.)

[13] For the concept of tools see T. Kotarbiński, *op. cit.*, pp. 55 ff. F. von Gottl-Ottilienfeld defines the tool of labour as follows: "The tool is the bodily intermediary of a given action by hand or machine on third objects." (*Wirtschaft und Technik. Grundriss der Sozialökonomik* [*Economy and Technology. Outline of Social Economy*], Part II, Tübingen, 1932, p. 94.) It is worth while drawing attention to this book, as it is so far the only systematic exposition of the praxeological principles applied in modern production techniques.

unprocessed objects found in nature (e.g. clubs and rock), tools of labour are always the product of human labour.[14] As a rule, tools of labour are objects which are specially adapted to carry out a specific operation (such as knives, axes, bows and arrows, files); all kinds of machinery and mechanical, optical and chemical equipment (such as boilers, microscopes, receptacles, pipes, etc.); electrical installations (such as transformers and wiring); means of transportation (such as horses, wagons, locomotives, ships and aeroplanes); and means for storing and preserving goods (e.g. warehouses and refrigerators). Such more or less specialized tools of labour are often called *instruments* (or *appliances*).

As the productive forces develop, so do the variants of specialized tools of labour and their number increases; as we say, there is an *instrumentalization* of the labour process. The development of the tools of labour (i.e. their growth in number, variety and efficiency) is the most dynamic factor in the development of productive forces. Man transforms his surroundings and shapes his environment with the tools of labour. The active relation of man to nature is seen in the use of the tools of labour; tools of labour are the most important means for the transformation of the surrounding environment.

Aside from tools of labour there are also means of labour which are necessary for the use of tools of labour. These indirectly transform the object of labour by enabling or making easier the use of tools of labour. Examples are land (to which the tools of labour are applied), all kinds of structures (buildings, fenced-off areas, etc.), roads, canals, bridges, etc. We call these means of labour *auxiliary facilities*.[15]

---

[14] We recall here the saying of Benjamin Franklin that man is a tool-making animal.

[15] The term is used by Kotarbiński (*op. cit.*, p. 57). He also uses the term "implement" in reference to all the means of labour, such as tools of labour and auxiliary facilities. In addition, Kotarbiński maintains that even though animals do not produce tools (although they occasionally use certain objects as tools), they do produce auxiliary facilities to make easier certain activity. Most often this equipment has the character of an enclosure (e.g. nests, burrowed-out dens, beavers' dams, etc.). Tools are produced by man alone (see *ibid.*, pp. 56–59).

The conclusion from the above considerations is that the difference between products and means of production—and within means of production, the difference between objects and means of labour—is not a material difference. It is rather a difference based on the function, or role, which a given material object plays in the labour process. The majority of means of production are products which are either produced or at least prepared or extracted by human labour. But not every product is a means of production; a significant number of products are consumption goods. The same object may be used either as an object of labour or as a means of labour. For example, water used to manufacture beverages is an object of labour, while water which turns the miller's wheel or which, as steam, powers a locomotive is a means of labour.

"Hence we see, that whether a *use-value* [i.e. a given material object — O. L.] is to be regarded as *raw material*, as ... [*means*] *of labour*, or as *product*, this is determined entirely by *its function in the labour process*, by the position it *there* occupies: as this varies, so does its character."[16]

Let us now discuss the way means of labour fulfil their role in the labour process. According to Marx, "A ... [*means*] *of labour* is a thing, or a complex of things, which the labourer interposes between himself and the ... [object] of his activity. He makes use of the mechanical, physical and chemical properties of some substances in order to make other substances subservient to his aims. ... The first thing of which the labourer possesses himself is not the ... [object] of labour but its ... [means]. Thus, Nature becomes one of the *organs* of his activity, one that he annexes to his own bodily organs, adding stature to himself in spite of the Bible."[17]

III

The use of means of labour, especially of tools of labour, consists in the skilful exploitation of the forces of nature by harnessing

---

[16] K. Marx, *op. cit.*, Vol. I, p. 162.
[17] *Ibid.*, p. 158.

these forces as aids to man in the labour process.[18] This takes place primarily by the extension, strengthening, acceleration and refinement of the operation of the organs of the human body. A club or rock thrown lengthens the reach of the human hand; a lever or crank strengthens the force of the human arm; a bicycle accelerates the result of the operations of the legs; a microscope refines the perceptive capabilities of the eye, etc. Such tools of labour are also usually modelled on the organs of the human body, and their operation is based on the same principles as those of the organs. "It is remarkable", says Kotarbiński, "that primitive and rudimentary tools are as if modelled on the organs, and are at the same time some kind of their extension and amplification: the mace—a fist; the knife—sharp incisors; the rake—fingers of the hand; stilts—pair of legs; tongs—the jaw, etc. Man succeeded in making a break through by producing tools—external products, as it were—on the model of and similar to man's own organs or those observed on other creatures."[19]

There are, however, certain tools of labour, particularly specialized tools, which strengthen rather than extend the operation

---

[18] The forces of nature are exploited in all areas of production. In the eighteenth century the Physiocrats falsely believed that the forces of nature participate in the production process only in agriculture. This view was still held in 1776 by Adam Smith, who wrote: "In agriculture too nature labours along with man ..." and, "in ... [manufactures] nature does nothing; man does all ... "(*An Inquiry into the Nature and Causes of the Wealth of Nations*, Vol. I, London, 1961, pp. 384, 385.) David Ricardo answered Adam Smith in the following way: "Does nature nothing for man in manufacture? Are the powers of wind and water, which move our machinery, and assist in navigation, nothing? The pressure of the atmosphere and the elasticity of steam, which enable us to work the most stupendous engines are they not the gifts of nature? To say nothing of the effects of the matter of heat in softening and melting metals, of the decomposition effects of the atmosphere in the process of dying and fermentation. There is not a manufacture which can be mentioned, in which nature does not give her assistance to man ..." (*On the Principles of Political Economy and Taxation*, London, 1819, pp. 61–62.) Ricardo's comments are even more applicable today when such forces of nature as electricity and atomic energy, not to mention a whole variety of chemical reactions, have been harnessed.

[19] T. Kotarbiński, *op. cit.*, p. 56.

of human organs, and replace them. The horse or automobile, for example, replaces the use of human legs. Other tools of labour carry out operations which no human organ could perform no matter how imperfectly. Such tools equip man, as it were, with new organs. Examples are the spindle, the electric power generator, or the cyclotron. The construction and the method of operation of such tools in no way bring to mind human organs, for they are constructed on other principles, derived from the laws of nature. A separate place is held by tools which supply energy, such as steam boilers, all kinds of motors, etc., which replace or aid the human organism in the labour process.

The turning point in the growing role of means of labour in the labour process was the introduction of machinery. The *machine* is a collection of specialized tools of labour—that is, instruments which are put into operation simultaneously or consecutively with the aid of one of these instruments (e.g. a starter in an automobile). As a rule a machine also possesses one or several instruments which control and regulate (e.g. the steering wheel and accelerator in the automobile) its operations.[20] A machine

---

[20] Regulating or controlling the operations of a machine means causing the machine to act on the object of labour in a given way selected by man at a given place and a given intensity. For example, controlling a machine tool consists in deciding whether the machine will cut or grind, in deciding the point at which the cutting or grinding edge will be applied to the metal (which is the object of labour), and in determining the number of revolutions per minute and the pressure of the cutting or grinding edge. Regulating means maintaining a machine in a given manner and place and with a given intensity regardless of outside influences which are external to the machine itself (e.g. temperature) or which result from the operation of the machine (e.g. vibrations). Regulating means preventing deviations in the manner, place and intensity of operation established by control (e.g. maintaining the given number of revolutions per minute and the given pressure of a machine tool, maintaining a constant temperature in a steam boiler, or maintaining a chosen direction for an aircraft). See B. I. Domanski, *Podstawy automatyki i telemechaniki* (*Principles of Automation and Telemechanics*), translated from Russian, Warsaw, 1954, p. 208; *Automatisierung. Stand und Auswirkungen in der Bundesrepublik Deutschland* (*Automation: State and Its Effects in the Federal Republic of Germany*), Munich, 1957, pp. 27–28; and W. Hornauer, *Automatyka przemysłowa* (*Industrial Automation*), translated from German, Warsaw, 1957, p. 18.

can be put into operation and maintained in motion by human muscles (e.g. hand- or pedal-operated machines), or by sources other than human energy. In the latter case, which is the rule today, there is a separate machine or part of a machine which we call the motor, or engine (e.g. an internal combustion or electric engine; the steam engine is also a motor).

A motor is a machine or part of a machine directly put in operation and maintained in operation by a source of energy drawn from nature. At first motors were operated by animal traction which replaced the muscular force of man (e.g. a treadmill operated by a horse or ox and attached to a thresher or pump). Next, use was made of non-organic sources of energy taken directly from nature, such as wind and water (e.g. in the operation of mills). Finally, forms of energy specially created by man were used, such as vapour pressure of steam or inflammable gases, electric power or nuclear energy. The motive power is transmitted to the machine by mechanical, electric, radio or other means. Transmission may be carried out by a separate machine or by part of a machine which is set in operation. Marx took this into consideration and distinguished between the motor mechanism, the transmitting mechanism and the tool, or working machine.[21] As we have seen, these can also be parts of one complex machine. The working machines act directly on the object of labour, transforming it according to the will of the person controlling the machine. Marx characterizes the method of operation of the machine in the labour process as follows: "The machine ... supersedes the workman, who handles a single tool, by a mechanism operating with *a number* of similar tools, and set in motion by a single motive power, whatever the form of that power may be."[22] To this it is necessary to add that instruments grouped together to form a machine operate not only simultaneously, but also in succession, in which case the successive operation of the various instruments "overlap" so that the operation of one instrument puts a second instrument in operation, the second in turn activates a third, etc.

---

[21] See K. Marx, *op. cit.*, Vol. I, p. 367.

[22] *Ibid.*, pp. 370–1.

We call this overlapping of operations of several instruments a *mechanism*. A mechanism is the joining together of the operations of a certain group of instruments in a chain of causes and effects with the operation of the instruments representing the links in the chain. The operation of one instrument sets in motion the operation of a second instrument (or a number of them), etc. This joining together may also be such that the operation of several other instruments is necessary to set in motion the operation of the instrument which is the successive link in the mechanism. Such cause and effect links connecting the operation of various instruments in a mechanism are called *coupling*.[23] We say that in a mechanism the operations of particular instruments are coupled in a specific way.

Similarly to the way simple tools were first modelled on the organs of the human body, working machines were at the beginning modelled on the simple tools of labour used directly by man. As Marx said: "On closer examination of the *working-machine* proper, we find in it, as a general rule, though often, no doubt, under very altered forms, the apparatus and tools used by the handicraftsman or manufacturing workman; with this difference, that instead of being human implements, they are the implements of a mechanism, or mechanical implements. Either the entire machine is only a more or less altered mechanical edition of the old handicraft tool, as, for instance, the power loom; or the working parts fitted in the frame of the machine are old acquaintances, as are spindles in a mule, needles in a stocking-loom, saws in a sawing machine, and knives in a chopping machine".[24] In the course of further development working machines gradually ceased to be modelled on the tools of labour used directly by man: they replaced them (e.g. an electrical surgeon's knife which burns tissue, or an acetylene torch which cuts and welds metal by melting it) or operated in ways no former

---

[23] The term "coupling" (*sprzężenie*) was introduced to Polish terminology by Henryk Greniewski. See his *Elementy cybernetyki sposobem niematematycznym wyłożone* (*Non-mathematical Exposition of Cybernetics*), Warsaw, 1959, pp. 32 and 77.

[24] K. Marx, *op. cit.*, Vol. I, p. 368.

tools could have operated (e.g. an X-ray for metal castings, an aircraft or an atomic reactor). From the very beginning motors were constructed in accordance with the requirements for exploiting the forces of nature (e.g. the steam-operated machine or electric motor) and not on the model of earlier tools of labour.

The machine replaces the direct action of man on the object of labour with the aid of a tool, and places the operation of a mechanism between man and the object of labour. This changes the character of human labour. The direct working of an object of labour by human force using tools is replaced by the *servicing of a machine* — that is, by placing it in operation, controlling and regulating its operation, and supervising the working of its mechanism. Instead of work on the object of labour, we are faced with work at a machine, with the transformation of the object of labour resulting from the activity of the machine's mechanism. Thus action of man on the object of labour is here indirect; man sets in motion a chain of causes and effects whose final effect is to transform the object of labour in a desired way. Marx quotes Hegel's well-known statement on the cunning of reason (*List der Vernunft*): "Reason is just as cunning as it is powerful. Its cunningness consists principally in its mediating activity, which by causing objects to act and re-act on each other in accordance with their own nature, in this way, without any direct interference in the process, carries out reason's intentions."[25] The "cunning" of human reason, as shown in the operation of the machine, consists in exploiting the law of causality at work in nature and in associating various forces and objects in a chain of causes and effects so that the final effect is the desired transformation of the object of labour.

IV

Indirect action by means of such a chain of causes and effects replaces the direct intervention of man with the object of labour. According to Kotarbiński there is seen here a minimization of

---

[25] K. Marx, *op. cit.*, Vol. I, p. 158.

intervention which is characterized as follows: "We try to arrange things so that what we need occurs to the greatest degree possible by itself, at least beginning from a certain point in the process. For example, instead of carrying down cut logs from mountain slopes, woodcutters simply push the logs down a stream which carries them further on and delivers them, as it were, to a pre-determined place".[26] This example indicates that the application of machines is not the only indirect activity within the labour process which acts as a substitute for direct intervention by setting in motion an appropriate chain of causes and effects in the processes of nature. This indirect activity is seen especially in chemical and agricultural production, even in the absence of machinery. What is more, this is the basic characteristic of these kinds of production.

In chemical production, for example, the appropriate ingredients are mixed together, the mixture is subject to a given pressure and temperature, and "nature alone" brings about a synthesis by an automatic chemical reaction. Thus, a chain of causes and effects, set in motion by man, produces as its final result the desired product. Direct intervention is replaced by servicing the chemical process: by starting, controlling, regulating and supervising it. Indirect activities preceded machines in various chemical processes, e.g. in preparing paints, bleaching linen, or fermenting wine. Even more ancient is this method in agricultural production: raising crops and breeding livestock are based outright on indirect activity. Here, from the very beginning the activity of man consists in setting up a chain of causes and effects whose final result is the desired product. Plants are sown or planted, but they grow by themselves and give the product in the form of grain or fruit. Human labour is thus reduced to servicing the biological process of growth and ripening (for example, by sowing or planting, appropriate irrigation, weeding, clipping unnecessary sprouts, grafting, cross-breeding, etc.). The situation is similar in livestock raising.

---

[26] T. Kotarbiński, *op. cit.*, p. 151. See also this author's *Sprawność i błąd (Efficiency and Error)*, Warsaw, 1960, pp. 56–57.

Thus, the operational mechanism of the machine amounts to applying in the tools of labour indirect activity which substitutes a cause-and-effect chain for direct intervention, in the same way as in agricultural or chemical production. In the mechanism of the machine, the ancient method of influencing biological and chemical processes is applied to mechanical and electro-mechanical processes.[27] Hence, this mechanism is a special case of the system of chains of causes and effects, or, as we say, of *the system of coupled operations.*[28]

The servicing of the system of coupled operations applied in the labour process, consists, as we have seen, in starting, controlling, regulating, and supervising that process. A further improvement of the labour process consists in reducing the servicing operations to setting up and supervising the system of coupled operations by built-in self-guiding and self-regulating mechanisms for the system. The introduction of such mechanisms, which replace direct intervention by man in controlling and regulating the activity of the system of coupled operations used in the labour process, is called *automation.* Automation always consists in introducing a special mechanism which controls and regulates the operations of the coupled set. This mechanism, either in the form of a separate machine or, more often, as an instrument connected to a group of instruments making up a machine, is called *the servo-mechanism.*[29] The servo-mechanism is indeed a mechanism in the

---

[27] Lewis Mumford draws attention to this by describing the worker servicing a machine in the following way: "... He is, so to say, a machine-herd, attending to the welfare of a flock of machines which do the actual work: at best, he feeds them, oils them, mends them when they break down, while the work itself is as remote from his province as is the digestion which fattens the sheep looked after by the shepherd." (L. Mumford, *Technics and Civilisation*, New York, 1943, pp. 410–11.)

[28] Research on the general sets of proprieties of the systems of coupled operations and the laws governing them is the domain of cybernetics. A good introduction is given by Ross Ashby, *Introduction to Cybernetics*, London, 1957.

[29] The term *control mechanism* is also often used. The discoverer of cybernetics, Norbert Wiener, uses the two terms interchangeably. See N. Wiener, *Cybernetics or Control and Communication in the Animal and the Machine*, New York–London, 1961, Chapter IV.

precise meaning of the word; it combines the action of mechanical (including hydro-mechanical and thermo-dynamic) and electro-mechanical forces. The servo-mechanism is usually powered by an auxiliary source of energy, in most cases electricity.[30]

The operation of the servo-mechanism depends on *feedback*,[31] or a closed chain of causes and effects. In feedback, the final link acts backwards on the preceding link or links in the chain. With automation of controlling and regulating processes, feedback must act in a given manner: any deviation of the final effect of the work of the machine (or chemical or biological process) from the desired effect, or the norm, must cause a change in earlier operations in such a way as to result in correcting the deviation in the final effect. Feedback which operates in this way is called *compensating* feedback.[32] It corrects, as it were, "mistakes" in the operation of the machine or any other coupling system used in the labour process.

One of the earliest servo-mechanisms is the centrifugal governor for steam-powered machinery invented by James Watt and patented in 1769. This instrument is attached to a wheel of the steam-powered machine and to a pipe channelling steam to the cylinder. If the wheel's r.p.m. exceed the established norm, the governor decreases the inflow of steam to the cylinder, causing a decline in the r.p.m. If, on the other hand, the r.p.m. are less than the norm, the governor increases the flow of steam and

---

[30] See *Automatisierung ...*, p. 30.

[31] This English term is also used in many other languages. See N. Wiener, *op. cit.*, Chapter IV.

[32] The compensating feedback mechanism operates in the following manner: if the final effect exceeds an established norm, then the intensity of the force causing this is reduced; the intensity is increased if the final effect falls below the norm. The cumulative feedback mechanism operates in an opposite manner: it increases the intensity of the force causing the final effect if this effect exceeds the norm, and diminishes it if it does not reach the norm. It is obvious that with this kind of coupling there can be no self-regulation; on the contrary, all deviations from the norm are cumulatively increased. This would be the case, for example, if the regulator of a steam-powered machine increased the inflow of steam when the machine's r.p.m. exceeded the norm.

thus increases the r.p.m. in this way the steam-powered machine automatically maintains the given r.p.m. The action of the servo-mechanism is purely mechanical here. Today, servo-mechanisms operate primarily electro-mechanically. An example is the automatic pilot maintaining a given direction of flight for an aircraft, or the gyrocompass maintaining a given direction of a ship.

Servo-mechanisms automate both the control and the regulation of the machine or other coupling system used in the labour process. Automation of control leads, however, to the automation of regulation,[33] which in turn consists of two levels. The manner, place and intensity with which the machine is to process the object of labour are established on the first level. This is called *programming* or establishing the norms for the machine's operations. The second level consists in regulating the machine's operations by a servo-mechanism in such a manner as to cause a correction of all deviations from the established norms, or, as we say, from the machine's programme. An example is the already mentioned automatic pilot of an aircraft or ship. Here the programme, or norm, is the direction of movement established by the pilot or captain; the servo-mechanism corrects all deviations. For many machines, programming affects most of the machine's operations. In this case, programming consists in establishing the norm of the order and intensity of various operations; then the servo-mechanism sets the various operations in motion according to the predetermined order and regulates the intensity of these operations (e.g. programmed control of the multi-use machine tool).

There are also machines in which programming itself is automatic. The programme, or the set of norms for the machine's operations, is in this case outlined in the form of changeable tasks which are adaptable to changes in the object of labour, or, in other words, in the form of relationship between the task and the condition of the object of labour. The simplest machine with automatic programming is the one whose operation automatically ceases when the programmed task is completed or

---

[33] See Ross Ashby, *op. cit.*, p. 213.

when the object of labour is damaged (e.g. yarn breaking off in a spinning frame). An example of highly complicated automation of programming is an automatic anti-aircraft gun, which aims, by automatic calculation, at the point in space the aircraft will reach after the passage of time necessary for a missile to strike it. The machine's programme here is for the missile to strike the aircraft, and the deviation from the established norm is the distance between the point of explosion of the missile and the position of the aircraft in space. The servo-mechanism of the anti-aircraft gun corrects this deviation after each shot with the aid of compensating feedback mechanisms. As is seen in this example, automated programming may be reduced to simple programming. The norm for the anti-aircraft gun instead of being defined as striking at a certain point in space, calculated by a special mechanism which programs the gun, can be formulated more simply, i.e. striking the aircraft. The automatic operations which program the servo-mechanism are now reduced to regulation correcting deviations from the norm.

Automatic control and regulation of the machine's operations is not new. It is the direct descendant of *mechanization*, or the substitution of a mechanism which couples the operations of the various instruments making up a machine in place of the direct use by man of the tools of labour. As early as the Middle Ages, the development of clockworks was related to the automation of many other operations. As a result, many complicated mechanisms were devised, with automated control and regulation, showing the hour, minute, day, month, phase of the moon, chiming the hour, playing a tune, setting a line of figures in motion, etc.[34] The fact that automation results from mechanization was

---

[34] Material technology saw automation for the first time in medieval clock mechanisms. This was pointed out by J. D. Bernal: "... the independently operating clock was created, which was the archetype of all modern self-regulating machines". (J. D. Bernal, *Science in History*, London, 1954, p. 234.) Automatic clock mechanisms were also known to the Arabs, who probably adopted them from Byzantium. Chinese authors describe such automatic mechanisms of the Arabs in the tenth century, and the Chinese themselves had built them as early as the seventh century. (See J. Needham, *Science and Civilization in China*, Cambridge, 1954, Vol. I, pp. 202–4.)

pointed out by Marx: "As soon as a machine executes, without man's help, all the movements requisite to elaborate the raw material, needing only attendance from him, we have an *automatic* system of machinery, and one that is susceptible of constant improvement in its details. Such improvements as the apparatus that stops a drawing frame whenever a silver breaks and the *self-acting stop* that stops the power-loom so soon as the shuttle bobbin is emptied of weft are quite modern inventions."[35]

Aside from automation or operations of a given machine, the co-ordination of a machinery system or an entire factory can also be automated. "A real *machinery system*, however," says Marx, "does not take the place of these *independent machines*, until the ... [object] of labour goes through a connected series of detail processes, that are carried out by a chain of machines of various kinds, one supplementing the other. ... Each detail machine supplies raw material to the machine next in order; and since they are all working at the same time, the product is always going through the various stages of its fabrication, and is also constantly in a state of transition, from one phase to another."[36] The result, as Marx colourfully stated, is that, "Here we have, in the place of the isolated machine, a mechanical monster whose body fills whole factories, and whose demon power, at first veiled under the slow and measured motions of his giant limbs, at length breaks out into the fast and furious whirl of his countless working organs."[37]

In the first stage of using mutually interacting machinery systems, the object of labour (or semi-product) is transferred from one machine to another by direct human intervention in the form of removal from one machine, transportation to another machine, providing working space, etc. Automation does away with the need of such direct intervention, because transfer from one machine to another is mechanized and automatically regulated and controlled. In this way, machines which operate automatically are joined to form automated machinery systems, and automated

---

[35] K. Marx, *op. cit.*, Vol. I, pp. 376–7.
[36] *Ibid.*, pp. 374–6.
[37] *Ibid.*, p. 377.

machinery systems are joined together to form automated factories. In the automated machinery system, or factory, various machines are coupled together to form one mechanism which is, properly speaking, one machine. This is the highest degree of automation of the production process. Modern terminology uses the appellation *complex*, or *full automation* of the production process, as opposed to partial automation covering only certain machines.[38] With full automation of the production process the role of labour amounts to pure supervision.

V

Mechanization of the labour process leads to the replacement of direct processing of the object of labour by mechanical processing; automation of control and regulation of the machine results in reduced human intervention in the operations of the machine and its greater supervision; and full automation of the production process eliminates entirely the need for direct human intervention in transferring the object of labour from one machine to another. The only thing that remains is supervision of the correct course of the automated process of production. Direct human intervention is needed only in the case of a breakdown of the process. But even here the introduction of self-repairing equipment for certain breakdowns of the machine or machinery systems reduces the need for human intervention.

The development trend of modern techniques leads to full automation of the production process. As we have seen, automation is a direct descendant of mechanization, and automation of various machines leads in turn to automated machinery systems and factories. Progress of this trend is dependent on technical possibilities alone. Wide possibilities are created by modern electro-mechanics and electronics. Since, historically, automation was brought about by mechanization, it was first introduced in those branches of production which are based on machines;

---

[38] In this connection, see *Automatisierung ...*, *ed.*, *cit.*, p. 10; and F. Pollock, *Automation: A Study of Its Economic and Social Consequences*, Oxford, 957, pp. 7–11.

machines thus became the object of automation. Automation next came to be introduced in chemical production in the form of servo-mechanisms which automatically regulate the conditions under which the chemical process takes place (temperature, pressure, humidity, flow of various liquids, intensity of fermentation, etc.). Automatic equipment is beginning to be applied in medicine. Up to the present, automation has been weakest in agricultural production, although even here there are some remnants of automatic regulation of the conditions under which the biological process takes place (e.g. temperature and humidity in a greenhouse), not to mention automation of secondary operations, executed by machines. In principle, automation may be applied to all feedback systems used in production, all biological and chemical systems, and all mechanisms.

With automation, the labour process leads to the programming of operations, the starting of operations of the automatic mechanism (or any other feedback system), and supervision of its proper functioning. This is the most extreme application of the principle of the minimization of intervention as used by Kotarbiński. "Minimization of intervention", says Kotarbiński, "leads to the postulate of pure surveillance, since what we are striving for is a process which is automatic, rather than a process in which we must intervene".[39] With the automation of various machines, surveillance is interrupted by direct intervention due to the necessity of transferring the object of labour from one machine to another; this is what is called "interventionary surveillance". It is only with full automation of the production process that it is possible to move away from pure surveillance, when the labour process consists entirely of supervision (with the exception of programming and setting in operation).

Thus, automation of the production process changes basically the very character of the labour process. With the direct use of tools, labour consists of the use of the force and skill of the muscles of the human body, controlled and regulated by the central nervous system. Mechanization of the labour process

---

[39] T. Kotarbiński, *Traktat* ..., p. 152.

replaces the direct work of human muscles by the operation of the machine's mechanism, and following the introduction of motors the physical force of the human organism is replaced by energy drawn from nature. Operating the machine (or other systems of coupled operations) requires a significantly smaller outlay of physical force and skill by the human organism than in the direct processing of the object of labour with the aid of tools. This continues to require, often to an even greater degree, the intensive operation of the central nervous system, especially the brain; this is particularly necessary for the control and regulation of the work of the machine. Thus, it is possible to say that automation of the production process will replace many of man's nervous and psychic operations to the same degree that mechanization of the labour process replaces the need for man's physical force and skill.

This is especially visible when the servo-mechanism automatically carries out operations in logic and mathematics (often very difficult for man), such as in modern computers. It plays a key role in the automation of the control and regulation of machine operations and other coupling systems used in the production process. Such devices are also called "artificial brains".[40]

J. D. Bernal draws attention to the change in the nature of the labour process caused by automation of the production process and states that automation is a new revolution in the labour process above and beyond mechanization: "The technical development of the twentieth century already shows that we are faced here with the second, and perhaps the third industrial revolution. ... In addition, although the original industrial revolution

---

[40] It is worth mentioning here that there is a close analogy between the operation of such devices and the central nervous system, based on the electrical character of the nervous system and the role of feedback in both the nervous system and in computers. It was Norbert Wiener (*op. cit.*, Chapters V and VII) who first pointed out this analogy and how this must facilitate an understanding of the operation of the central nervous system. This analogy— and differences—were discussed in detail by the eminent mathematician, John von Neumann (*The Computer and the Brain*, New Haven, 1958). A layman's discussion is given by W. Sluckin, in *Minds and Machines*, Penguin Books, 1960.

primarily concerned manufacturing and energy transmission, which, in principle, free man from heavy physical labour, the twentieth century revolution consists to a large degree in substituting the machine or electrical equipment for the capabilities of man, and should thus free him from the burden of monotonous office work or servicing the machine".[41] Or, according to another well-known automation expert, Frederick Pollock: "For the first time since the dawn of the industrial age machines are being invented which displace not only man's muscular effort but also the functions performed by his sensory organs and by his brain."[42] This was pointed out already before him by Norbert Wiener, who wrote: "... the first industrial revolution, the revolution of the dark satanic mills was the devaluation of the human arm by the competition of machinery .... The modern industrial revolution is similarly found to devalue the human brain, at least in its simpler and more routine decisions".[43]

Whether or not the revolution involved in the automation of the production process can be properly called a second industrial revolution is to some extent simply a question of terminology. However, there are important reasons against using this term.[44]

---

[41] J. D. Bernal, *op. cit.*, p. 497.

[42] F. Pollock, *op. cit.*, p. 39.

[43] N. Wiener, *op. cit.*, p. 27.

[44] The term "industrial revolution" was used by Engels in 1845 in *Die Lage der arbeiten Klasse in England*, Berlin, 1952. This term is used in connection with the widespread process of mechanization of labour which took place in England at the end of the eighteenth century and beginning of the nineteenth century and which was the technological base for the shift from manufactures to large-scale industry. The term was next used by Marx (*Capital*, Vol. I, pp. 367, 370). It was, however, Arnold Toynbee who popularized this term in his book, *Lectures on the Industrial Revolution*, published in 1884. It is possible that Toynbee took the term "industrial revolution" from Marx; according to Herbert Heaston in his article "Industrial Revolution" (*Encyclopaedia of the Social Sciences*, Vol. VIII, New York, 1948, p. 53), Toynbee knew Marx's *Capital*, and had studied the German socialist movement. Nevertheless, in those days much was written about the "revolution" in industrial production, so that Toynbee could have borrowed this term from another source. As we have seen, automation of production had been called a "second industrial revolution" by Wiener, Bernal and

others. The term has become very much in vogue today. We should keep in
mind, however, that it had already been used earlier, in the 1920's, in connection with the large-scale technological changes which were taking place
as part of what was then called "rationalization of production". This consisted in introducing and spreading mass-production methods, primarily by
introducing the assembly line and using scientific methods in organizing production. See Otto Bauer, *Kapitalismus und Sozialismus nach dem Weltkriege*,
Vol. I, *Rationalisierung und Fehlrationalisierung*, Berlin, 1931, pp. 161-9. In
this connection, Bernal, as we have seen above in his quotation, is not sure
whether to speak of two or three industrial revolutions. The first would be
widespread use of the machine and the shift from manufactories to modern industry; the second would be the spreading of mass production; and the third
would be automation of the production process. (*Science in History, ed. cit.*,
pp. 497-8, 590-1.) There can be no doubt that the development of the modern
production techniques has passed through more or less clearly defined stages,
and as each new stage is entered there is something of a revolution in the
production process. This is pointed out by Schumpeter in his *Business Cycles*,
which contains a history of the development of capitalism presented against
the background of changes in production techniques. Schumpeter maintains
that at the close of the nineteenth century and early in the twentieth century
there was an industrial revolution which consisted in the use of electricity
in industry as a source of energy (the first industrial revolution, according
to him, was the use of steam). In addition, according to Schumpeter, in the
1920's there was a third industrial revolution, based on the use of oil and
gasoline in internal combustion engines (see J. Schumpeter, *Business Cycles*,
New York and London, 1939, Vol. I, pp. 397-8, and Vol. II, pp. 753-4). As
we see, Schumpeter considered the use of new kinds of energy rather than
changes in the nature of the social process of labour as a criterion for differentiating between various "industrial revolutions". For this reason, his views
are of little use, since they overlook the most essential aspects of the social
process of production. Calling automation a "second industrial revolution"
is justified to the extent that we are talking about a real revolution in the character of the social process of labour. This revolution, however, results in
less pervasive changes in the production process than the revolution at the
end of the eighteenth and the beginning of the nineteenth centuries which
was brought about by mechanization of the labour process. Modern industry,
created at that time, was the basis for the historical process of industrialization. But automation of the production process is a revolution carried out
within the framework of already-existing modern industry which is merely improved upon. For this reason, speaking of automation as a second industrial
revolution would appear to be incorrect, for this term refers to the specific
historical features of the industrial revolution, which were the basis for industrialization. It should also be pointed out that the industrial revolution is
closely connected with the formation of the capitalist mode of production,

There can be no doubt, however, that automation of the production process is a qualitative "change", and is thus a revolution in the character of the social process of production. Using tools and specialized instruments in the labour process increases the scope and efficiency of human organs and creates new, artificial means for use by man. The introduction of machines, or the mechanization of the labour process, increases the efficiency and power of the tools of labour and permits operations which it was not possible to carry out with the old tools. It also increases the scope and efficiency of the operations of man's nervous system, allowing new operations to be carried out which it had previously not been possible to do. Mechanization of the labour process increases the physical power and efficiency of the entire human organism, while automation of the production process increases the power and efficiency of the human intellect.

VI

Making use of means of labour usually requires joint activity of many people. Only very simple tools can be used by a single individual; in this case, we call the production process handicrafts. With more complicated tools, especially instruments, machines, machine systems, and other systems of coupled operations (e.g. agriculture and chemical production), so many various operations are involved that a single individual is not equal to the task. The need then arises for collective performance of such operations, or group labour. This is the reason that there are groups of individuals in the production process who make use of a given reserve of means of labour (tools and auxiliary equipment) to process objects of labour; taken together these means are called

---

that is, with the creation of a new social system. The revolution created by automation is being carried out in countries with both socialist and capitalist modes of production. This process is most intensive in the Soviet Union and the United States, although its social and historic significance differs in the two countries.

the *plant*.[45] Plants are also given many other names, such as farm, workshop,[46] industrial plant, transportation plant, etc.

In the plant, the object of various operations, or of specific types of work, is the common goal of producing a product or products; this joint striving to achieve a certain goal by these various operations is called *co-ordination*. This includes the various activities of each person and of several persons. Co-ordination of the activities of several persons is called *co-operation*. We distinguish, on the one hand, between simple co-operation, which simply consists of a joint effort of several persons to achieve a given result in the production process (e.g. transporting heavy objects, ditch-digging, etc.), and, on the other hand, co-operation as the *division of labour*. With division of labour, the activities of various persons are specialized; each person undertakes some of the activities involved in production. In this way, with co-operation, the work of various persons in the plant becomes an integral part of the work of the human group. The individual becomes, according to Marx, "detail labourer", and is part of the "collective labourer"—i.e. the sum total of those working in the plant.[47]

The need to co-ordinate various operations in the plant leads to the creation of special kinds of operations and special kinds of work—namely, *management*. "The labour of superintendence and management will naturally be required whenever the direct process of production assumes the form of a combined social process, and does not rest on the isolated labour of independent producers."[48]

This is indispensable because "all labours, in which many individuals operate, necessarily require for the connection and unity of the process one commanding will, and this peforms

---

[45] In Polish, *zakład produkcyjny*; in German, *Betrieb*; in Russian, *zavod*.

[46] Workshops account for industrial production based on simple tools and small machines operated by a few people or sometimes even one person.

[47] See K. Marx, *op. cit.*, Vol. I, p. 330. Marx uses the German term *Teilarbeiter* and *Gesamtarbeiter*. In *Capital*, Vol. III (Chicago, 1919, p. 124) Marx speaks of the "combined labourer" (*kombinierter Arbeiter*).

[48] K. Marx, *op. cit.*, Vol. III, p. 451.

the function, which does not refer to fragmentary operations but to the combined labour of the workshop, in the same way as does that of a director of an orchestra."[49]

Management work may be performed by a single individual (one-man management) or by a group of persons (collegial management). Persons performing the management function often make use of the help of other persons who gather, store and transmit information on the operations within the plant. Such persons (e.g. bookkeepers, secretaries, messengers) are called auxiliary management personnel. Their activities are necessary for management work and for this reason they are considered as part of this work.[50]

Management is characterized by the fact that its direct object of labour is not a material object transformed in the production process, but the activities of those who transform the object of labour.[51] Management influences, determines and co-ordinates the activities of these persons. Hence, management indirectly influences the process of transforming the object of labour; thus, in the plant it is productive work in the same way as is the work of those who directly transform the object of labour. "This is a kind of productive labour"—Marx says—"which must be performed in every mode of production requiring a combination of labours."[52] However, the influence of management on the transformation of the object of labour is indirect, and is therefore *indirectly productive.*

---

[49] *Ibid.* Engels gives a similar justification for the need of management in "On Authority" (K. Marx, F. Engels, *Selected Works,* Vol. I, Moscow, 1962, pp. 636–7).

[50] Auxiliary management personnel are often also called administrative personnel, and their work—administrative work.

[51] This was pointed out by Kotarbiński: in discussing the broader problem of non-manual labour he concludes that the state of man as an experiencing individual is the product of management and the condition of such a person before undertaking his non-manual activity is management's material. (See *Traktat* ..., p. 277.) In the specific case of management the material or object of labour are the operations of other individuals, and the product are the operations of these same individuals who are subordinate to management.

[52] K. Marx, *op. cit.,* Vol. III, p. 451.

Also connected with management is *conceptual work*, i.e. determining or *programming* the operations of various persons employed in transforming the object of labour. Such programming includes establishing which products are to be produced, the material to be used as the object of labour, the tools to be used and the method of using and operating them. This kind of conceptual work is part of the work of management. Often, however, another group of people are appointed to carry out conceptual work; in this case, there is a separation of management into executive and conceptual work. Marx calls conceptual work "universal labour", and includes in it all scientific work, discoveries and inventions as part of it.[53]

Within the plant, to separate management and perhaps also conceptual work is part of the division of labour among those employed in the plant. Division of labour within the plant is the basis for the modern development of the productive forces. This was recognized by Adam Smith, who remarked: "The greatest improvements in the productive powers of Labour, and the greater part of the skill, dexterity and judgement with which it is anywhere directed, or applied, seem to have been the effects

---

[53] See K. Marx, *op. cit.*, Vol. III, p. 124. Distinctions are often drawn between non-manual and manual labour. However, in reality it is difficult to make this division, for all labour, including manual labour, involves the use of the force and skill of the muscles of the human body, and also requires the operation of the human central nervous system, and a consciousness of the goal, a will, and concentration of attention. "Besides the exertion of the bodily organs", according to Marx, "the process demands that, during the whole operation, the workman's will be steadily in consonance with his purpose. This means close attention." (*Capital*, Vol. I, p. 157.) Consequently, Marx correctly defines labour as the "productive expenditure of human brains, nerves, and muscles". (*Ibid.*, p. 11.) At best one can say that different, specific types of labour are more or less "mental" or "physical". However, with mechanization, and even more so with automation of the production process, all work becomes increasingly non-manual as it becomes progressively more similar to supervision. On the other hand, management and conceptual work are based on very exact criteria—which result from the fact that management's object of labour (including conceptual work) are the activities of other individuals, not the direct material object which is transformed in the production process.

of the division of labour."[54] Adam Smith also listed the factors which cause the growth of output as a result of the division of labour: "This great increase of the quantity of work which the same number of people are capable of performing, in consequence of the division of labour, is owing to three different circumstances; first, to the increase of dexterity in every particular workman; secondly, to the saving of the time which is commonly lost in passing from one species of work to another; and lastly, to the invention of a great number of machines which facilitate and abridge labour and enable one man to do the work of many."[55] Mechanization of the production process and automation are especially closely connected with the development of the division of labour in the plant.

There has been a certain division of labour for ages in agriculture and in handicrafts employing several people, but the great development of the division of labour is connected with the development of modern industry whose creation, as we know, is connected with the creation and development of the capitalist mode of production. The beginning of this development is marked by the creation of *manufactories*—plants which employ large numbers of people and in which there is a change from simple co-operation to co-operation based on the division of labour with the use of simple tools, instruments, and a few manually operated machines.[56] A highly developed division of labour within the

---

[54] Adam Smith, *An Inquiry into the Nature and Causes of the Wealth of Nations*, Vol. I, *ed. cit.*, p. 7.

[55] *Ibid.*, p. 12.

[56] Some see the beginnings of manufactories in the Greek *ergasteria*—handicraft workshops employing several or even several hundreds of workers, primarily slaves (Lujo Brentano, *Das Wirtschaftsleben der antiken Welt* [*Economic Life in Antiquity*], Jena, 1929, pp. 36, 47–50, 81). Evidence of this can be seen in Ksenofont's remarks on the detailed specialization of handicraft production. It would seem, however, that these remarks concern more specialization among workshops, and not, as is the case with manufactories—within workshops. Max Weber characterizes the *ergasteria* in the following way: "The *ergasterion* may be freely *divided* (by selling off some of the slaves) like a block of lead, since it is an undifferentiated collection of forced labourers, not a differentiated organization of labour" (*Agrarverhältnisse im Altertum, Gesammelte Aufsätze zur Sozial- und Wirtschaftsgeschichte*, Tübingen, 1924,

framework of manufactories created a basis for the mechanization of the production process, made possible the introduction
of machines and encouraged inventiveness. As a result, the fac-

p. 9; see also M. Weber, *Wirtschaftsgeschichte*, Berlin, 1958, p. 121). The
ergasteria are similarly seen by N. Mashkin: "The Greek *ergasterion* has
nothing in common with the factory. Only appearances remind one of manufactories because in ancient times we do not find that which is characteristic
for manufactories: the collective worker made up of many detail workers"
(*K voprosu ob ekonomicheskoy zhizni Gretsii klasicheskogo peryoda*: *Drevnyaya
Gretsia*: [*The Economic Life of Greece of the Classical Period: Ancient
Greece*] Moscow, 1956, p. 248). Along with the fall of the ancient social system
and the disappearance of mass slavery, the *ergasteria* also disappeared, for
there was shortage of workers. In the Middle Ages, production took place
in small handicraft workshops. The guild system sanctioned this state of affairs,
forbidding more than a small number of apprentices and journeymen. Manufactories made their appearance only in the fourteenth and fifteenth centuries in textile manufacturing in Italy and Flanders. In the second half of
the sixteenth, and especially throughout the seventeenth and eighteenth centuries, there was a growth of manufactories in Scotland, England and France.
Manufactories represent the first step in the development of the capitalist
mode of production; they are organized by capitalists and are based on the
employment of hired labour. The development of manufactories is connected
with the process which Marx called primitive accumulation (K. Marx, *Capital*, Vol. I, p. 736). The result of this process is the creation of a numerous
class of hired workers. The basic role was played here by the expulsion of
the peasants from the land in the seventeenth and eighteenth centuries. The
expulsions in England in the eighteenth century were especially intensive in
connection with expropriation of common lands by land owners (these lands
were enclosed by the owners: hence the term *enclosure of commons*). This
process was described by Marx (*Capital*, Vol. I, pp. 740–58). See also M. Dobb,
Studies in the Development of Capitalism, London, 1947, pp. 221–42; on pages
142–61, Dobb describes the process of creating manufactories. The problem
of supplying workers for manufactories was one of the central problems treated
in the mercantilist economic literature of the seventeenth and eighteenth centuries. In some countries, which attempted to reach the level of development
of industrial production of Western Europe, there was a shortage of hired
workers, and serfs were used, as, for example, in Russia in the seventeenth
and eighteenth centuries. Nevertheless, capitalist production relations gradually began to be introduced in manufactories, as was pointed out by S. G.
Strumilin (*Ocherki ekonomicheskoy istorii Rossii* [*Essays on the Economic History of Russia*], Moscow, 1960, Chapter IV). In eighteenth-century Poland,
so-called magnate manufactories were created which were based on serf-
labour. A description of these manufactories is given by Witold Kula in *Szkice*

tory was formed, characteristic of modern industry, in which various kinds of machines are used in the production process.[57]

---

o manufakturach w Polsce w XVIII wieku (Essays on Manufactories in Poland in the Eighteenth Century), Vols. I and II, Warsaw, 1956. But even in these manufactories serfs became more independent as the bonds of serfdom weakened, and they gradually became hired workers (see *ibid.*, p. 28). Thus, serf manufactories were a transition stage to capitalist manufactories, although, as a rule, they ended in failure. In China, where social development differed from that in Europe as early as the time of the Northern Dynasties of the Sungs (from the end of the tenth to the beginning of the twelfth century), there were manufactories, primarily royal, which employed hired labour. During the Ming Dynasties (from the second half of the fourteenth to the mid-seventeenth century) there was a blossoming of manufactories, including private ones, especially for silk fabrics and porcelain, which were based on hired labour. See *Dzieje Chin (The History of China)* (Szang-Jüe, Ed.), Warsaw, 1960, pp. 293, 446–51 (translated from Chinese). This would indicate that there were self-generated beginnings of capitalists development in China which, however, did not lead to a full development of the capitalist mode of production.

[57] The creation and development of the factory is the basis for the industrial revolution, mentioned above (footnote 44). This is connected with a series of inventions which made possible the mechanization of the labour process used in manufactories. The most important inventions occurred in England in the textile industry; they followed one another in a very short space of time. Around 1765 James Hargreaves invented a spinning machine called the *spinning-jenny*, patented in 1770. In 1760 Richard Arkwright invented a spinning frame operated by water power (the *water-frame*). Both these inventions were perfected by Samuel Crompton in 1779 into a new spinning frame, called *spinning mule*. And, finally, in 1792 William Kelly introduced the automatic spinning frame, called *self-actor*. Mechanization came somewhat later for weaving. Although John Kay invented the automatic shuttle as early as 1773, a real breakthrough was made only with the construction of the power loom in 1787 by Edmund Cartwright. All these machines, however, required a driving force, which appeared in the form of the steam engine, patented by James Watt in 1769 (but used even earlier). Steam machines had been known earlier, for as early as the latter part of the seventeenth century they were used for water pumps. But it was only with Watt's invention that they were widely adapted to industry, first in the textile industry and then in iron production. As Marx remarked, events occurred in this order because it was only with the working machines that the need arose for the widespread application of steam machines. See K. Marx, *Capital*, Vol. I, pp. 368–70. ("The tool or working-machine is that part of the machinery with which the industrial revolution of the eighteenth century started. And to this day it constantly serves as such a starting point, whenever a handicraft, or a manufacture, is turned into an industry

Large-scale mechanization of the production process and the creation of the factory as a new kind of plant meant that, from that moment on, the development of the productive forces was based not on improving the capabilities and skills of the workers by the division of labour, as was the case with manufactories, but on improving and introducing new means of labour in the form of machines. As Marx pointed out, "In manufacture, the revolution in the mode of production begins with the labour-power, in modern industry it begins with the instruments of labour."[58] In the factory, the need for the worker's capabilities and skills usually is reduced to operating machines, and the division of labour is adapted to the specialization of the machines.[59] And finally, mechanization of the production process in the modern factory allows automation. The result of automation, as we know, is reducing the labour process to pure supervision of the operation of the automatic plant.

---

carried on by machinery. ... It was ... the invention of machines that made a revolution in the form of steam engines necessary.") The development of machines caused a demand for iron. Increased iron production was made possible by Abraham Darby's invention in 1735 of iron smelting based on coke instead of formerly used charcoal. In 1784, Henry Cort introduced *pudding* as a new method of steel refining, at the same time introducing rolling in place of the former process of forging. This made possible the mass production of high-quality iron and the development of machine production. However, machines continued to be built by hand. It was only with Henry Mandslay's invention in 1717 of the metal working machine tool powered by a lead-screw that the road was opened for the mechanization of the machine building industry. This was the last of a series of inventions which were the technological basis for the industrial revolution. This industrial revolution called to life the factory, which replaced manufactories (often by transforming the manufactory into a factory) and gradually ousted handicrafts. The creation of the factory represents the next step (after the manufactory) in the development of the capitalist mode of production. As a result, the factory became the basic model for the plant in the capitalist mode of production— nearly the only kind of plant in capitalist industry. The socialist mode of production inherited the factory from the capitalist mode of production, and also creates new plants in the form of factories.

[58] K. Marx, *op. cit.*, Vol. I, p. 366.

[59] "So far as division of labour reappears in the factory, it is primarily a distribution of the workmen among the specialized machines." (*Ibid.*, p. 419.)

VII

The plant turns out a given product or products. The plant is part of various divisions of production (e.g. agriculture, industry, transportation, warehousing), and, additionally, it is part of various sub-divisions, or branches of production (e.g. electrotechnical, chemical and textile industries), based on given products. There is a division of labour and co-operation among various plants; one plant uses the product of another plant as its raw material. Thus aside from the division of labour within the plant, there is also a broader division of labour on a society-wide scale which appears in the form of a division of labour and co-operation among plants. The division of labour among plants and within the plant are different levels of the overall division of labour among members of human society[60]—of the *social division of labour*. Marx characterizes these two levels as follows: "If we keep labour alone in view, we may designate the separation of social production into its main divisions or *genera*—viz., agriculture, industries, etc., as division of labour *in general*, and the splitting up of these families into species and sub-species, as division of labour *in particular*, and the division of labour within the workshop as division of labour *in singular*, or *in detail*."[61]

----

[60] By "society" we mean all people connected by relations of simple co-operation and division of labour. The scope of society changes with the historical development of the scope of production relations. In the primitive tribe, the jointly hunting "society" includes all the members of the tribe; in primitive economies of the self-sufficient village commune, the "manse" of ancient times, and the feudal manor of the Middle Ages, everyone is included in the "society". Modern society, in principle, includes all members of the nation—hence the term "national economy". Nevertheless, the term reaches beyond, because of international division of labour. See O. Lange, *Political Economy*, Vol. I, *ed. cit.*, p. 15.

[61] K. Marx, *op. cit.*, Vol. I, pp. 343–4. Marx often uses the term "social division of labour". On p. 9 of *Capital*, Vol. I, this term is used very broadly, covering both the division of labour among plants and within the plant itself. As Marx says, "This division of labour is a necessary condition for the production of commodities, but it does not follow, conversely, that the production of commodities is a necessary condition for the division of labour. In the primitive Indian community there is social division of labour, without *production of commodities*. Or, to take an example nearer home, in every fac-

The development and differentiation of the social division of labour and its various levels is tied up not only with the development of productive forces, but also with the development of social modes of production. In the primitive economy which is dominant in pre-capitalist modes of production, neither division of labour nor co-operation exists as yet among plants. The entire primitive community, rural commune (e.g. in ancient India), manse (e.g. the Greek *oikos* or the Roman *familia*), or feudal manor represent the plant. All production operations take place within the community, commune, manse or manor; this is called *household economy*. The production operations, which are determined consciously and purposefully, are co-ordinated by the household head, and the products are consumed within the household itself; there is only an occasional exchange of products among different households. It is only with the development of commodity relations that there arises a differentiation of various plants from the whole; as a result, there appear various levels of social division of labour. Aside from co-operation and division of labour within the plant, there comes about a division of labour and co-operation among plants.

Co-operation and division of labour within the plant, and earlier, within the household economy, designed to satisfy directly the needs of those employed, are, as we have already emphasized, conscious and purposeful, with all operations being co-ordinated by the plant or household head. However, division of labour and co-operation among plants, which form along with the development of commodity relations, are spontaneous. This is especially true in the capitalist mode of production, in which

tory labour is divided according to a system, but this division is not brought about by the operatives mutually exchanging their individual products." On the other hand, on p. 343, Marx speaks of the difference between "the division of labour in manufacture" (*manufakturmässige Teilung der Arbeit*) and "the social division of labour, which forms the foundation of all production of commodities". The same differentiation appears on p. 345, but here, "social division of labour" is used narrowly to include only the division of labour between plants. I use "social division of labour" broadly to cover all levels of the division of labour among members of society.

commodity relations attain full development. It is also in the capitalist mode of production that the contradiction between the division of labour within the plant and among plants is fully apparent. Marx defines this contradiction as "the *a priori* system on which the division of labour within the workshop is regularly carried out, and [which] becomes in the division of labour within the society an *a posteriori* nature-imposed necessity, controlling the lawless caprice of the producers, and perceptible in the barometrical fluctuations of the market prices."[62] Engels, on the other hand, characterizes this state of affairs as *"the antithesis between the organization of production in the industrial factory and the anarchy of production in a society as a whole."*[63]

Certain efforts at overcoming this contradiction can even be observed in the capitalist mode of production in the form of agreements which co-ordinate the activities of several plants (e.g. cartels), or join together several plants under common administration (trusts), and also in co-ordination by state intervention. Nevertheless, private ownership presents a roadblock to such efforts, as a result of which division of labour and co-operation among groups of plants remain spontaneous. There can only be full co-ordination of the operations of all plants in society in a socialist mode of production as part of *planning of the social economy.*[64] Planning gives the same conscious and purposeful character to division of labour and co-operation among plants as to co-operation and division of labour within the individual plant.

VIII

Social division of labour at various levels leads to the specialization of various human activities—that is, to specialization of various kinds of concrete labour. These various kinds of con-

---

[62] K. Marx, *op. cit.*, Vol. I, p. 349.

[63] F. Engels, *Herr Eugen Dühring's Revolution in Science (Anti-Düring)*, London, 1955, p. 301.

[64] See O. Lange, *op. cit.*, Vol. I, pp. 151–3.

38 *Political Economy*

crete labour are carried out by given groups of people—or occupations such as farmers, shoemakers, weavers, metal workers, engineers in various specializations, bookkeepers, factory managers, etc. Thus, social division of labour is in fact an *occupational division of labour.*[65]

The separation of various occupations leads to a separation of specific kinds of labour. The work done by various members of society ceases to be a collection of similar, homogeneous operations. Various occupations develop pronounced differences;

---

[65] The earliest division of labour occurring in the history of human societies is not an occupational, but a natural division of labour, i.e. a division which occurs between man and woman, and also to a lesser degree between younger and older people. Women take up agriculture and gardening (so-called "digging", the most primitive form of land cultivation), while men are concerned with hunting or fishing (see L. Krzywicki, *Ustroje społeczno-gospodarcze w epoce dzikości i barbarzyństwa* [*Socio-economic Systems in the Period of Savagery and Barbarity*], Warsaw, 1914, pp. 147–69). This was the basis for a division between "masculine" and "feminine" occupations which lasted for centuries. M. J. Herskovitz (*Economic Anthropology*, New York, 1952, pp. 127–42) indicates that although "masculine" and "feminine" occupations differed greatly in various societies, they were, nevertheless, always precisely determined and sanctified by habit and tradition. See also R. Thurnwald, *Werden, Wandel und Formen der Wirtschaft. Die menschliche Gesellschaft in ihren ethnosoziologischen Grundlagen*, Vol. III, Berlin–Leipzig, 1932, pp. 7–8. The development of the occupational division of labour is discussed by Engels; he differentiates three stages. *The first great social division of labour* was the separation of shepherd tribes; this occurred with the primitive commune. It led to a regular exchange of products of shepherding for other objects, primarily agricultural products. At that time, livestock often served as money. *The second great social division of labour* is connected with the beginnings of the production and use of iron, at which time handicrafts (i.e. industrial production) were separated from agriculture. Tool and weapon making from iron, the processing of other metals (silver and gold), and, to some degree, weaving, all became separate occupations. Towns were thus founded and they separated the urban areas from the countryside. And, finally, *the third great social division of labour* consists in the separation of commerce. The merchant is thus formed; he becomes the middle-man in the exchange of products of various occupations. The merchant is in particular the middle-man between handicrafts and agriculture, between the town and the countryside, and between towns. At this time, metallic money also occurs. The merchant is the first great occupation not concerned with production. See F. Engels, *The Origins of the Family, Private Property and the State*, Moscow, 1948, pp. 235–6.

they differ from the point of view of the necessary capability, adroitness, training, and physical and mental effort. This is expressed by saying that various kinds of work require appropriate *qualifications*. The qualification for work in a particular occupation is gained by learning the work and gaining skill in practice. However, not all work requires learning and gaining qualifications; there are some operations which are so simple (e.g. ditch-digging, carrying heavy objects, operating simple machines, etc.) that any normal healthy person can perform them without any learning. Such operations are called *simple* or *unskilled labour*. Simple labour, as Marx said, "is the expenditure of simple labour-power, i.e. of the labour-power which, on an average, apart from any special development, exists in the organism of every ordinary individual. *Simple average labour*, it is true, varies in character in different countries and at different times, but in a particular society it is given."[66] Marx goes on to speak of skilled labour.[67] Labour associated with specific occupations is always skilled. Simple labour can always be done by any normal person capable of working and is not peculiar to any particular occupation; it can be done by people who do not possess any occupation.

IX

Management is an integral part of the occupational division of labour. As we saw above, it results from the need to co-ordinate various operations in the plant, and as such is indispensable in all social modes of production.[68] Management also has another

---

[66] K. Marx. *op. cit.*, Vol. I, p. 11.

[67] *Ibid.* In the original German, the term *komplizertere Arbeit* (more complicated labour) is used, while later the term *kompliziertestte Arbeit* (the most complicated labour) is used. Marx thus did not speak of just one kind of skilled labour, as may be assumed from the English text; he is talking rather about varying degrees of skilled labour, which is appropriate to the higher or lower degree of qualifications needed in a given occupation.

[68] This was strongly emphasized by Engels in discussing the necessity for co-ordinating all the operations in the cotton-spinning mill or the railroad. In discussing the railroad, he wrote as follows: "Here too the co-operation of an infinite number of individuals is absolutely necessary, and this co-oper-

significance which is connected with the characteristics of the means of production—i.e. with the specific features of a given historical mode of production. In antagonistic modes of production, management serves not only the social need of co-ordinating operations in the production process, but also subordinates this process to the interests of the owners of the means of production. Management becomes a tool by which the owners of the means of production exploit the workers. Marx describes this in the following manner: " ... this labour of superintendence necessarily arises in all modes of production, which are based on the antagonism between the labourer as a direct producer and the owner of the means of production. To the extent that this antagonism becomes pronounced, the role played by superintendence increases in importance. But it is indispensable also under the capitalist mode of production since then the process of production is at the same time the process by which the capitalist consumes the labour-power of the labourer."[69]

This double character of management in antagonistic modes of production results from the fact that the owner of the means of production or his agent (the *villicus* in the ancient slave economy, the overseer of the feudal manor, and the manager in the capitalist factory) is also the organizer of the production process. Thus, he fulfils a double role, i.e. of the socially necessary co-ordinator of the production process and of the organizer of the exploitation of workers. But he is co-ordinator in the production process because he is the owner of the means of production or the owner's agent. The crucial fact here is the ownership of the means of production, while the co-ordinating role is a consequence.[70]

---

ation must be practised during precisely fixed hours so that no accidents may happen. Here, too, the first condition of the job is a dominant will that settles all subordinate questions, whether this will is represented by a single delegate or by a committee charged with the execution of the resolutions of the majority of persons interested. In either case there is very pronounced authority." (F. Engels, "On Authority", *ed. cit.*, p. 638.)

[69] K. Marx, *op. cit.*, Vol. III, pp. 451–2.

[70] "It is not because he is a leader of industry that a man is a capitalist; on the contrary, he is a leader of industry because he is a capitalist. The leadership of industry is an attribute of capital, just as in feudal times the

This is connected with the existence of two kinds of production relations and their mutual relationship. Production relations are the social inter-human relations which are formed within the production process. They result from the fact that the production process is a social process in which people co-operate and work for each other. There are both co-operation (simple co-operation and the division of labour) and various forms of ownership of means of production within this social process, from which there result two kinds of production relations. The first are relations of production which are created and formed as part of co-operation in the labour process; they are called *co-operation relations*. The second are relations of production which are based on the forms of ownership of the means of production existing in a given society; they are called *ownership relations*. Co-operation relations are the direct result of simple co-operation and division of labour. They last as long as there are people engaged in simple co-operation and division of labour, and are connected with the techniques used in the production process. This is well illustrated in the following example of labour relations in the railroad, given by Krzywicki: "At the proper time there must be someone to sell tickets, to weigh packages, to follow the train's current position, to fill the duties of engineer, to inspect cars, and to send and receive telegrams. The operations of each person are exactly attuned to the operations of all. Each person, as it were, is a living addition to one or another part of dead objects: to the train, ticket-wicket, the train's make-up, etc. This collection of people and the entire railroad line represent one entity; it is impossible to understand these human actions without keeping in mind the time-tables, their technical equipment, and the flow of commodities."[71]

---

functions of general and judge were attributes of landed property." (K. Marx, *op. cit.*, Vol. I, p. 323.)

[71] L. Krzywicki, "Rozwój społeczny wśród zwierząt i u rodzaju ludzkiego" (The Social Development of Animals and Humans), *Studia Socjologiczne* (*Sociological Studies*), Warsaw, 1951, pp. 201–2. See also O. Lange, *op. cit.*, Vol. I, p. 12.

The co-operation relations described here are to a large extent independent of ownership relations and of whether the railroad is private property or some kind of social property. But they do exclude the possibilities of certain kinds of private ownership (e.g. small-scale ownership of the various types of railroad transportation); this kind of ownership would make impossible co-operation and division of labour involved in the technical conditions of the railroad. However, whether the railroad is capitalist private property or socialist social property will influence the level and way of paying wages, the relationship of management to personnel, the existence of workers' self-government and its rights, the conditions for hiring and firing, etc. The form of ownership can also influence production techniques, i.e. the degree of mechanization of various operations, and can thus influence the formation of co-operation relations.

Co-operation and ownership relations involve a mutual relationship. Co-operation relations are determined by the technical conditions of production and the state of the productive forces, while ownership relations are determined by co-operation relations. Ownership relations, in turn, influence co-operation relations, either directly by the fact that they determine which co-operation relations will be possible within the framework of the given ownership relations, or indirectly by their influence on the techniques used in the production process. The main instrument for the direct influence of ownership relations on co-operation relations is the fact that ownership relations determine who is to co-ordinate the various operations in the production process, i.e. who will be manager of the productive process, and in whose interest he will perform his functions.

X

A certain period of time is required to produce a given object. Various operations, or specific kinds of labour, which make up the production process require more or less time. In addition, all operations are not carried out at the same point in the production process. Some operations are delayed over time, some follow directly upon others, and, what is more, the conclusion of some later operations is often conditioned by the effective conclusion of earlier operations. This subsequent effect of one operation upon the other is established by the techniques for transforming the object of labour with the aid of given means of labour. Thus, the order of operations in agriculture is determined by the techniques for cultivating a given crop; the order of operations in the production of electric bulbs is determined by the kind of machinery, the way it is used, and the operations carried out by the machinery, etc. As we see, co-ordination of the various operations in production also affects co-ordination.

The time needed to carry out all the operations in producing a given object is called the *working period*.[72] The working period varies in the production of various objects. As Marx said: "In one ... [branch] a definite quantity of finished product, cotton yarn, is completed daily, or weekly; in the other, the productive process may have to be repeated for three months in order that the finished product, a locomotive, may be ready. ... These differences in the duration of the productive performance are found not only in two different spheres of production, but also within one and the same sphere of production, according to the intended volume of the product. An ordinary residential house is built in less time than a large factory, and therefore requires a smaller number of consecutive labour processes."[73]

However, the working period does not cover all the time needed for production. As we know, production makes use of indirect activity; it sets in motion a cause and effect chain which replaces man's direct intervention on the object of labour, and it relies on coupled sets, such as various kinds of biological and chemical processes, and the machine. In addition, these coupled sets require a certain amount of time in order to achieve the result desired by man, even though they do not always require man's

[72] "But if we speak of a working period, then we mean a number of consecutive working-days required in a certain branch of production for the completion of the finished product." (K. Marx, *op. cit.*, Vol. II, Chicago, 1919, p. 262.)

[73] *Ibid.*, p. 260.

service, or labour, throughout the period. Marx gives several examples: "For instance, grape juice, after being pressed, must ferment for a while and then rest for some time, in order to reach a certain degree of perfection. In many branches of industry the product must pass through a drying process — for instance, in pottery — or be exposed to certain conditions which change its chemical nature — for instance, in bleaching. Winter grain needs about nine months to mature. Between the sowing and harvesting time the labour-process is almost entirely suspended. In timber raising, after sowing and incidental preliminary work are completed, the seed may require about 100 years in order to be transformed into a finished product. ..."[74] We should add that processing a given object on an automatically operated machine requires a certain period of time after the worker has put the raw material into the machine. The overall time needed to produce a given product is called the *production time* or *production period*.[75] As can be seen, the production period as a rule is longer than the working period; in any case, it cannot be shorter.

Means of production (both the object and means of labour) are consumed in the production process. Some are completely used up in the course of one production period, as is the case of the objects of labour, which are transformed into products. In the language of technology, the objects of labour are the material from which the product is processed; the material is entirely

---

[74] K. Marx, *op. cit.*, Vol. II, p. 272.

[75] In planning and economic administration, the term *production cycle* is usually used to designate the production period. The production period, or production cycle, under discussion here concerns the production process in a given plant. It should not be confused with the production period in Böhm-Bawerk's theory. In the theory of this eminent autority of the Austrian school of political economy, the production period concerns not a particular plant, but the entire social economy. Böhm-Bawerk sees production as a process occurring in consecutive stages, beginning with raw material extraction, passing through the production of various semi-products, tools and equipment needed to process objects of labour in their various stages, and ending finally with consumer goods. Some processing is performed at each stage of the process. Böhm-Bawerk defines a production period as the average time between labour outlays at various stages and the final output of consumer goods.

transformed into the product. We also give expression to this when we say that the objects of labour "are entirely absorbed by the product". At the conclusion of the production process they are entirely used up, and no longer exist in their original form. Some of the means of labour are also completely used up in one production period because this is the way they are used (e.g. coal, oil or electric power for the motor, oils and greases for machines, electric power for factory lighting, etc.). They are not materials of which the product is made, but they are nevertheless entirely used up in the production period.[76] Means of production completely used up in one production period are called *working capital means.*

As a rule, however, means of labour have a longer lifetime. They remain in their original, natural state, and thus may be used over a longer period, exceeding one production period. Such means of production are called *fixed capital means.* It is clear that the period of use of means of production is not unlimited; all means of labour (tools, machines and various kinds of auxiliary equipment) are gradually used up, until they can no longer be used, and must finally be replaced. The reasons for this vary. Means of labour are eventually used up; the rapidity with which this occurs depends on the frequency and intensity of their use. For example, a machine operating 16 hours per day will be used up more rapidly than a machine used only 8 hours. The internal combustion or steam engine is used up more rapidly with heavier duty, and railroad tracks are used up more rapidly on lines with more freight and traffic (especially in railroad yards).

Means of labour are gradually used up even when not used in production. Buildings and various installations are exposed to wind and rain; the material used in a building or equipment is

---

[76] "Some portions of the means of production do not yield their substance to the product. Such are auxiliary substances, which are consumed by the instruments of labour themselves in performance of their functions, such as coal consumed by a steam engine; or substances which merely assist in the operation, such as gas for lighting, etc. ... But they are entirely consumed in every labour process which they enter and must therefore be replaced by new specimens of their kind in every new labour process." (K. Marx, *op. cit.*, Vol. II, p. 180.)

destroyed in the course of time; iron and steel used in machinery are subject to corrosion or otherwise lose their usefulness. In addition, as a result of technical progress, improved means of labour become available, especially better new machinery and equipment. This is called *moral wear and tear,* or *economic obsolescence,*[77] as opposed to the physical wear and tear discussed above. Often, means of labour cease to be useful due to accident (e.g. destruction of a factory by fire, destruction of buildings by flooding, the sinking of a ship, the loss of railroad cars in an accident, etc.).

It should be mentioned that whether given means of production are working or fixed capital depends on the manner in which they are used in the production process, and on whether they are used up in the course of one production period or in the course of several such periods; it does not depend, however, on their actual physical nature. The ox used as a working animal is fixed capital; when fattened for slaughter it becomes an object of labour, and thus working capital.[78] In the first case, the production period is the annual period of cultivation of crops and the ox is used over a large number of such periods; in the second case the production period is the time needed for fattening the ox before it is slaughtered, and it is utilized as an object of labour for one such period only.

The period of use of the means of production in the production process is called the *utilization period.* The utilization period

---

[77] Marx used the term "moral depreciation", on the understanding that the adjective "moral" is not strictly correct, but is used as a distinction from physical wear and tear: "But in addition to the material wear and tear, a machine also undergoes what we may call *moral depreciation.*" (K. Marx, *op. cit.,* Vol. I, p. 402.) S. Strumilin has the following remarks on this term in his *Ocherki ob khozyaystvye SSSR,* Moscow, 1957: "It is not correct to use the term moral wear and tear. It was only in a society with the categoric rule of 'Look after your own pocket' (as Shchedrin said) that the concepts of economic and moral losses were not differentiated. In Soviet conditions it would be more correct to oppose the concept of physical wear and tear to the designation '*economic obsolescence*', replacing the term 'moral wear and tear' as one of many survivals of capitalism in human consciousness." Today, the designation "economic wear and tear" is also often used.

[78] See K. Marx, *op. cit.,* Vol. II, p. 184.

may be numerically expressed as either a unit of time (the production period) or a calendar unit of time (e.g. a month or year). If we measure the utilization period taking the production period as our unit of measure, then the utilization period of working capital means always equals unity, while the utilization period of fixed capital means is a multiple of the production period. However, this method of measurement makes it impossible to directly compare utilization periods of means of production in various divisions and branches of production. For this reason, the utilization period is usually measured in calendar units of time.

Thus, means of production are used up in the course of time, and, as we have seen, this is the result of either utilization in the production process (as is usually the case) or for other reasons which over the course of time cause them to lose their usefulness. The pace at which means of production wear out is measured by their rate of wear and tear, which is the reciprocal of the utilization period. As with the utilization period, the rate of wear and tear can be measured either as a unit of time appropriate to the production period, or as a calendar unit of time. If, for example, the production period is 3 months and a machine is utilized for 10 years in a given production process, then working capital means which are used up in the course of one production period have a utilization period equal to one production period; the rate of consumption is equal to one. The machine, on the other hand, has a utilization period equal to forty production periods; its rate of wear and tear is one-fortieth of one production period. However, if we calculate according to the calendar, then the utilization period of working capital means is one-quarter of a year, while the annual rate of consumption is four (i.e. it is necessary to renew working capital means four times a year); the utilization period of the machine is 10 years and its rate of wear and tear is one-tenth annually (i.e. it will be necessary to replace the machine after 10 years of service).

XI

The production process does not end with the completion of one production period. It is constantly repeated, for material goods are repeatedly needed to satisfy human needs: "Whatever the form of the process of production in a society, it must be a continuous process, and must continue to go periodically through the same phases. A society can no more cease to produce than it can cease to consume. When viewed, therefore, as a connected whole, and as proceeding with incessant renewal, every social process of production is, at the same time, a *process of repro-duction*."[79] Reproduction is a continually repeated process of production; it is a social process, like production, and it is there-fore called the *social* process of reproduction.

Since, as we know, means of production are used up in the production process, there is a need *to renew* the used-up means; otherwise the production process could not be continued. The means used up are renewed by producing other means of produc-tion as replacements. This means that a certain quantity of prod-ucts must have the physical properties of the used-up means of production, since it is only as such that they can serve as re-placements. According to Marx: "The conditions of production are also those of reproduction. No society can go on producing — in other words, no society can reproduce — unless it constantly reconverts a part of its products into means of production, or elements of fresh products. All other circumstances remaining the same, the only mode by which it can reproduce its wealth and maintain it at one level is by replacing the means of pro-duction—i.e. the [tools] of labour, the raw material, and the auxiliary substances consumed in the course of the year—by an equal quantity of the same kind of articles; these must be sepa-rated from the mass of the yearly products, and thrown afresh in-to the process of production."[80]

Making use of renewed means of production requires a repe-tition of the various operations which make up the production

---

[79] K. Marx, *op. cit.*, Vol. I, pp. 577–9.
[80] *Ibid.*, p. 578.

process. The reproduction process is a continual repetition of given labour processes. For this to be possible the capability of the various members of society to carry out their work must be maintained. That is, the number of people performing given work and their capacity to do so must be sustained. In addition, people who lose their capacity to do given work due to old age, and also the deceased, must be replaced by new people who have these capacities. These people equipped with the capacities to do given work are called *labour-power*.[81] Hence, aside from the need for renewal of the used-up means of production, there is also the need for constant renewal of the labour-power available in society.

The renewal of labour-power is made up of two processes. First, the available labour-power must be constantly maintained. Labour-power is exhausted in the labour process, and must be constantly renewed by nourishment, rest, appropriate leisure facilities, housing conditions and efforts to maintain skills (or occupational qualifications). This renewal of the available labour-power requires that several biological, social and cultural needs of the working members of society be met. Failure to fully or adequately meet these needs leads to a decline in capacity, i.e. to a decline in labour-power.

Nevertheless, the available labour-power cannot be maintained —or constantly renewed—for an indeterminate period of time. This is so because of natural biological processes of ageing and dying, as a result of which after a certain period of time the available individual labour-power declines and, finally, ceases entirely due to old age or death. In the end, each individual withdraws from participation in the social process. Secondly, thus, the renewal of society's available labour-power entails the replacement of individuals withdrawing from the social labour process by new individuals suitably skilled. This renewal of working human

---

[81] The term "labour-power" was introduced by Marx to distinguish between it and the work actually carried out: "By *labour-power* or *capacity for labour* is to be understood the aggregate of those mental and physical capabilities existing in a human being, which he exercises whenever he produces a use-value of any description." (K. Marx, *op. cit.*, Vol. I, p. 145.)

generations in society requires primarily further procreation to replace in future the older generation; this is the process of *human reproduction.*[82] But this alone is not sufficient. The new generation must for a certain period of time be nursed, raised and then taught the skills and proficiency needed for specific work in the production process—that is, it must gain a given occupational qualification. This is all part of the process of renewal of those working in society. Hence, the renewal of generations also involves satisfying the many biological, social and cultural needs of the new generation and of those older persons who are engaged in nursing, raising, teaching and shaping the new generation.

The renewal of society's labour-power, consequently, includes both the renewal of available labour-power and the renewal of each generation of working people.[83] Both of these two processes, making up the renewal of society's labour-power, are connected with the necessity of meeting various biological, social and cultural needs. This, in turn, requires the production of goods which meet these needs; they are called *consumption goods* (which also include various service facilities, such as medical treatment, educational and recreational facilities, etc.).[84] A certain quantity of products must therefore be consumption goods, needed for the renewal of society's labour-power. These consumption goods

---

[82] Human reproduction is defined as follows: "Human reproduction is the continual renewal of departing generations by the new." (A. Boyarskii and P. Shusherin, *Demograficheskaya statistika* [*Demographic Statistics*], Moscow, 1955, p. 90.)

[83] K. Marx presents it in the following way: "The labouring power of a man exists only in his living individuality. A certain mass of necessaries must be consumed by a man to grow up and maintain his life. But the man, like the machine, will wear out, and must be replaced by another man. Beside the mass of necessaries required for his own maintenance, he wants another amount of necessaries to bring up a certain quota of children that are to replace him on the labour market and to perpetuate the race of labourers." (K. Marx, *Value, Price and Profit*, Chicago [n.d.], p. 75.) Engels presents this question in a similar way. (See *Engels on 'Capital'*, New York, 1937, pp. 3–7).

[84] On services, see O. Lange, *op. cit.*, Vol. I, pp. 3–4.

are called the *means of subsistence necessary for the maintenance of labour-power.*[85]

XII

In consequence, it turns out that the reproduction process requires constant production of a certain quantity of means of production allocated to replace used-up means of production; reproduction also constantly calls for a certain quantity of products in the form of subsistence means, necessary for the maintenance of society's labour-power. At a certain level of development of productive forces, above primitive conditions, the quantity of products produced in the social production process is more than that needed to renew means of production and labour-power.[86] This surplus quantity of products is called surplus production, i.e. production over and above that necessary for renewal in the reproduction process. Taken as a whole, this is the *surplus product* of the social production process.[87]

---

[85] The term is from Marx (see *Capital*, Vol. I, p. 149). It should be remembered, however, that these means are necessary not only to sustain life biologically, but also to sustain those social and cultural conditions which are necessary to maintain society's labour-power.

[86] According to Engels, this surplus began to appear at the middle level of barbarity (in L. H. Morgan's classification of the stages of social development), i.e. after the introduction of livestock raising, metal working, weaving and crop raising. See F. Engels, *Origin of the Family, Private Property and the State*, ed. *cit.*, p. 38. (This was confirmed by Ludwik Krzywicki in "Rozwój stosunków gospodarczych" [Development of Economic Relations], *Świat i Człowiek* [*The World and Man*], paper III, Warsaw, 1912, p. 294.) Melville J. Herskovits gives the example of modern tribes which still do not produce a surplus of products over and above that needed to renew the means of production and labour-power; included are Bushmen, Hotentots, Eskimos, aborigines of the Tierra del Fuego, and certain Indian tribes in Bolivia and the Gran Chaco Plateau. All other so-called primitive peoples known to ethnographers produce surplus products. (See M. J. Herskovitz, *op. cit.*, Chapter 18.)

[87] The term was first used in this sense by Marx (see *Capital*, Vol. I, p. 213). The Physiocrats had used a similar term earlier (*produit net*), as did the classical economists (surplus product) who attempted to express the same concept as Marx did. However, these earlier definitions of surplus product

The various individual products making up the surplus product may vary in form and use. If they all are used exclusively for consumption, then production of the means of production will be just adequate to renew the means of production used up in the production process. This is called *simple reproduction*.[88] If, however, some of the products making up the surplus product are the means of production, there will be an increase in the stock of means of production used in the production process. This is called *expanded reproduction*.[89] In expanded reproduction the stocks of the means of production are increased; as a rule, this leads to an increase in the level of production. Increasing the stock of means of production generally requires an increase in the number of concrete operations carried out by the surplus means of production. This, in turn, requires an increase in society's labour-power. As a result, the surplus means of consumption become necessary means of subsistence, with which their material form is often connected (e.g. special foods, or accessories and equipment for occupational training). Thus, in expanded reproduction some of the products making up the surplus product are the means of production, while others, which are the means of consumption, become the necessary means of subsistence.

In certain circumstances, such as war, or natural disasters (earthquakes, floods, harvest failures, etc.), the products turned out in the production process may be insufficient for the renewal of means of production and labour-power. This may be the result of a significant decline in production (e.g. in the case of harvest

lacked in precision. An exact definition was given only by Marx on the basis of his differentiation between the concepts of labour and labour-power. The history of earlier usages of the term "surplus product" is given in Marx's *Theory of Surplus Value*, London, 1951. Many modern authors use the term economic surplus. So does, for example, M. J. Herskovitz (*op. cit.*, p. 395), using it as a synonym for the Marxian term "surplus product". Paul Baran (*The Political Economy of Growth*, New York, 1957, pp. 25–43) also uses the term "economic surplus"; for him, economic surplus is partly narrower and partly wider a concept than the Marxian surplus product. Baran points this out himself (pp. 25–26).

[88] The term is from Marx; see *Capital*, Vol. I, pp. 577 ff.

[89] See K. Marx, *op. cit.*, Vol. I, pp. 592, 598; Vol. II, p. 521.

failure) or of a strong increase in the wear and tear of the means of production used for renewal (e.g. due to war destruction or earthquakes). In this case the stock of the means of production used in the production process and/or labour-power declines, as a result of which there is a decline in the level of production. This is called *contracted reproduction.*[90]

As we can see, there are various numerical relationships in the production process. There is the relation of the quantity of the necessary means of subsistence to the quantity of products needed to renew the used-up means of production (which, in turn, depend on the stock of the means of production being utilized and the rate of wear and tear). There is also a relation between the quantities of products produced and their differing use (in production or consumption). There are also given relations for the amount of used-up means of production, the number of specific operations carried out, and the level of production. There is also the problem of what part of the various products constitutes jointly the surplus product; what is the physical make-up of the surplus product; and to what degree the various products making up the surplus product are allocated to increasing the stock of means of production or to increasing the necessary means of subsistence of the labour-power. And finally, the question arises of the rate of growth of production under various conditions of expanded reproduction. All these quantitative relations require close examination.

---

[90] To the best of the author's knowledge this concept was first introduced by Bukharin; he used the term, "negative expanded reproduction" (N. Bukharin, *Die Oekonomik der Transformationsperiode* [*The Economy of the Transition Period*], Hamburg, 1922, p. 43). In the capitalist mode of production contracted reproduction may also be the result of certain phases of the trade cycles, i.e. during crises and depressions.

CHAPTER II

Quantitative Relations in Production

I

Production is a collection of co-ordinated labour processes in which conscious and purposeful human activity or labour transforms objects of labour, making use of means of labour. In other words, in production human labour and means of production are brought together; the result is the product. According to Marx, "*In the labour process*, therefore, man's activity, with the help of the [tools] of labour, effects an alteration, designed from the commencement, in the material worked upon. The process disappears in the *product*. ... Labour has incorporated itself with its [object]: the former is materialized, the latter transformed. That which in the labourer appeared as movement now appears in the product as a fixed quality without motion. The blacksmith forges and the product is a forging. If we examine the whole process from the point of view of its result, *the product*, it is plain that both the [*tools*] and the [*object*] *of labour* are *means of production*."[1]

Both labour and means of production are factors of the production process; they are *production factors*. These factors are specific kinds of labour, such as weaving, spinning, metalworking, ploughing, carrying objects, etc., as well as various concrete means of production such as wool, iron ore, sulphuric acid, shovels, metal-working machines, electric motors, locomotives, etc. The various specific kinds of labour are *personal factors of production*, and require not only that there be available people

[1] K. Marx, *Capital*, Vol. I, London, 1918, p. 160.

54

capable of working but also that they have appropriate skills. Various other means of production are *material factors of production* and their concrete character and form are expressions of production techniques, i.e. material techniques used in various labour processes.[2]

In order to turn out the product, personal and material factors of production must be brought together. The manner in which this is brought about differs in various social production processes and, what is more, this is the characteristic trait of a given historical mode of production. Nevertheless, a necessary condition for production in all social systems is that these factors are more and more brought together. This was stated clearly by Marx: "Whatever the social form of production, labourers and means of production always remain factors of it. But in a state of separation from each other either of these factors can be such only potentially. For production to go on at all they must unite. The specific manner in which this union is accomplished distinguishes the different economic epochs of the structure of society from one another."[3] Nevertheless, in this grouping together, the roles of the personal and material factors of production are different. The personal factors, or human labour in its various concrete forms, are active, creative factors of the production process, while the means of production, or the material factors of production, are the material objects which human labour sets in motion and transforms. "In so far then as labour is such specific productive activity, in so far as it is spinning, weaving, or forging, it raises, by *mere contact*, the means of production from the dead, makes them living factors of the labour process, and combines with them to form the new products."[4]

For this reason, human labour which is an active factor in the production process is called *living labour*, as opposed to means of production which are the result of earlier work which

---

[2] The terms "personal" and "material" factors of production were introduced by Marx (*Capital*, Vol. II, Chicago, 1919, p. 44).

[3] *Ibid.*, pp. 36–37.

[4] K. Marx, *op. cit.*, Vol. I, p. 182.

is, as it were, *stored up* in them.[5] Marx characterizes the active role of living labour in the production process as follows: "A machine which does not serve the purposes of labour is useless. In addition, it falls a prey to the destructive influence of natural forces. Iron rusts and wood rots. Yarn with which we neither weave nor knit is cotton wasted. Living labour must seize upon these things and rouse them from their death-sleep, change them from mere possible use-values into real and effective ones."[6] The means of production become "bathed in the fire of labour's organism, and, as it were, made alive for the performance of their functions in the process."[7] In this way, living labour sets and maintains the production process in motion, and represents the conscious and purposeful human activity which makes use of the results of prior labour which is stored up in the means of production. Means of production are the means used by human activity (living labour) to achieve the goal: the product.[8]

The production process described above (a collection of labour and means of production which leads to the turning out of a product) may be shown schematically:

---

[5] See K. Marx, *op. cit.*, Vol. I., p. 160: "Though a use-value, in the form of a *product*, issues from the labour process, yet other use-values, products of previous labour, enter into it as *means of production.*"

[6] *Ibid.*, pp. 162–3.

[7] *Ibid.*, p. 163.

[8] The lack of distinction between the active role of personal factors of production (i.e. human labour) and the auxiliary role of material factors of production which are material means for human activity is the basis for the theory of production factors, which originated with J. B. Say (*Traité d'économie politique*, Paris, 1803). This theory has been widely accepted by representatives of the Austrian and neo-classical schools as equal factors of production which together turn out the product. Each of these factors of production has an equal "share" in the product which is their joint creation. This theory makes a fetish of the production process, seeing it as a natural automatic process whereby the factors of production are transformed into the product. In setting human labour equal to the material factors of production, this theory disregards the humanist character of the production process as conscious and purposeful human activity. In practice, this theory serves as a basis for apologists of that distribution of the social product which is specific to the capitalist mode of production as being the result of the natural character of the production process. (See O. Lange, *Political Economy*, Vol. I, Oxford–Warsaw, 1963.)

$$\begin{bmatrix} \text{labour} \\ \text{means of production} \end{bmatrix} \rightarrow \text{product.}$$

We introduce the letter **L** to represent labour, **Q** to represent the means of production, and **P** to represent the product; this diagram may now be shown as follows:

$$\begin{bmatrix} L \\ Q \end{bmatrix} \rightarrow P.$$

In this diagram **L** is a collection of various kinds of specific labour (e.g. spinning, weaving, metal-working, assembling, masonry, sowing, ploughing, etc.). In a similar manner, **Q** is a collection of various specific means of production, e.g. coal, iron ore, tools and machines, various kinds of land, i.e. arable land, grassland or woodland, etc. The various specific types of labour or means of production making up **L** or **Q** are called the *components* of a given set.[9]

---

[9] The components of set L, i.e. the various specific kinds of labour, are represented by $L_1, L_2, ..., L_m$, and the components of set Q, or the various specific means of production, by $Q_1, Q_2, ..., Q_n$. These sets can now be presented symbolically as follows:

$$L = \begin{bmatrix} L_1 \\ L_2 \\ \vdots \\ L_m \end{bmatrix} \quad \text{and} \quad Q = \begin{bmatrix} Q_1 \\ Q_2 \\ \vdots \\ Q_n \end{bmatrix}.$$

The above diagram, representing the production process, may then be written in a more developed form:

$$\begin{bmatrix} L_1 \\ L_2 \\ \vdots \\ L_m \\ Q_1 \\ Q_2 \\ \vdots \\ Q_n \end{bmatrix} \rightarrow P.$$

This diagram shows the various components of sets **L** and **Q**, thus making clear the group character of labour and of means of production.

Product **P** at the right-hand side of the diagram may be a single commodity turned out in the production process. Often, however, a larger group of products is produced simultaneously in the same production process. For example, various types of radio and television sets, various grades of gasoline, paraffins, asphalt and oils, and various kinds of meat, fat, leather, and bristles — are all produced as part of the same process of pig-breeding. In such cases we speak of *joint production*. Sometimes, in joint production a main product for which production is carried out is distinguished from by-products. For example, the main product in pig-breeding is meat, while fat, leather and bristles are by-products; gasoline is the main product in oil-refining. However, it is often difficult to make a distinction between the main products and by-products; all products appearing in the joint production process are equally the goal of productive activity. This is true in the case of the joint production of radios and television sets, or of motor-cycles, bicycles and motor-boats. If it is a joint production process we are dealing with, then **P** in the above diagram represents a set of various products turned out in the joint production process; the individual products are the components.[10]

The specific kinds of labour, the means of production and the product (or products in case of joint production) are quantities expressed by compound numbers stating the units by which they are measured. Labour is usually measured in units of time (man-hours), i.e. in the number of hours worked by a worker performing a given operation. Products are measured either in units of weight, volume, length, energy (e.g. kilowatts), or simply by the number of pieces. As far as means of production are con-

---

[10] In this case the various components of products **P** can be denoted by $P_1, P_2, \ldots P_k$, or

$$\mathbf{P} = \begin{bmatrix} P_1 \\ P_2 \\ \vdots \\ P_k \end{bmatrix}.$$

This expression can be placed at the right-hand side of the diagram given in footnote 9.

cerned, units of measurement vary for working and fixed capital means. Working capital means are entirely used up during one production period. They are measured in units similar to those used for products: weight, volume, length, power, number of pieces, etc. However, fixed capital means maintain their natural form for more than one production period; they are used in the course of the production period and maintain their usefulness later. Thus, what we need is not a measure of their being used up, as is the case with working capital means, but a measure the duration of use. Utilization is measured in units of time, i.e. in terms of hours a given machine, building, or car is utilized (thus, in terms of machine-hours, building-hours, car-hours, etc.). These units of measurement of various kinds of labour, of means of production and of products are called *physical units*.

The amount of labour put into the production process, the quantity of used-up working capital means of production, and the utilized quantity of fixed capital means of production are jointly called *outlay*.[11] The quantity of products turned out is called the *return*[12] of a given production process. As we see, the outlay (or outlays) and return are measured in physical units. Outlays and returns are given for a specific period of time, e.g. for the production period, or for a calendar unit of time (month, quarter, year, etc.). Thus, they are measured as "so-and-so" many physical units per "such-and-such a period of time", i.e., a quantity of physical units in a given time period. If the time period under consideration changes, the levels of outlays or returns change proportionately. This is expressed by saying that outlays and returns are flows of physical units over a given time. However, the amount of fixed capital means active in the production process (as opposed to its utilization) is measured in physical units, disregarding the time factor, e.g. the quantity of machinery, buildings, area of cultivated land, etc. Such magnitudes defined without reference to time are called *stocks*.[13] There are also stocks

---

[11] In French, *dépense*; in German, *Aufwand*; in Russian, *zatraty*.

[12] In French, *rendement*, in German, *Ertrag*; in Russian, *pryikhod*.

[13] As is known, all physical magnitudes can be expressed in units of length, mass and time (denoted by L, M, T), or, in terms of the metric system,

of working capital means (as opposed to their outlay, or utilization in the production process, which is a flow).

Outlays of various kinds of labour and means of production and the return on a given production process may be established for specific plants or for a group of plants (e.g. a trust or an amalgamation of enterprises), or even for an entire branch of production (e.g. the steel industry). Outlays and returns for a group of plants or for an entire production branch are calculated by adding up the outlays and returns of the individual plants. The outlays of the various specific kinds of labour or of the various concrete means of production (and in the case of joint production, also of the various products) are added up separately. The result is a set of totals which represents either outlays of labour or of means of production, or the returns of a group of plants or of a production branch. These sums are the components of the set.

The sets representing outlays of labour, outlays of means of production, and returns may be subject to further refinements. Such sets can be added together by summing up their compo-

---

i.e. centimetres, grams, seconds (cm, g, sec). The units in which the physical magnitude is expressed are dimensions. For example, the dimension of speed is symbolically $\dfrac{L}{T} = LT^{-1}$; the dimension of acceleration, LT^{-2}; the dimension of force, MLT^{-2}; the dimension of mechanical work ML^2T^{-2}, etc. In an analogous manner we can speak of the dimensions of economic magnitudes. If we consider, for the time being, magnitudes measured in physical units and we denote the physical units by N, stocks have N as their dimension, and flows NT^{-1}. W. S. Jevons was first to use systematically in economics the concept of the dimension of a specific quantity. (See W. S. Jevons, *The Theory of Political Economy*, London, 1871, Chapter 3.) Certain errors in Jevons's treatment of the problem were corrected by P. H. Wicksteed (*The Common Sense of Political Economy*, London, 1946, Vol. II, Appendix, "Dimensions of Economic Quantities"). This Appendix is a reprint of an article in *Palgrave's Dictionary of Political Economy*, London, 1894. See also S. C. Evans, *Mathematical Introduction to Economics*, New York–London, 1930, Chapter 2; for the more recent works, see A. Boyarski, *Matematiko-ekonomicheskiye ocherki* (*Mathematical and Economic Notes*), Moscow, 1962, Chapter 7. See also O. Lange, *The Theory of Reproduction and Accumulation*, Oxford–Warsaw, 1969, pp. 8–11.

nents; the result is a new set whose components are the sums of the components in the sets added up. In addition, since outlays and returns are flows, the sets may be multiplied by real (not compound) numbers. In this case, each component is multiplied by a given number, and the results form the components of a new set. With multiplication there is a change in the accepted period of time, e.g., in changing from time measured in production periods to time measured by the calendar, or on changing from one calendar unit to another (e.g. from months to years). It follows that the sets can also be divided by a real number (multiplication by its reciprocal) and subtracted (by adding a set multiplied by -1).

Magnitudes expressed by arbitrarily ordered sets of real numbers, which can be added by summing up their various components, and which can be multiplied by a real number, multiplying the various components by this number, are called *vectors*.[14] The real numbers of which the set is formed are the

---

[14] Let $(x_1, x_2, ..., x_n)$ and $(y_1, y_2, ..., y_n)$ be ordered sets of n real numbers. Such sets are said to be n-dimensional vectors and the numbers $x_1, x_2, ..., x_n$ and $y_1, y_2, ..., y_n$ are the components of the vectors. If

$$\mathbf{x} = \begin{bmatrix} x_1 \\ x_2 \\ \cdot \\ \cdot \\ x_n \end{bmatrix} \quad \text{and} \quad \mathbf{y} = \begin{bmatrix} y_1 \\ y_2 \\ \cdot \\ \cdot \\ y_n \end{bmatrix},$$

then

$$\mathbf{x} + \mathbf{y} = \begin{bmatrix} x_1 + y_1 \\ x_2 + y_2 \\ \cdot \\ \cdot \\ x_n + y_n \end{bmatrix};$$

also

$$\lambda \mathbf{x} = \begin{bmatrix} \lambda x_1 \\ \lambda x_2 \\ \cdot \\ \cdot \\ \lambda x_n \end{bmatrix} \quad \text{and} \quad \lambda \mathbf{y} = \begin{bmatrix} \lambda y_1 \\ \lambda y_2 \\ \cdot \\ \cdot \\ \lambda y_n \end{bmatrix},$$

where λ is any real (scalar) number. The vectors' components may also be written in rows instead of in columns, as $\mathbf{x} = (x_1, x_2, ..., x_n)$ and

vector's *components*. Magnitudes expressed by a single real number (not by a set of numbers), as opposed to vectors, are called *scalars*. Scalars may be measured according to a given "scale" (e.g. length or weight). But vectoral magnitudes cannot always be measured according to a given scale, for each component may be changed in a different proportion. It can be measured according to a given scale only in the special case when all components change in the same proportion (i.e. are doubled or tripled). Outlays of labour and of means of production (**L** and **Q** in the above diagram) are vectors. Return **P** is a scalar if only one kind of product is turned out; it is a vector with joint production.

II

The basic quantitative relation in production is the relation between return and labour outlays on the one hand and the means of production on the other. This relation depends on what Marx called the productiveness of labour, "whereby the same quantum of labour yields, in a given time, a greater or less quantum of product, dependent on the degree of development in the conditions of production."[15] Productivity of labour is dependent on the overall development of productive forces in given historical conditions. As Marx said: "This productiveness is determined by various circumstances, among others, by the average amount of skill of the workmen, the state of science and the degree of its practical application, the social organization of production, the extent and capabilities of the means of production, and by *physical*

$y = (y_1, y_2, ..., y_n)$. In addition, vectors x and y are equal, i.e. x = y when all their components are equal $(x_1 = y_1, x_2 = y_2, ..., x_n = y_n)$.

[15] K. Marx, *op. cit.*, Vol. I, p. 528. On the concept of labour productivity see S. Strumilin, *Problemy proizvodityelnosti truda* (*Problems of Labour Productivity*), Moscow, 1956 and F. D. Markuzon, "Izmyenyeniye proizvoditelnosti truda v kapitalisticheskikh gosudarstvakh", *Uchenye zapisky po statistikie* (Changes in Labour Productivity in Capitalist Economies, *Scientific Statistical Papers*), Moscow, 1957, Vol. III, p. 249. See also B. Minc, *Ekonomia polityczna socjalizmu* (*The Political Economy of Socialism*), Warsaw, 1963, pp. 190–3.

conditions."[16] The concrete result of a change in labour productivity is a change in the quantity of the product, or return, connected with a given outlay of labour (i.e. living labour), and of means of production.

In order to investigate this connection more closely we will examine outlays of various kinds of labour and of various specific means of production per unit of production. This is called *unit outlay*. It is calculated by dividing total outlays by the level of production; the resultant quotients are the components of unit outlays. Using the same symbols as introduced in the above diagram (page 57) showing the production process, unit outlay may be expressed as follows:[17]

$$\begin{bmatrix} \dfrac{L}{P} \\[2mm] \dfrac{Q}{P} \end{bmatrix}$$

In this diagram L/P is a set (vector) of unit outlays of various specific kinds of labour, and Q/P is the set (vector) of unit outlays

---

[16] K. Marx, *op. cit.*, Vol. I, p. 7. "By *increase in the productiveness of labour*, we mean, generally, *an alteration in the labour-process*, of such a kind as to shorten the labour-time socially necessary for the production of a commodity, and to endow a given quantity of labour with the *power* of producing a greater quantity of use-value." (*Ibid.*, p. 303.)

[17] In this diagram, L/P and Q/P are the product of vectors L and Q multiplied by the real number $\dfrac{1}{P}$. Let $L_1, L_2, ..., L_m$ and $Q_1, Q_2, ..., Q_n$ be the components of these vectors. Then

$$\frac{L}{P} = \begin{bmatrix} \dfrac{L_1}{P} \\[1mm] \dfrac{L_2}{P} \\[1mm] \vdots \\[1mm] \dfrac{L_m}{P} \end{bmatrix} \quad \text{and} \quad \frac{Q}{P} = \begin{bmatrix} \dfrac{Q_1}{P} \\[1mm] \dfrac{Q_2}{P} \\[1mm] \vdots \\[1mm] \dfrac{Q_n}{P} \end{bmatrix}$$

and the above diagram may be presented in the form of clearly visible components.

of various specific means of production. The components of these sets, or, in other words, the various unit outlays, are often called *technical coefficients of production*,[18] for they depend on the technical conditions in which the production process takes place. The production coefficients are thus the outlays of means of production (i.e. of specific kinds of labour and of specific means of production) which under given technical conditions are necessary for producing one unit of production.[19]

Unit outlays, or coefficients of production, are measured in physical units, i.e. a given number of tons of ore per ton of steel, so many tons of coal per kilowatt of electricity; so many machine-hours or man-hours per metre of cloth, etc. They express the relation of two flows (of outlays and the product) to each other in a given period of time; when we divide, the time-period is shortened and the relation of physical units remains (e.g. tons of ore to tons of steel).[20]

Dividing outlays by the quantity of products turned out is possible, of course, only when the return is scalar. With joint production, the return is a vector, i.e. a collection of various products. In this case, we choose one of the products according to conventions as a "product of reference" and then calculate the various unit outlays, or coefficients of production, in relation to it. In this case, in addition to coefficients of production we also have additional coefficients which indicate the quantity of the

---

[18] See O. Lange, *Introduction to Econometrics*, 3rd ed., Oxford–Warsaw, 1966, pp. 224–5, and O. Lange, *Theory of Reproduction ...*, pp. 54–55. Production coefficients were systematically introduced in the economic analysis of Leon Walras, *Éléments d'économie politique pure* (*Elements of Pure Political Economy*), Paris, 1874, Chapter 4. Walras used the term *coéfficients de fabrication*.

[19] In the practice of economic planning production coefficients are called *technical norms*.

[20] Let $N_f T^{-1}$ be the dimension of outlays of the factor of production, and let $N_p T^{-1}$ be the product (or return). Then the dimension of unit outlays is

$$\frac{N_f T^{-1}}{N_p T^{-1}} = \frac{N_f}{N_p}.$$

various products turned out with one unit of the reference product.[21]

In place of unit outlays of factors of production, or coefficients of production, we may also use their reciprocals. The reciprocal of a unit outlay is the productivity of the given factor of production. Thus, we speak of the productivity of labour and the productivity of means of production. Productivity of labour is a collection (vector) of the productivities of various specific kinds of living labour used in the production process, while productivity of means of production is a collection (vector) of the productivities of various specific means of production. Each specific kind of labour and each specific means of production has its own productivity.[22] These productivities depend on the given production technique, although there is a connection between the productivity of labour (i.e. of living labour) and outlays of means of production. As a rule, a higher level of labour productivity requires greater outlays of means of production connected with labour, and results in the processing of more raw material and in equipping living labour with a greater quantity of means of labour. This was pointed out by Marx: "The degree of *productivity of labour*, in a given society, is expressed in the *relative extent of the means of production* that one labourer, during a given time, with the same tension of labour-power, turns into products. The mass of the means of production which he thus transforms, increases with the productiveness of his labour. ... The *increase* of [the productiveness of labour] appears, therefore, in *the diminution of the mass of labour in proportion to the mass of means of production*

---

[21] Let $P_1, P_2, ..., P_k$ be the components of vector $\mathbf{P}$ expressed as the returns on a joint production process, and let, for example, P_1 be the component representing the product of reference. Thus,

$$\frac{P_2}{P_1}, \frac{P_3}{P_1}, ..., \frac{P_k}{P_1}.$$

For a detailed discussion, see O. Lange, *Optimal Decisions*, Oxford–Warsaw, 1971, pp. 149–50.

[22] On the productivity of the means of production, see K. Marx, *op. cit.*, Vol. I, pp. 7, 618–19. He used the term "efficacy [*Wirkungsfähigkeit, Wirksamkeit*] of the means of production."

moved by it, or in the diminution of the subjective factor of the labour process as compared with the objective factor."[23]

A given production technique is characterized by a collection (vector) of unit outlays, or coefficients of production; or, what amounts to the same thing, it is a collection of the productivities of the various factors of production. A product may usually be produced according to various production techniques, or, in other words, *technical processes.* Each of these processes is characterized by its own vector of unit outlays (or coefficients of production). If a given product can be produced by *r* various technical processes, the situation is as shown in the diagram on page 67:[24]

---

[23] K. Marx. *op. cit.*, Vol.I, pp. 635–6: "But those means of production play a double part. The increase of some is a *consequence*, that of the others a *condition* of the increasing productivity of labour. For example, with the division of labour in manufacture, and with the use of machinery, more raw material is worked up at the same time, and, therefore, a greater mass of raw material and auxiliary substances enter into the labour process. That is the *consequence* of the increasing productivity of labour. On the other hand, the mass of machinery, beasts of burden, minerals, manures, drain-pipes, etc., is a condition of the increasing productivity of labour. So also is it with the means of production concentrated in buildings, furnaces, means of transport, etc. But whether condition or consequence, the growing extent of the means of production, as compared with the labour-power incorporated with them, is an expression of the growing productiveness of labour." (p. 636.)

[24] This table may be written in a more developed form which clearly shows the unit components of outlays of labour and the means of production. Thus:

$$
\begin{bmatrix}
\dfrac{L_{11}}{P} & \dfrac{L_{12}}{P} & \cdots & \dfrac{L_{1r}}{P} \\[2ex]
\dfrac{L_{21}}{P} & \dfrac{L_{22}}{P} & \cdots & \dfrac{L_{2r}}{P} \\[2ex]
\cdots & \cdots & \cdots & \cdots \\[1ex]
\dfrac{L_{m1}}{P} & \dfrac{L_{m2}}{P} & \cdots & \dfrac{L_{mr}}{P} \\[2ex]
\dfrac{Q_{11}}{P} & \dfrac{Q_{12}}{P} & \cdots & \dfrac{Q_{1r}}{P} \\[2ex]
\dfrac{Q_{21}}{P} & \dfrac{Q_{22}}{P} & \cdots & \dfrac{Q_{2r}}{P} \\[1ex]
\cdots & \cdots & \cdots & \cdots \\[1ex]
\dfrac{Q_{n1}}{P} & \dfrac{Q_{n2}}{P} & \cdots & \dfrac{Q_{nr}}{P}
\end{bmatrix}
$$

$$\begin{bmatrix} \dfrac{L_1}{P} & \dfrac{L_2}{P} & \cdots & \dfrac{L_r}{P} \\[2ex] \dfrac{Q_1}{P} & \dfrac{Q_2}{P} & \cdots & \dfrac{Q_r}{P} \end{bmatrix}.$$

In this diagram each column represents a collection (vector) of unit outlays specific to a given technical process. Each row gives the unit outlay of the factor of production needed in various technical processes. This diagram is called the *matrix of production techniques.*[25]

Technical processes may also differ from the point of view of the production period, which, however, can be reduced to differences in unit outlays. If in two technical processes the quantity of the used-up or utilized factors of production and the quantity of the product produced are the same, but one process lasts longer than the other, then the quantity of the product produced in one unit of time (i.e. the return) is less from the process having a longer production period; unit outlays are also correspondingly greater. This difference is expressed in the matrix of production technique. Outlays of factors of production may also be variously distributed over time in different technical processes. Outlays made in different time periods may in this case be treated as outlays

Here, the first subscript is the outlay of a given means of production; the second is the technical process. For example, L_{ij} is the outlay of the ith kind of labour in the jth technical process.

[25] Matrices are rectangular tables of numbers which may be subject to various algebraic calculations, such as addition or multiplication by a real number (scalar). As above, the matrix may also be seen as a collection of vectors. (See Appendix, "Mathematical Note", at the end of this chapter.) The presentation of various production techniques of a given product in matrix form was first introduced by T. C. Koopmans in "Analysis of Production as an Efficient Combination of Activities" in T. C. Koopmans (ed.), *Activity Analysis of Production and Allocation*, New York, 1951. A more thorough analysis is found in T. C. Koopmans, *Three Essays on the State of Economic Science*, New York, 1957, pp. 68–79. Koopmans calls the various technical processes *activities*; an analysis of the production process by examining the various technical processes, shown in the matrix columns, is called *activity analysis*. This latter term is now in general use. On activity analysis, see O. Lange, *Optimal Decisions, ed. cit.*, and R. G. D. Allen, *Mathematical Economics*, London, 1954.

of various factors of production. The time schedule for outlays
may thus be shown in the matrix of production technique.

The matrix of production technique pictures the multiplicity
of technical processes by which the product may be produced.
If the product is produced by one of the technical processes,
equivalent to one column of the unit outlays in our matrix, the
product is said to have been produced by a *pure* technical process.
It is possible, however, to produce a given product so that a certain
quantity of it is produced by one technical process, another
quantity by a second technical process, perhaps a third quantity
by yet another technical process, etc. In this case the product is
produced by a *mixed* technical process. The mixed process consists
in the production of various quantities of the same product by
different technical processes. When a mixed process is used,
unit outlays (coefficients of production) of the various factors
of production are the weighted average of all the unit outlays
making up the mixed process. The weights used are the quantities
of products produced by each technical process.

Let a_{i1} be the unit outlays of a given (the ith) factor of production in the first technical process and let a_{i2} be the unit outlays
of the same factor in a second technical process. Further, let
x_1 be the quantity of a given product produced by the first process,
and x_2 the quantity produced by the second process. Thus
outlays in the first technical process will be $a_{i1}x_1$, and in the
second process $a_{i2}x_2$. Total outlays of the factor of production
are then $a_{i1}x_1 + a_{i2}x_2$. A total of $x_1 + x_2$ of the product will be
produced in both technical processes. The unit outlays of the
production factor in the mixed technical process are thus:

$$\frac{a_{i1}x_1 + a_{i2}x_2}{x_1 + x_2}. \tag{1}$$

This is the weighted average of unit outlays in both processes.
The same holds true for all factors of production (i.e. all possible
indices of i). The same reasoning may be applied to any number
of technical processes. In this way, unit outlays specific to all
mixed technical processes may be deduced from the matrix of
production technique.

Within certain limits set by the character of each technical process, it is possible to change the dimensions of production, i.e. the quantity of the product. There are processes in which a change in the dimensions of production does not cause changes in unit outlays of the factors of production, i.e. of the coefficients of production; here, outlays are proportionate to the dimensions of production, and production coefficients (i.e. unit outlays) are constant. Such processes are thus *divisible*,[26] that is, they can be freely reduced to processes with small production dimensions in which the same proportions are maintained between outlays and returns, among the various outlays, and with joint production also among the various products. Divisible pure technical processes are characterized by the fact that they may also be replaced by mixed processes made up of pure processes of a smaller production dimension; each mixed process is also divisible, i.e. its production coefficients are not dependent on the production dimensions. This results from the fact that the weighted average of unit outlays in formula (1) is only dependent on the relation x_2/x_1, i.e. on the proportion in which the dimensions of production were distributed in the various production processes making up the mixed process. It is not dependent on the absolute dimensions of production. The joining together of mixed technical processes also gives a divisible process. Divisible technical processes thus can be freely mixed; the result will always be a divisible process.

III

In the various technical processes (pure or mixed) used to produce a given product certain connections are evident. Let us assume that the unit outlays of all factors of production in one technical process are greater than in any other process, or that unit outlays of at least one of the factors of production are higher while outlays of no other factor are less. This process is *inefficient*.

---

[26] Divisible technical processes are also called *linear* processes because the quantitative relation between outlays and returns is a simple proportion, i.e. a linear function.

An inefficient technical process will not be used in the production process, for it requires greater outlays of all factors of production, or of at least one of them without lower outlays of the other factors. Thus, inefficient technical processes should be removed from the technical production matrix; the corresponding columns should be crossed off. Two or more technical processes which require the same unit outlays of production factors are equivalent. Such technical processes may be treated as one process. If there are equivalent technical processes in the matrix of production technique, it is sufficient to leave one of them in the matrix and remove the rest as redundant, crossing off the appropriate columns.

Removing inefficient or equivalent technical processes from the matrix of production technique gives us an *effective* matrix of production technique. The effective matrix of production technique is the result of a process of selection in which inefficient or equivalent redundant technical processes are removed. The technical processes remaining after selection are the effective ones. In the production process, only effective technical processes (or perhaps mixed ones) are chosen.

Effective technical processes are characterized as follows. For any two processes unit outlays of at least one factor of production must be greater, and lower for at least one other factor, in one process than in the other. If unit outlays of all factors are equal, then the two processes are equivalent; and if unit outlays of one of the factors in one process were more or less than in a second process, and unit outlays of all the other factors were equal in both processes, then one of the processes would be inefficient. Therefore, a greater unit outlay of one factor of production must be accompanied by lower unit outlays of at least one other factor (and vice versa). This property of effective technical processes is called the *law of substitution of outlays*. Along with a change in the technical process used to produce a certain quantity of a given product, there is always an increase in unit outlays of at least one factor of production and a decrease of the unit outlays of at least one other factor; i.e. there is a substitution of outlays.

The law of substitution of outlays can be also expressed as follows: with a change of a technical process there is a change of at least two factors of production. The proportions of the unit outlays of the other factors may either change or remain constant. Thus, substitution must include the outlays of at least two factors; it may, but not necessarily, include other factors. An especially important role is played in practice by substitution between personal and physical factors of production, i.e. between outlays of labour and of means of production. We shall return to this problem later.

In certain conditions, joint production is accompanied by the *law of substitution of returns* (i.e. of the quantities of the various products). This occurs when in two different technical processes unit outlays of factors of production are equal, but the processes differ in the quantities of products produced at given outlays of production factors; otherwise they would be equivalent. If with equal outlays of production factors one process produces more (less) of a given product than another process, then it must produce less (more) of at least one other product; otherwise, one process would be inefficient (with the same outlays of production factors one process would produce less of a given product than the second process with the same level of outlays for all other products). As with outlays of production factors, substitution here must also concern at least two products; it may, but not necessarily, concern more.

When the effective technical processes are divisible, we are faced with the *law of an increasing rate of substitution of outlays* in addition to the law of simple substitution; with joint production we are additionally faced with the *law of a decreasing rate of substitution of returns*.

Let us consider three effective technical processes. Let a_{i1}, a_{i2}, and a_{i3} be the unit outlays (coefficients of production) of the ith factor of production in each of the three processes; unit outlays of the jth factor of production will then be a_{j1}, a_{j2} and a_{j3}. Let us assume that the outlays of these two factors are subject to substitution. Substituting the second process for the first will increase unit outlays of the ith factor by $a_{i2}-a_{i1}$ and decrease

unit outlays of the *j*th factor by $a_{j2}-a_{j1}$.[27] The absolute value
of the relation of these changes in unit outlays, or

$$\left|\frac{a_{i2}-a_{i1}}{a_{j2}-a_{j1}}\right|$$

expresses the increase of unit outlays of the *i*th factor of production
per unit decrease of unit outlays of the *j*th factor. This expression
is called the *rate of substitution*. If we replace the second technical
process by a third, and assume that unit outlays of the *i*th factor
will be increased while outlays of the *j*th decrease, we arrive at
the following rate of substitution:

$$\left|\frac{a_{i3}-a_{i2}}{a_{j3}-a_{j2}}\right|.$$

If, as we assume, the processes are divisible, the following
inequality must be satisfied:

$$\left|\frac{a_{i2}-a_{i1}}{a_{j2}-a_{j1}}\right|<\left|\frac{a_{i3}-a_{i2}}{a_{j3}-a_{j2}}\right|, \qquad (2)$$

i.e. in the substitution of outlays related to a consecutive chain
of technical processes, the rate of substitution increases. This
follows from the reasoning outlined below.

As we know, divisible technical processes can be mixed in an
arbitrary way. Let us take then any process being a mix of the
first and the third processes and producing the same quantity of
commodity (volume of production) as the second process. Let
us denote by a_{i2} and a_{j2} the unit outlays of the *i*th and the *j*th
factors of production in this mixed process. We have then according
to formula

$$\bar{a}_{i2}=\frac{a_{i1}x_1+a_{i3}x_3}{x_1+x_3} \quad \text{and} \quad \bar{a}_{j2}=\frac{a_{j1}x_1+a_{j3}x_3}{x_1+x_3},$$

where x_1 and x_3 denote the volume of production of the first and
the third processes being part of the mixed process. It follows that

[27] Since the factors are numbered in an arbitrary way, we may assume
that the unit outlays of the *i*th factor are increased while the unit outlays of
the *j*th factor are decreased.

$$\frac{\bar{a}_{i2}-a_{i1}}{\bar{a}_{j2}-a_{j1}} = \frac{a_{i1}x_1+a_{i3}x_3-a_{i1}(x_1+x_3)}{a_{j1}x_1+a_{j3}x_3-a_{j1}(x_1+x_3)} = \frac{a_{i3}-a_{i1}}{a_{j3}-a_{j1}}$$

and

$$\frac{a_{i3}-\bar{a}_{i2}}{a_{j3}-\bar{a}_{j2}} = \frac{a_{i3}(x_1+x_3)-a_{i1}x_1-a_{i3}x_3}{a_{j3}(x_1+x_3)-a_{j1}x_1-a_{j3}x_3} = \frac{a_{i3}-a_{i1}}{a_{j3}-a_{j1}}.$$

Thus we have

$$\frac{\bar{a}_{i2}-a_{i1}}{\bar{a}_{j2}-a_{j1}} = \frac{a_{i3}-\bar{a}_{i2}}{a_{j3}-\bar{a}_{j2}},$$

i.e. both these rates of substitution are equal.

If the second technical process is effective we have either

$$a_{i2} < \bar{a}_{i2} \quad \text{and} \quad a_{j2} \leqslant \bar{a}_{j2}$$

or

$$a_{i2} \leqslant \bar{a}_{i2} \quad \text{and} \quad a_{j2} < \bar{a}_{j2},$$

i.e. the unit outlay of one factor of production must be smaller in the second process than in the mixed process and the unit outlay of the second factor cannot be greater (otherwise the second process would be equivalent to the mixed one or would be inefficient). After substituting in this expression a_{i2} and a_{i3} for $\bar{a}_{i2}$ and $\bar{a}_{j2}$ and after taking into account these inequalities it turns out that on the left-hand side we decrease the numerator or increase the denominator or both. Instead, on the right-hand side we decrease the numerator or increase the denominator or both. In consequence, we obtain

$$\left|\frac{a_{i2}-a_{i1}}{a_{j2}-a_{j1}}\right| < \left|\frac{a_{i3}-a_{i2}}{a_{j3}-a_{j2}}\right|.$$

It turns out that in consecutive switching to other technical processes the rate of outlay substitution increases. This is the law of the increasing rate of substitution of outlays.[28] This law expresses growing difficulties in substitution: substitution of each subsequent unit of a given factor of production requires a greater and greater increase of the outlay of the second factor. This can also be expressed in the following way: in consecutive replace-

---

[28] A graphical interpretation of the law of the increasing rate of substitution is given in Section 6 of the Appendix, "Mathematical Note" at the end of this chapter.

ments of one factor of production by the other the relative productivity of the second factor decreases.

In an analogous way it can be shown that, in joint production
under conditions in which the law of substitution of returns
operates, the effective and divisible technical processes satisfy
in relation to the products the law of the decreasing rate of substitution.[29] Substitution of products becomes more and more
difficult: a decrease of one product by consecutive units results
in ever-smaller increases in the second product. It should be
noted that the law of the increasing rate of substitution of outlays
and the law of the decreasing rate of substitution of returns which
operate under certain conditions in joint production pertain
only to those factors of production or products which are included
in substitution. These laws express certain further limitations on
substitution: even where substitution occurs it takes place under
conditions of increasing difficulties.

The result of increasing difficulties in substitution, characteristic of divisible effective technical processes, is the *law of
increasing additional outlays*. This law operates when the volume
of production (the quantity of the product) is increased by consecutive switching from one technical process to another, the
outlays of all factors of production, except for one, remaining
unchanged. An increase in the volume of production under such
conditions requires an increase in the outlays of the factor which
is being changed or otherwise technical processes would not be
effective (we could increase production without increasing the
outlay of any factor, i.e. obtain the same quantity of product
with a lower unit outlay of at least one factor of production).
As to the relationship between outlay and product, this is equivalent to the law of substitution of outlays or returns in joint production.[30] It turns out that if effective technical processes are

---

[29] See on this subject Section 6 of the Appendix, "Mathematical Note".

[30] This becomes immediately apparent if the return is defined as a negative
outlay. Then an increase in outlay related to an increase in the quantity of
the product can be interpreted as an increase in outlay combined with a decrease
in another (negative) outlay, i.e. as the substitution of outlays. In a similar
way, we can interpret it as a substitution of returns if the outlay is treated as
a negative return.

divisible, consecutive unit increases in production require ever-greater additional outlays of the given factor.

Let the outlay of the ith factor be variable. Let us denote by a_{i1}, a_{i2}, a_{i3} its unit outlay in three processes and by x_1, x_2, x_3 the volume of production in these processes. We assume $x_1 < x_2 < x_3$. The outlay of a given factor in particular processes is $a_{i1}x_1, a_{i2}x_2, a_{i3}x_3$. In switching from the first to the second process, the outlay increases by $a_{i2}x_2 - a_{i1}x_1$, and in switching from the second to the third process by $a_{i3}x_3 - a_{i2}x_2$. Increases in outlay, i.e. additional outlays per unit of increase in the product, are:

$$\frac{a_{i2}x_2 - a_{i1}x_1}{x_2 - x_1} \quad \text{and} \quad \frac{a_{i3}x_3 - a_{i2}x_2}{x_3 - x_2}.$$

Instead of the second process we now consider a mixed process in which the quantity of product x_2 is obtained so that the quantity $\dfrac{x_1(x_3 - x_2)}{x_3 - x_1}$ is produced by the first process and the quantity $\dfrac{x_3(x_2 - x_1)}{x_3 - x_1}$ by the third process. Altogether we produce in the mixed process

$$\frac{x_1(x_3 - x_2)}{x_3 - x_1} + \frac{x_3(x_2 - x_1)}{x_3 - x_1} = x_2.$$

The outlay of a factor in such a mixed process is

$$\bar{a}_{i2}x_2 = \frac{a_{i1}x_1(x_3 - x_2) + a_{i3}x_3(x_2 - x_1)}{x_3 - x_1},$$

where $\bar{a}_{i2}$ denotes the unit outlay. We have then

$$\frac{\bar{a}_{i2}x_2 - a_{i2}x_1}{x_2 - x_1} = \frac{a_{i3}x_3 - \bar{a}_{i2}x_2}{x_3 - x_2}.$$

Since by assumption the second process is effective, then $a_{i2} < \bar{a}_{i2}$. Substituting this in the equation arrived at, we find that

$$\frac{a_{i2}x_2 - a_{i1}x_1}{x_2 - x_1} < \frac{a_{i3}x_3 - a_{i2}x_2}{x_3 - x_2}. \tag{3}$$

In consequence, it turns out that in consecutive switching from the first to the second process and from the second to the third process, etc., the initial outlay of the factor of production per unit increase in the product increases. This is the law of increasing additional outlays. Instead of additional outlays per unit increase in the commodity, we can consider its reciprocal. This reciprocal denotes an increase in the product corresponding to a unit of additional outlay, i.e. the productivity of additional outlay. Thus to increasing additional outlays there corresponds their decreasing productivity. The law of increasing additional outlays can then be formulated also as the law of decreasing productivity of additional outlays. Both these formulations are equivalent.

The law of substitution of outlays and, under certain conditions of joint production, the law of substitution of returns, as well as the law of the increasing (or eventually decreasing) rate of substitution operating in divisible technical processes and the law of increasing additional outlays, are related to the selection of technical processes. In connection with the selection of effective technical processes there operates the law of substitution of outlays and, under certain conditions, the law of substitution of returns. When technical processes are divisible, there operate also in connection with this selection the law of the increasing rate of substitution of outlays and, under certain conditions, the law of the decreasing rate of substitution of returns as well as the law of increasing additional outlays. These laws confirm *praxeological regularities* resulting from a certain praxeological rule of behaviour, namely from the rule of excluding inefficient technical processes and redundant equivalent processes. These laws are not, as is sometimes erroneously maintained, universal laws of production techniques. The acceptance of such universal laws of production techniques, allegedly appearing in every process of production and of technique peculiar to it and of the historical development of social productive forces, is a generalization going beyond the scope of empirically verifiable factors and bordering on metaphysical speculation.[31]

---

[31] The view which perceives in the law of the increasing rate of substitution of outlays (and eventually decreasing rate of substitution of returns)

Technical processes corresponding to a given level of historical development of productive forces and a given branch of production are of very different kinds: some make possible sub-

---

and in the law of increasing additional outlays a universal law of production techniques is related to the question of the law of decreasing returns, i.e. decreasing productivity of production factors. This law states that additional units of a factor of production consecutively applied to the process of production while the outlays of the other factors remain unchanged are characterized by a decline in productivity after exceeding a certain initial outlay. The law of the increasing rate of substitution of outlays is interpreted as a conclusion from this law. For in consecutive substitution of factors, because the consecutively withdrawn units of the replaced factor have an ever-greater productivity, in order to offset them, it is necessary to use greater and greater consecutive quantities of the factor that is being substituted for the first one. Moreover, consecutive units of the factor that is being substituted are characterized by decreasing productivity which necessitates additionally increasing consecutive outlays of this factor. Similarly, in the case of joint production, the decline in productivity of the factors of production causes that consecutive units of the factors freed owing to a decline in the quantity of one product result in a declining increase in the second product. The law of decreasing productivity of the factors of production, however, is not a necessary and not even always sufficient condition of the law of increasing (or with reference to products—decreasing) rate of substitution. The necessary condition is only that the productivity of consecutive units of the factor that is being substituted for the other one increase at a lower rate than the productivity of consecutively withdrawn units of the factor that is being replaced. This is a much broader condition than the requirement that the law of decreasing productivity be satisfied by both factors of production. Anyway, the fact that the law of decreasing productivity of the factors of production is satisfied is not always sufficient to ensure an increasing rate of substitution of the factors. The result may be thwarted by the dependence of the productivity of additional units of one factor upon the outlay of another factor; it may happen that the productivity of consecutive units of the factor that is being substituted for the other one increases owing to a decrease in the outlay of the factor that is being replaced. On the other hand, if the productivity of consecutive units of the factor that is being substituted for the other one declines rapidly owing to a decline in outlay of the replaced factor, the rate of substitution may increase even without a decline in productivity of the consecutive units of the particular factor of production. It turns out that the law of the increasing rate of substitution of outlays (as well as the law of the decreasing rate of substitution of returns) and the laws of decreasing returns do not coincide. (See on this matter the Section 7 of the Appendix, "Mathematical Note".) The statement that the increasing (or decreasing) rate of substitution does not coincide

stitution of outlays of production factors and of products, others
do not or make it possible only in one area and do not in another:
if substitution is possible, it may occur in various ways: under

---

with the law of decreasing returns is important because this alleged law,
accepted as universal, is empirically unverifiable. This law was first formulated
only for the outlay of labour and of the means of production for an unchanging
area of land in agriculture. The first to formulate it was A. Turgot (*Observation
sur un mémoire de G. de Saint-Péravy* [*Comment on G. de Saint-Péravy's Report*],
Paris, 1768). It was later formulated independently by E. West (*Essay on the
Application of Capital to Land*, London, 1815). Ricardo introduced this law
into his theory of rent on land, thus popularizing it. An eminent specialist in
chemistry, Justus Liebig, attempted in the middle of the nineteenth century
to justify the law of decreasing productivity of outlays on land. E. A. Mitscher-
lich (1909) derived it from empirical studies on the productivity of outlays on
fertilizing soil. Marx, in contradistinction to Ricardo, did not relate the rent
on land to the law of decreasing return from land (see *Capital*, Vol. III, *ed. cit.*,
Chapters XL–XLIV), and Lenin criticized it as an abstraction contrary to
historical experience and disregarding the fact that an increase in outlays of
labour and means of production for a given area of land is related, as a
rule, to technical progress. (See V. Lenin, "Kwestia agrarna a krytycy Marksa",
Dzieła ["The Agrarian Question and the Critics of Marx", *Works*], Vol. 5, p.
113.) The founder of the American fraction of the subjectivist school in political
economy, J. B. Clark, expanded the law of diminishing returns to cover all
factors of production (*The Distribution of Wealth*, New York, 1899), and
used it as a basis for the theory of marginal productivity of factors of production, thus making out of it a universal law of production techniques. In this
form, the law of decreasing productivity of factors of production was generally
accepted by the neo-classical and related schools. It was most distinctly formulated by P. H. Wicksteed (*The Common Sense of Political Economy*, London,
1902, 2nd ed., 1933, Vol. I) and K. Wicksell (*Lectures on Political Economy*,
translated from Swedish, London, 1934 [first Swedish edition 1901], Vol. I).
The modern interpretation of the law of decreasing productivity was given
by E. Schneider (*Theorie der Produktion* [*Production Theory*], Vienna, 1934)
and S. Carlson (*A Study in the Pure Theory of Production*, London, 1939).
It should be noted, however, that the founder of the neo-classical school—
Alfred Marshall, used in his theoretical analysis the universal law of decreasing
productivity of production factors with great restraint. He felt that substitution of production factors is not a common phenomenon but is fairly limited
in its application. He also confined the operation of the law of decreasing
returns mainly to agriculture and the production of raw materials. (See
A. Marshall, *Principles of Economics*, London, 1958, pp. 318 ff. and 387.)
The law of decreasing productivity of factors of production is of no major

the conditions of increasing, decreasing or constant rates of sub-stitution. The variety of technical processes is enormous; however, not all technical processes are applied in production; there is a selection—a rejection of inefficient processes or of redundant equivalent processes.

If there is more than one technical process by which a given commodity can be produced, then alternative technical processes remain after such a selection only in case when the increased unit outlay is offset by a decrease in some other outlay (or a de-creased return is offset by an increase in another return). This means that only the processes that obey the law of substitution remain. With respect to divisible processes in which the volume of production can be changed in an arbitrary way without changing unit outlays the difficulty in substitution constitutes a criterion of selection. From among alternative processes we select first the one in which substitution is the easiest, then the process in which it is more difficult, then the one in which it is even more

---

importance also in the theories expounded by the Lausanne School. L. Walras based his theory of production on the assumption of constant factors of production; in producing every commodity there is only one technical process and there is no possibility of substitution of the factors of production. (See L. Walras, *Éléments d'économie politique pure*, Chapter 4.) Later, in the fourth edition of his work (1900), Walras supplemented his analysis by admitting the possibility of a general substitution of the factors of production in accord-ance with the theory of marginal productivity (Chapter 7). Pareto treated sub-stitution of the factors of production as a special case of no general appli-cation. (See V. Pareto, *Manuel d'économie politique* [*Manual of Political Economy*], Paris, 1907.) This history of the problem is given by J. Schumpeter, *History of Economic Analysis*, London, 1954, pp. 1026–53. A critical analysis was given by the well-known mathematician K. Menger, "The Laws of Return. A Study in Metaeconomics" (in the collective work edited by O. Morgenstern, *Economic Activity Analysis*, New York, 1954) and by S. Kruszczyński, *Problem kształtowania się przychodów i kosztów* (*Problem of the Structure of Returns and Costs*), Poznań, 1962. As we point out in the text, all these pseudo-problems, bordering on metaphysics, are of no consequence to the quantitative relations prevailing in the process of production. Substitution of production factors and of products as well as its growing difficulty with continuously changing technical processes do not result from the nature of production techniques but are generally a consequence of selection of technical processes. This is a problem in praxeology and not in technology.

difficult, etc. In this way the rate of substitution of outlays increases (and the rate of substitution of returns decreases) in consecutive switching from one process to another. An increase in the volume of production by increasing the outlay of one factor is accomplished by first switching over to the process in which the additional outlay of the factor is most productive, then to the one in which it is less productive, then to the one in which it is even less productive, etc. The selection of technical processes causes then the remaining processes, i.e. the effective ones, to satisfy the above-mentioned laws of substitution, of the rate of substitution and of the productivity of additional outlays.

Observation of technical processes used in the process of production may create the impression that these properties are related to the nature of production techniques because in the process of production one usually does not encounter technical processes which do not have these properties. This, however, does not follow from the "nature" of technical processes but results from the fact that the processes which do not have the properties mentioned above have been eliminated by rejecting inefficient and superfluous equivalent processes. This is the result of the principle of praxeological behaviour used in production.[32]

IV

In the form given above, the matrix of production techniques does not yet give us a complete picture of technical possibilities of production because it takes into account only unit outlays corresponding to particular technical processes. Technical processes not only differ from one another in unit outlays of production factors, but they also differ in the stock of fixed capital means required for a given technical process. Fixed means are involved in the process of production not only in the form of outlays,

---

[32] The praxeological nature of the results of empirical studies of relations between outlays and returns was pointed out also by Z. Bosiakowski in his review of the study by S. Kruszczyński. See *Ekonomista*, No. 2/1963, pp. 428–32.

i.e. in the form of utilization over a long period of time. As we know, their utilization is a sort of flow and is measured by the quantity of natural units in a given period of time, e.g. machine-hours, or truck-hours per month or per year. Fixed capital means are also involved in the process of production in aggregate stock, regardless of the extent of their utilization. A machine can be used for a few or for more hours, and consequently it produces a smaller or greater quantity of the commodity. For instance, with a weaving machine we can produce a smaller or greater quantity of a fabric, depending upon the number of hours of its operation; a truck may be used over a varying number of hours and correspondingly may carry a varying number of goods (ton-kilometres); in the same way, a building may be used over varying numbers of hours and if a certain process of production takes place in it, then the quantity of commodity depends upon the number of hours of utilization of the building. However, not a single unit of commodity can be produced without the whole machine or without the whole building; we cannot even carry a single ton of goods over a single kilometre without the whole truck (we disregard here, of course, the possibility of using substitute means of transportation). This was emphasized by Marx: "At the same time, though with diminishing vitality, the machine as a whole continues to take part in the labour process. Thus it appears that *one factor of the labour process*, a means of production, *continually enters as a whole into that process. ...*"[33]

Fixed capital means of production retain their natural form and their usefulness over more than one production period. Therefore, once introduced into the process of production, they are involved in it as a whole, indivisible stock. A machine, a car or a building may only be utilized for several hours of a day but we cannot do without a whole machine, a whole car or a whole building. The stock of fixed capital means used in the process of production is usually called the *technical equipment of production.*

---

[33] K. Marx, *op. cit.*, Vol. I, *ed. cit.*, p. 186. On page 187 Marx quotes the following comment on the stocking frame: "for the machine makes many pairs [of stockings—O. L.], and none of those pairs could have been done without any part of the machine".

In a full description of the conditions of production it is necessary to mention, in addition to unit outlays of production factors, also the technical equipment, i.e. the stock of fixed capital means. Particular production processes differ also in the technical equipment involved.

Every technical process involves, as a rule, a specific stock of various fixed means—buildings, equipment, machines, means of transportation, etc.—which are needed for a given process and constitute the necessary technical equipment. In producing steel by a specific technical process, furnaces must have a given capacity, heat resistance, thickness of the walls; they must also be equipped with the requisite number of ladle cars, an appropriate building, etc. Any change in these requirements corresponds to a change in the technical process. Similarly, for a given technical process in crude oil processing we need an appropriate number of installations, tanks, pipes, heating and cooling equipment, etc., as well as a suitable site. The diversity, extent and size of these installations depend upon the technical process used. Each method of producing sulphuric acid or aluminium requires different equipment and machinery. Different methods of metal-working require different machines (e.g. different types of machine tools) of different capacities and efficiency. Various technical processes used for producing a given commodity thus require different equipment, strictly defined for every case. The amount of technical equipment, i.e. the stock of particular fixed capital means, is independent of the use it is to be put to and therefore also of the quantity of commodities to be produced. It is a fixed quantity defined for each technical process.

To obtain a full picture of technical possibilities of production we should introduce in our matrix of production techniques the technical equipment, needed for particular technical processes. For this purpose, we must distinguish among the means of production between the fixed capital means and the working capital means. Let us denote the outlay of working capital means by $Q^{(0)}$ and the outlay of fixed capital means by $Q^{(1)}$ and let S denote the stock of fixed capital means. Then the matrix of production techniques can be written in the form of the following table:

$$\begin{bmatrix} \dfrac{L_1}{P} & \dfrac{L_2}{P} & \cdots & \dfrac{L_r}{P} \\[2mm] \dfrac{Q_1^{(0)}}{P} & \dfrac{Q_2^{(0)}}{P} & \cdots & \dfrac{Q_r^{(0)}}{P} \\[2mm] \dfrac{Q_1^{(1)}}{P} & \dfrac{Q_2^{(1)}}{P} & \cdots & \dfrac{Q_r^{(1)}}{P} \\[2mm] S_1 & S_2 & \cdots & S_r \end{bmatrix}$$

In this table each column denotes a set (vector) of unit outlays and of technical equipment corresponding to a given technical process. Technical equipment (the stock of fixed capital means) is shown at the bottom of each column; the last row of the matrix shows the technical equipment required for particular production processes.[34] We call this table a *full matrix of production technique*.

Taking into consideration technical equipment, we can expand the notion of inefficient and equivalent technical processes. A technical process is inefficient if it requires a greater unit outlay of one or more factors of production *or* larger technical equipment by one or more components[35] while no other unit outlay or other component of technical equipment is smaller. Technical processes are equivalent if unit outlays and corresponding components of technical equipment are of the same size. Eliminating inefficient

[34] Technical equipment is a set, i.e. a vector, whose components are the stocks of particular fixed capital means. For a given technical process, let us say the *j*th, the vector representing technical equipment can be written in the following form:

$$S_j = \begin{bmatrix} S_{1j} \\ S_{2j} \\ \vdots \\ S_{ij} \end{bmatrix}.$$

In this case *j* is an index of the technical process, i.e. $j = 1, 2, \ldots, r$.

[35] These components are the components of the vector of technical equipment S corresponding to a given technical process, with appropriate machines, buildings, installations, etc.

technical processes and equivalent superfluous processes, we obtain the expanded notion of effective technical processes. By reasoning similarly as above it can be shown that effective (in the expanded sense) technical processes satisfy the law of substitution.

Substitution may thus take place between particular unit outlays, between particular components of technical equipment or between components of technical equipment and unit outlays. Particularly worth noting is the last-mentioned kind of substitution. According to the law of substitution at least two quantities must be involved. Then, there is no substitution of outlay and no substitution of components of technical equipment; there must be substitution between at least one unit outlay and at least one component of technical equipment. This fact is confirmed by experience which shows that an increase in technical equipment is accompanied by a decrease in operating outlays, i.e. unit outlays of factors of production. This fact, however, does not follow from the "nature" of production techniques, as many erroneously thought, but is a result of selection eliminating inefficient technical processes and superfluous equivalent processes. If a certain technical process requires a greater quantity of one or several components of technical equipment and is not combined with a decrease in any unit outlay, i.e. with a decrease in operation outlays, such a process is not used in production, because it is inefficient. The regularity, confirmed by experience, that to a greater amount of technical equipment there correspond smaller operation outlays (and vice versa) is not a mysterious, "natural" property of production techniques. It is simply a praxeological regularity, the result of a specific selection of technical processes.

As we have seen, Marx has noted that a decrease in unit labour outlays, i.e. an increase in the productivity of labour, coincides, as a rule, with increased technical equipment in the production process. Substitution of more technical equipment for direct labour is the main lever of the historical process of increasing productivity of human labour. It is usually combined with the substitution of unit outlays of means of production, particularly of working capital means, for unit outlays of labour, because an increase in production due to a unit outlay of labour requires a greater number of objects of labour to be transformed into a product.[36]

Technical equipment appropriate to a given technical process determines the maximum outlay, i.e. the maximum extent of utilization of fixed capital means. The outlay of a fixed capital means must be within the limits of uninterrupted use of this means in the process of production, i.e. it is impossible to use a fixed capital means for more than 24 hours a day. The use of the stock of ten machines cannot exceed 240 machine-hours per day, and the use of the stock of five cars cannot exceed 120 car-hours per day, etc. Frequently, a fixed capital means cannot be used without interruption because breaks are required for checking, mainte- nance and repairs. Some of these breaks, e.g. for checking and maintenance, are strictly defined by the technical conditions and if they are disregarded a loss in the utility of a given technical means may result. Other breaks, e.g. for repairs, are of a random nature, but their average duration can be determined from exper- ience. In this way, a given fixed capital means has a maximum utilization time during a given period (day, month, year). With a given stock of fixed capital means it is impossible to exceed a certain maximum extent of utilization of this stock, i.e. of a cer- tain maximum outlay.

In consequence, to each technical process there corresponds a certain maximum quantity of the product (volume of produc- tion) that can be obtained (during a given period) by using a given process. This quantity is determined by the maximum use of the technical equipment needed for a given process; we call it the *productive capacity* of a given technical process. Each technical

---

[36] See above, footnote 23. It follows from the text quoted that Marx combined an increase in labour productivity both with the substitution of technical equipment for unit labour outlay ("the mass of machinery, beasts of burden, minerals, manures, drain-pipes, etc., is a condition of the increasing productivity of labour. So also is it with ... buildings, furnaces, means of transport, etc.") and with the substitution of unit outlays of means of production, particularly of working capital means ("more raw material is worked up at the same time ...") for unit outlays of labour. These two kinds of substitution related to increased productivity of labour should be distin- guished from one another. A great deal of confusion in economic literature was due to the lack of strict distinction.

process has then its specific productive capacity. If the volume of production is smaller than the productive capacity of the process, we say that the productive capacity is not fully utilized. The ratio of the actual volume of production to the productive capacity of the technical process is called the *degree of utilization of productive capacity*. Frequently, this ratio is expressed as a percentage, and we say that the productive capacity is utilized to 70 per cent, 90 per cent, etc. The maximum degree of utilization is, of course, 100 per cent. Under-utilization of productive capacity may be due to the fact that the stock of fixed capital means of production is not used over its maximum time of utilization or to the fact that not all stock (i.e. not all fixed capital means) is being used. The first case occurs when, for example, buildings and machinery are used only over part of a day, say, over 8 hours, because the production establishment employs only one shift. The second case occurs when part of the machinery (or building) is idle, e.g. because of a shortage of raw materials or because engines are only partially utilized.[37] In both cases the stock of fixed capital means of production (i.e. technical equipment) is not utilized to its maximum capacity.[38]

---

[37] In this connection we speak of the degree of extensive or intensive utilization of productive capacity. The first pertains to the time of utilization of technical equipment, the second to the part of stock that is being utilized. (See A. Gozulov, *Ekonomicheskaya Statistika* [*Economic Statistics*], Moscow, 1958.)

[38] Besides a maximum extent there may also exist a minimum extent of utilization of fixed capital means of production. Utilization may be indivisible, i.e. its degree, for technical reasons, cannot be less than a certain lower limit. For instance, a 100 h.p. engine cannot work if its load is only 10 h.p. A blast furnace cannot be operated for an arbitrarily short period of time but must be used without interruption over the whole period of its life span, which lasts several years. For this reason the furnace must have a certain minimum capacity and, therefore, we cannot smelt in it less than a certain definite quantity of pig iron per day. In this connection some authors speak of a "minimum productive capacity" of the technical process in contradistinction to a maximum productive capacity discussed above. (See, for example, E. Gutenberg, *Grundlagen der Betriebswirtschaftslehre*, Berlin, 1957, Vol. I, pp. 56–67.) However, a minimum productive capacity is usually strictly defined. This is pointed out by Gutenberg: "The notion of minimum capacity is not so precisely

It may happen that the stocks and the maximum time of utilization of a particular fixed capital means are such that each of them enables us to produce the same quantity of the commodity. We say then that technical equipment has a *harmonious structure*. Frequently, however, particular components of technical equipment enable us to produce different quantities of the commodity. We say then that technical equipment has a *non-harmonious structure*. With a non-harmonious structure of technical equipment the productive capacity of the technical process is determined by the component of equipment which, in comparison with other components, enables us to obtain the smallest quantity of the product; this component is regarded as a *limiting* one. The remaining components of technical equipment are then not utilized to their maximum possible capacity and are partly idle.

The structure of technical equipment may be harmonious or non-harmonious, depending upon a given production technique; this structure constitutes a feature of a specific technical process. Particular technical processes may thus result in partial idleness of certain components of technical equipment even when the productive capacity is fully utilized. However, a non-harmonious structure of technical equipment can be transformed into a more harmonious one by appropriate joining of technical processes. Suppose that we have two technical processes in which the same technical fixed capital means are used. Let us have in the first process three components of technical equipment which enable us to produce (in a given period) 100, 120, 150 units of a commodity respectively. Here, the first component is a limiting one and the remaining two are not fully utilized. In the second process let technically the same components enable us to produce respectively 200, 180 and 150 units of the commodity, i.e. the third component of technical equipment is a limiting one, and the first and second components are not fully utilized. By joining both these processes we obtain a mixed process in which 300 units of the

defined technically as the notion of maximum capacity" (*ibid.*, p. 58). For this reason we use the term "productive capacity" in the sense of maximum capacity, speaking, if need be, of minimum utilization of this capacity.

commodity are produced and all the components of technical equipment are fully utilized. The structure of the technical equipment of this mixed process is harmonious. Such joining of technical processes is called the *harmonization of the structure of technical equipment.*

The harmonization of technical equipment by joining technical processes is then possible in cases in which in various technical processes the same technically fixed capital means are used and the components of technical equipment which are limiting ones in one technical process are partly idle in another process. The joining of technical processes decreases disharmony in the structure of technical equipment but does not always lead to its full harmonization because idleness of particular components of technical equipment in various processes may not always be eliminated by joining these processes. Full harmonization can, however, always be achieved by a *multiplication* of the technical process, i.e. by increasing the volume of production to the multiple quantity of the product which can possibly be achieved, considering the components of technical equipment. When the volume of production is so increased, not all components of technical equipment must be multiplied in the same ratio. For instance, if in the first of the above-mentioned processes the volume of production is increased six times, i.e. to 600 units of the commodity, then the first component of the technical equipment must be multiplied six times, the second component five times, and the third four times only. Then, every component would enable us to produce 600 units of the commodity and the structure of technical equipment would be fully harmonized. Similarly, in the second process, mentioned as an example, the structure of technical equipment can be harmonized when the volume of production reaches 1800 units. Then the first component of technical equipment must be multiplied 9 times, the second component 10 times, and the third 12 times. Any volume of production being a multiple of the quantity of the product that can be achieved by the particular components of technical equipment leads to harmonization of the structure of technical equipment: the least multiple is sufficient for this purpose. The least multiple deter-

mines the lowest volume of production (and in this way the productive capacity of the multiplied process) at which the structure
of technical equipment is harmonized. It turns out then that by
appropriate joining of technical processes we can reduce disharmony and by multiplying the technical process we can achieve
a full harmonization of technical equipment. Both these methods
can be joined for the purpose of achieving complete harmonization at the lowest possible volume of production.[39]

Harmonization of the structure of technical equipment is always related to an increase in productive capacity. In harmonization by joining technical processes the productive capacity of
the new mixed process equals the lowest quantities of the commodity which the particular components of the combined technical equipment enable us to achieve. After multiplying the technical process its capacity equals the multiple of the quantity of
the commodity which the particular components of technical
equipment enable us to achieve; thus it is greater than the quantity
of the commodity which the limiting component enables us to
attain and which determines the productive capacity of the process before multiplication. Frequently the structure of technical
equipment can be harmonized by joining technical processes
by which various commodities are produced if in these processes
technically the same fixed capital means are used (fully or partially).
The result is then the joint production of two or more commodities. Very often joint production is the result of joining different

---

[39] See Section 3 of the Appendix, "Mathematical Note", at the end of
this chapter. The problem of harmony of technical equipment was mentioned by the Danish engineer–economist Ivar Jantzen in the work "Voxende
Udbytte i Industrien", *Nationalokonomisk Tidskrift*, Copenhagen, 1924, Vol. 62.
English translation of the book by the same author: *Basic Principles of Business
Economics*, Copenhagen, 1939. A German translation is given as an appendix
to the book by E. Schneider, *Theorie der Produktion* [*Production Theory*], *ed.
cit.* (See also Ivar Jantzen, "Laws of Production and Costs", *Econometrica*,
Vol. 17, Supplement 1949 [Report on Washington Meeting].) As far as we
know, Jantzen was the first to state that by multiplying the volume of production the structure of technical equipment can be harmonized. This statement
he defined as *the law of harmony*. (See F. Zeuthen, *Economic Theory and
Method*, London, 1955, pp. 117–18.)

technical processes in order to harmonize the structure of technical equipment.

It can be seen that the harmonization of the structure of technical equipment either by increasing the quantity of a particular commodity produced (by joining or multiplying the processes), or by transition to joint production (possibly also by increasing the quantity and the variety of the commodity), requires more technical equipment. Thus, it is related to an increase both in the amount of technical equipment and in the productive capacity of the production establishment, i.e., as we say, of the "size" of the establishment.[40] It may possibly necessitate combining a great number of production establishments into a new, "larger" establishment possessing more technical equipment and greater productive capacity (or a more diversified productive capacity in the case of shifting to joint production, or in the case of increasing its diversity). Moreover, it may turn out that the harmonization of technical equipment in one branch of production depends upon increased production in another branch. Such a dependence may result from the fact that increased production in another branch is the condition of the utilization of increased productive capacity that would be created in consequence of the harmonization of technical equipment. This may be the consequence of the fact that the second branch of production supplies raw materials or buys the commodity produced.[41]

The necessity of taking into consideration technical equipment limits considerably the impact of the growing rate of substitution of outlays (and the declining rate of substitution of returns) and the laws of increasing additional outlays. These laws, as we know, are the result of applying to the process of production the praxeological principle of eliminating inefficient processes. The processes that do not satisfy these laws are inefficient if they are divisible

---

[40] The harmonization of technical equipment constitutes a technical basis for the law of concentration of production which appears both in the capitalist and in the socialist systems of production. It is also combined with the phenomenon known as *increasing returns of scale* or *economies of scale*.

[41] This is a basis for the phenomenon which Marshall calls *external economies*. (See A. Marshall, *Principles of Economics, ed. cit.*, p. 226.)

because then there are available one or more mixed processes, which give the same production result with a smaller outlay of at least one factor of production. Technical equipment, on the other hand, determines the productive capacity of particular technical processes. In consequence, joining two or more processes in order to produce a given quantity of the commodity may result in unutilized productive capacity of these processes or in a non-harmonious structure of their technical equipment. Under these conditions technical processes are indivisible and the use of mixed processes cannot be considered. Mixed processes do not "compete" for their application. In consequence, the processes that do not satisfy the above-mentioned laws concerning the rate of substitution and additional outlays do not have to be inefficient.

In this situation these laws do not operate. They may operate only in a special case when the technical equipment and the productive capacity of the processes of which the mixed process is composed are relatively low. Then, the processes are approximately divisible and the mixed process does not result in unutilized capacity or in a serious lack of harmony in the structure of technical equipment. For this reason these laws operate only in the branch of production in which technical equipment and the productive capacities of technical processes are relatively small. These laws cease to operate, however, as the amounts of technical equipment and of productive capacity are increased and as, in consequence, the "size" of production establishments is also increased.[42] The law of the increasing rate of substitution of outlays

---

[42] It follows that these laws, being praxeological regularities, apply mainly to agricultural production and to certain kinds of raw-material production where technical equipment is relatively small, but they do not apply to industrial production characterized by a greater amount of technical equipment. This is consistent with empirical observations mentioned by A. Marshall (*Principles of Economics, ed. cit.*, pp. 318–19 and 137–54). However, as the amount of technical equipment in agriculture and in extracting industries increases in consequence of technical progress, these laws cease to operate also in these fields. This explains Lenin's empirical results pertaining to the law of diminishing return on land against the background of capitalist development of agriculture (see V. Lenin, "Kwestia agrarna a krytyty Marksa", *Dzieła,* [The

(and eventually of the decreasing rate of substitution of returns) and the law of increasing additional outlays are then not a universal principle of selection of technical processes.

V

The selection of technical processes, as discussed above, is confined to the choice of effective processes. In a certain fairly special situation, in which technical equipment does not play any major part, it results in the choice of the processes that satisfy the laws of the increasing (or decreasing) rate of substitution and increasing additional outlays. After selection, as a rule, there remains more than one technical process by which a given commodity (or a given set of commodities) can be produced. It is also possible to use mixed processes, but this can be limited because of the productive capacity and because of the harmony of the structure of technical equipment. A further reaching selection of technical processes is impossible on the basis of calculations in physical units only because there are no criteria available.

In practical experience in a natural economy the application of specific technical processes (pure or mixed ones) for producing particular commodities is determined by collective experience in the social process of labour. This takes place in a protracted and spontaneous process of "trial and error" which leads to a certain "natural selection" of technical processes. The result of such a selection is usually consolidated into a custom and is transmitted by tradition.[43] The process of selection has no unique criterion; it takes place spontaneously in conditions of mutual influence of traditional and customary ways of behaviour and of slowly occurring changes in the social productive forces, i.e. in technical production methods, in means of production and in man's skill of

---

Agrarian Problem and the Critics of Marx", *Works*], Vol. 5, pp. 112–25). L. Krzywicki ("Kwestia rolna", *Dzieła* ["The Agrarian Problem", *Works*], Vol. 8, Warsaw, 1967, pp. 166–7) emphasized in this context the importance of technical equipment in agriculture.

[43] See O. Lange, *Political Economy*, Vol. 1, Oxford–Warsaw, 1963, pp. 151–2.

using them (as well as in the number of men possessing such
skills). Therefore, in our further considerations we shall assume
for the time being that the production of each commodity takes
place by a specific technical process which emerges from the above
described process of selection and is sanctioned by custom and
tradition. Only the discussion of a money-commodity economy
will provide us with a unique criterion for the selection of technical processes in the form of value-money accounting and of
the principle of rational management.

APPENDIX TO CHAPTER II

MATHEMATICAL NOTE

1. The matrix of production techniques

We denote, as in the text, by:

$$\mathbf{L}_j = \begin{bmatrix} L_{1j} \\ L_{2j} \\ \vdots \\ L_{nj} \end{bmatrix}, \quad \mathbf{Q}_j^{(0)} = \begin{bmatrix} Q_{1j}^{(0)} \\ Q_{2j}^{(0)} \\ \vdots \\ Q_{kj}^{(0)} \end{bmatrix}, \quad \mathbf{Q}_j^{(1)} = \begin{bmatrix} Q_{1j}^{(1)} \\ Q_{2j}^{(1)} \\ \vdots \\ Q_{lj}^{(1)} \end{bmatrix}$$

where $j = 1, 2, \ldots, r$, the vectors of labour outlays, working capital outlays and fixed capital outlays in the jth technical process.
The number of particular kinds of labour is h, the number of
particular working capital means is k and the number of particular fixed capital means is l. We consider r possible technical
processes. We denote by P the quantity of the product (return)
obtained. Outlays and outputs are measured in physical units
for a given period of time (they are flows). We assume that outlays
are non-negative quantities (and at least some of them are positive) and that the output is a positive quantity.

The vectors mentioned form *the outlay matrix*:

$$\begin{bmatrix} \mathbf{L}_1 & \mathbf{L}_2 & \ldots & \mathbf{L}_r \\ \mathbf{Q}_1^{(0)} & \mathbf{Q}_2^{(0)} & \ldots & \mathbf{Q}_r^{(0)} \\ \mathbf{Q}_1^{(1)} & \mathbf{Q}_2^{(1)} & \ldots & \mathbf{Q}_r^{(1)} \end{bmatrix}.$$

This matrix can also be written in the developed form emphasizing the components of the particular vectors:

$$
\begin{bmatrix}
L_{11} & L_{12} & \cdots & L_{1r} \\
L_{21} & L_{22} & \cdots & L_{2r} \\
\cdots\cdots\cdots\cdots\cdots \\
L_{h1} & L_{h2} & \cdots & L_{hr} \\
Q_{11}^{(0)} & Q_{12}^{(0)} & \cdots & Q_{1r}^{(0)} \\
Q_{21}^{(0)} & Q_{22}^{(0)} & \cdots & Q_{2r}^{(0)} \\
\cdots\cdots\cdots\cdots\cdots \\
Q_{k1}^{(0)} & Q_{k2}^{(0)} & \cdots & Q_{kr}^{(0)} \\
Q_{11}^{(1)} & Q_{12}^{(1)} & \cdots & Q_{1r}^{(1)} \\
Q_{21}^{(1)} & Q_{22}^{(1)} & \cdots & Q_{2r}^{(1)} \\
\cdots\cdots\cdots\cdots\cdots \\
Q_{l1}^{(1)} & Q_{l2}^{(1)} & \cdots & Q_{lr}^{(1)}
\end{bmatrix}.
$$

The columns of this matrix show the outlays of particular factors of production in a given technical process, and the rows show the outlays of a given factor of production in various technical processes. Writing $n = h+k+l$, we state that the outlay matrix (in the developed form) has n rows and r columns.

For the sake of simplicity, we denote the elements of the developed form of the outlay matrix by X_{ij}, i.e. X_{ij} is the element located at the intersection of the ith row and jth column $(i = 1, 2, ..., n; j = 1, 2, ..., r)$. Then the outlay matrix assumes the following form:

$$
\mathbf{X} = \begin{bmatrix}
X_{11} & X_{12} & \cdots & X_{1r} \\
X_{21} & X_{22} & \cdots & X_{2r} \\
X_{n1} & X_{n2} & \cdots & X_{nr}
\end{bmatrix}. \tag{1.1}
$$

The unit outlay of the ith factor of production in the jth technical process we denote as

$$
a_{ij} = \frac{X_{ij}}{P} \quad (i = 1, 2, ..., n; j = 1, 2, ..., r). \tag{1.2}
$$

The unit outlays are also called *coefficients of production*. Their dimension is independent of time, i.e. it is a ratio of two stocks.

The coefficients of production form a *matrix of production techniques*.

$$A = \begin{bmatrix} a_{11} & a_{12} & \cdots & a_{1r} \\ a_{21} & a_{22} & \cdots & a_{2r} \\ a_{n1} & a_{n2} & \cdots & a_{nr} \end{bmatrix}. \tag{1.3}$$

The columns of this matrix denote the unit outlays of particular factors of production for a given technical process and the rows denote the unit outlays of a given factor of production for various technical processes.

The stocks of particular fixed capital means required for the *j*th technical process constitute a vector which we denote by:

$$S_j = \begin{bmatrix} S_{1j} \\ S_{2j} \\ \vdots \\ S_{lj} \end{bmatrix} \quad (j = 1, 2, \ldots, r).$$

This vector is called the *technical equipment* of a given process. The quantities $S_{1j}, S_{2j}, \ldots, S_{lj}$ are non-negative and are components of the technical equipment. The dimension of the stocks is independent of time. The technical equipments form a matrix with *l* rows and *r* columns. We denote this matrix by S.

By introducing into the production technique matrix the technical equipment corresponding to particular technical processes, we obtain a *complete matrix of production techniques*:

$$\begin{bmatrix} A \\ S \end{bmatrix} = \begin{bmatrix} a_{11} & a_{12} & \cdots & a_{1r} \\ a_{21} & a_{22} & \cdots & a_{2r} \\ \cdots\cdots\cdots\cdots\cdots \\ a_{n1} & a_{n2} & \cdots & a_{nr} \\ S_{11} & S_{12} & \cdots & S_{1r} \\ S_{21} & S_{22} & \cdots & S_{2r} \\ \cdots\cdots\cdots\cdots\cdots \\ S_{l1} & S_{l2} & \cdots & S_{lr} \end{bmatrix} \tag{1.4}$$

or, in abbreviated form:

$$\begin{bmatrix} A \\ S \end{bmatrix} = \begin{bmatrix} a_1 & a_2 & \cdots & a_r \\ S_1 & S_2 & \cdots & S_r \end{bmatrix}, \tag{1.4a}$$

where

$$\mathbf{a}_j = \begin{bmatrix} a_{1j} \\ a_{2j} \\ \vdots \\ a_{nj} \end{bmatrix} \quad (j = 1, 2, \dots, r).$$

In the complete matrix of production techniques, the columns denote unit outlays *and* technical equipment for a given technical process, and the rows denote unit outlays of a given factor of production or the stock of a given fixed capital means in various technical processes.

2. *Joint production*

We can include joint production in the matrix of production techniques, treating only one of the joint products as the product of reference. The remaining products are treated then as *sui generis* factors of production whose outlays have a negative value. Negative unit outlays of these "factors of production" express the quantities of the particular product obtained by a given technical process per unit of the product of reference.[1]

Another way of including joint production in the matrix of production techniques consists in denoting all products by positive numbers and outlays of factors of production by negative numbers (these outlays are, in a sense, negative products). This enables us to place all the products and outlays in the matrix of production techniques. Because of the accepted rule of signs, this matrix assumes then the character of a balance table in which the outputs are positive and outlays are negative items.[2] This

---

[1] See O. Lange, *Optimal Decisions*, Oxford–Warsaw, 1971.

[2] Examples of such matrices performing the functions of balance tables are given by P. Pichler in: "Anwendung der Matrizenrechnung bei Betriebskostenüberwachung" ("Use of Martix Calculation in the Control of Operation Costs") in the collective work *Anwendung der Matrizenrechnung auf wirtschaftliche und statistische Probleme* (*Use of Matrix Calculations in Economic and Statistical Problems*), Würzburg, 1959, and the collective work: *Matematicheskiye metody planirovaniya proizvodstva* (*Mathematical Methods of Production Programming*), edited by M. Fedorovitch, Moscow, 1961.

procedure has obvious advantages. We do not apply it because for our purposes it is more convenient to express outlays of production factors by positive numbers. We also express the components of technical equipment by positive numbers.

3. *Productive capacity and the structure of technical equipment*

S_{ij} is the stock of the ith fixed capital means in the jth technical process. We denote by t_{ij} the maximum time of its utilization during a given period of time. The maximum feasible outlay of this means, during a given period of time, is:

$$(X_{ij})_{\max} = t_{ij}S_{ij} \ (i = 1, 2, ..., l; j = 1, 2, ..., r).$$

Considering also (1.2), we find that the stock S_{ij} enables us to produce (during a given period of time) the quantity of the product amounting, at the most, to

$$(P_{ij})_{\max} = \frac{t_{ij}S_{ij}}{a_{ij}} \ (i = 1, 2, ..., l; j = 1, 2, ..., r). \quad (3.1)$$

For a given, say jth, technical process, the particular components of the technical equipment $S_{1j}, S_{2j}, ..., S_{lj}$ determine the maximum quantities of the products $(P_{1j})_{\max}, (P_{2j})_{\max}, ..., (P_{lj})_{\max}$, respectively. The smallest of them constitutes *the productive capacity* of the given technical process, which we denote by $\hat{P}_j$. We have then

$$\hat{P}_j = \min_i (P_{ij})_{\max} \quad (j = 1, 2, ..., r). \quad (3.2)$$

In a special case when $(P_{1j})_{\max} = (P_{2j})_{\max} = \cdots = (P_{lj})_{\max}$, the structure of technical equipment is harmonious. When this is not the case, the structure is in disharmony and then the ith fixed capital means which satisfies condition (3.2) is a limiting component of technical equipment. As a measure of disharmony of the structure of technical equipment we can use the difference

$$\max_i(P_{ij})_{\max} - \min_i(P_{ij})_{\max},$$

i.e.

$$\max_i(P_{ij})_{\max} - P_j \quad (j = 1, 2, ..., r). \quad (3.3)$$

This is the difference between the greatest potential productive capacity made possible by the particular components of the technical equipment and the actual productive capacity determined by the limiting component.

The joining of k technical processes $(k \leqslant r)$ produces a process whose productive capacity is:

$$\min_i \sum_{j=1}^{k} (P_{ij})_{\max}.$$

This diminishes the disharmony in the structure of technical equipment if

$$\max_i \sum_{j=1}^{k} (P_{ij})_{\max} - \min_i \sum_{j=1}^{k} (P_{ij})_{\max} < \max_i (P_{ih})_{\max} - \min_i (P_{ih})_{\max} \tag{3.4}$$

for all $h = 1, 2, \dots, k$.

Let us denote by W_j the multiple of the numbers $(P_{ij})_{\max}$, $(P_{2j})_{\max}, \dots, (P_{lj})_{\max}$ in the jth technical process. Then

$$\lambda_{ij} = \frac{W_j}{(P_{ij})_{\max}} \tag{3.5}$$

is a whole number for all $i = 1, 2, \dots, l$. Multiplying in this process the component of technical equipment S_{ij} by $\lambda_{ij} (i = 1, 2, \dots, l)$, we obtain the multiplied jth technical process. In the multiplied process the components of technical equipment are

$$\lambda_{ij} S_{ij}, \lambda_{2j} S_{2j}, \dots, \lambda_{lj} S_{lj}.$$

In accordance with (3.1) these components enable us to produce the quantities of the product equal to

$$\lambda_{ij} (P_{ij})_{\max} = \lambda_{2j} (P_{2j})_{\max} = \dots = \lambda_{lj} (P_{lj})_{\max} = W_j, \tag{3.6}$$

because of (3.5). The multiplication of the technical process leads to a full harmonization of the structure of its technical equipment.

4. Substitution

The following geometric interpretation illustrates the law of substitution of outlays. We present technical processes as vectors $W(n+1)$-dimensional Euclidean space. The components of these vectors are the elements of the columns of the effective, complete matrix of production technique. Every vector has $n+l$ components, namely n unit outlays (coefficients of production) and l components of technical equipment. Obviously, some components may equal 0 (when a certain factor of production is not used in a given technical process). The ends of these vectors determine a certain joint hyper-surface consisting of $(n+l-1)$-dimensional simplexes. The law of substitution of outlays states that this hyper-surface "slopes" towards at least one of the co-ordinates, i.e. what amounts to the same thing, the projection of this hyper-surface on at least one wall of the system of coordinates is a "sloping" line.

Since the numbering of factors of production and of components of technical equipment is arbitrary we draw this projection as in Fig. 1.

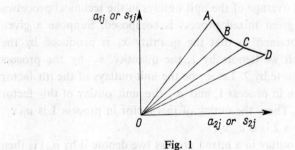

Fig. 1

This graph presents the wall of the system of co-ordinates determined by two co-ordinates representing the outlays or the components of technical equipment. The vectors OA, OB, OC, OD, etc., are projections on this wall of the vectors representing various technical processes. The vertexes A, B, C, D, etc., of these vectors determine the angular line $ABCD$, etc. This line is a projection, on the above-mentioned wall of the hyper-surface determined by the ends of $(n+1)$-dimensional vectors representing technical processes. According to the law of substitution of outlays this angular line is "declining". Indeed, if this line were rising, then, as can easily be checked from the graph, the technical processes corresponding to the vectors *OB, OC, OD* would require greater unit outlays of both factors, or greater components of technical equipment than the process corresponding to vector *OA*. These processes would then be inefficient. Similarly, these processes would be inefficient if the line *ABCD* were horizontal because then the processes represented by the vectors *OB, OC* and *OD* would require a greater unit outlay a_{2j} or a greater component of technical equipment S_{2j} than the process represented by the vector *OA* for the same quantity of the unit outlay a_{1j} or the component of technical equipment S_{1j}. If two or more vertexes *ABCD* etc., coincided, the technical processes would be equivalent. In consequence, the line *ABCD*, etc., must be "declining". This is a geometrical expression of the law of substitution of outlays.

5. *Mixed processes*

When mixed technical processes are used, unit outlays are the weighted average of the unit outlays in the technical processes of which a given mixed process is composed. Suppose a given output is obtained so that the quantity x_1 is produced by the process which we denote by 1, the quantity x_2 by the process which we denote by 2. Let a_{i1} be the unit outlays of the ith factor of production in process 1, and a_{i2} the unit outlay of this factor in process 2. Then, the outlay of this factor in process 1 is $a_{i1}x_1$, and in process 2 it is $a_{i2}x_2$.

The unit outlay in a mixed process (we denote it by $\bar{a}_{ix}$) is then

$$\bar{a}_{ix} = \frac{a_{i1}x_1 + a_{i2}x_2}{x_1 + x_2}.$$

We denote by $x = \dfrac{x_1}{x_1 + x_2}$ the share of the first process in production by the mixed process. The share of the second is $\dfrac{x_2}{x_1 + x_2} = 1 - x$. The unit outlay of the ith factor in the mixed process can be presented in the form

$$\bar{a}_{ix} = a_{i1}x + a_{i2}(1-x). \tag{5.1}$$

It can easily be seen that it depends upon parameter x, determining in what proportion the product is obtained by each of the two technical processes.

Let us now take the wall of the system of co-ordinates determined by the unit outlays of the first and second factors of production (the numbering of factors is arbitrary), i.e. by the co-ordinates a_{1j} and a_{2j}. In Fig. 2 are shown the projections on this wall of the vectors representing technical processes 1 and 2.

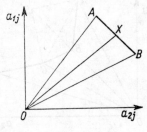

Fig. 2

They are the vectors OA and OB. The ends of these vectors A and B have the co-ordinates (a_{11}, a_{21}) and (a_{12}, a_{22}). To the mixed process composed of the above-mentioned two technical processes there corresponds the vector (projection) whose end has the co-ordinates (a_{1x}, a_{2x}). We denote it in the graph by OX. Because of (5.1) we have

$$\bar{a}_{1x} = a_{11}x + a_{12}(1-x)$$
$$\bar{a}_{2x} = a_{21}x + a_{22}(1-x),$$

i.e. a parametric equation of the straight line intersecting the point with the co-ordinates (a_{11}, a_{21}) and (a_{12}, a_{22}), i.e. the points A and B. It turns out then that point X, i.e. the end of the vector OX, representing (in the projection on the wall of the system of co-ordinates) the mixed process is located on the segment AB. The location of point X on this segment depends upon parameter x. If $x = 1$, then point X coincides with point A (only process 1 is used), and if $x = 0$, then point X coincides with point B (only process 2 is used); for $0 < x < 1$ point X is located between point A and point B at a distance determined by the proportion of the division of production between the two technical processes.

6. Properties of the rate of substitution

We consider three divisible technical processes denoted by 1, 2, 3, whose vectors—the projections on the wall of the system of co-ordinates determined by the first and second factor of production—are shown in Fig. 3.

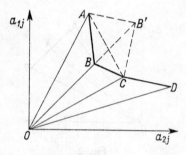

Fig. 3

They are vectors OA, OB and OC. Also shown in Fig. 2 is vector OX, corresponding to a mixed process composed of processes 1 and 3. If vector OB, representing the technical process 2 is longer than vector OX (e.g. its length is OB'), then this process requires a greater unit outlay of both factors of production than the mixed process, i.e. it is inefficient in relation to the latter. If the length of vector OB equals OX, then process 2 requires the same unit outlay as the mixed process, i.e. it is equivalent to it. Therefore, process 2 is effective only if vector OB is shorter than vector OX, corresponding to the above-mentioned mixed process.

A similar reasoning can be applied to the technical processes 2, 3, and 4 and to vectors OB, OC and OD, etc., of Fig. 3 corresponding to them. In consequence, it turns out that the angular line $ABCD$, etc., determined by the ends of the vectors (projections), representing effective technical processes, is concave to the origin of the system of co-ordinates. It turns out also that only the mixing of the "neighbouring"[3] technical processes, e.g. processes 1 and 2, 3 and 4, etc., is effective. It can be seen directly from the graph that any process resulting from mixing processes 1 and 3 is represented by the segment *AC*. Such a mixed process requires a greater unit outlay of both factors of production than process 2. Similarly, the joining of processes 2 and 4 requires a greater unit outlay of both factors than process 3; the joining of processes 1 and 4 requires a greater unit outlay of both factors than processes 2 and 3.

The angular line *ABCD*, etc., is "declining" and at the same time it is concave to the origin of the system of co-ordinates. It follows that the slope of its particular segments (*AB*, *BC*, *CD*, etc.) with respect to the axis of abscissae decreases (Fig. 3). The slope coefficients (tangents) of the consecutive segments *AB*, *BC*, *CD*, etc., form then a decreasing sequence:

$$\left|\frac{a_{11}-a_{12}}{a_{21}-a_{22}}\right| > \left|\frac{a_{12}-a_{13}}{a_{22}-a_{23}}\right| > \left|\frac{a_{13}-a_{14}}{a_{23}-a_{24}}\right| > .... \qquad (6.1)$$

This is illustrated in Fig. 4. The first term of this sequence is equal to the tangent of the angle *ABR*, i.e. to the slope coefficient of the segment *AB*.

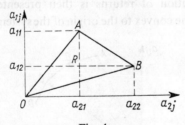

Fig. 4

---

[3] According to the law of substitution the angular line *ABCD*, etc. is "declining". The vertexes *A*, *B*, *C*, *D*, etc., can then be monotonically arranged according to their heights and the vectors *OA*, *OB*, *OC*, *OD*, etc., can be arranged according to the vertexes. The "neighbouring" technical processes are defined as the processes to which there correspond neighbouring vectors in the system of vectors thus arranged.

In the same way it can be shown that further terms of the above sequence are equal to the slope coefficients of the segments *BC*, *CD*, etc. We express the slope by absolute values because otherwise they would be negative since the segments *AB*, *BC*, *CD*, etc., are "declining".

The reciprocals of the slope coefficients (6.1) form an increasing sequence:

$$\left|\frac{a_{21}-a_{22}}{a_{11}-a_{12}}\right| < \left|\frac{a_{22}-a_{23}}{a_{12}-a_{13}}\right| < \left|\frac{a_{23}-a_{24}}{a_{13}-a_{14}}\right| < \ldots \quad (6.2)$$

These reciprocals are *the rates of substitution* of outlays and they measure a unit increase in the outlay of one factor of production per unit decrease in the unit outlay of the other factor. The sequence of inequalities (6.2) states that in consecutive switching from one technical process to another (neighbouring one) the rate of subsitution of outlays increases. This property is called the *law of the increasing rate of substitution of outlays*.

Treating returns as negative outlays we obtain the law of the decreasing rate of substitution of returns as a direct conclusion from the law of the increasing rate of outlays. Transforming negative outlays into positively counted returns we change the sign in the sequence of inequality (6.2). The law of the decreasing rate of substitution of returns is then presented geometrically by an angular line convex to the origin of the system of co-ordinates.

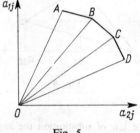

Fig. 5

This is shown in Fig. 5 in which the axis of co-ordinates Oa_{1j} and Oa_{2j} denote unit returns, i.e. the return (the quantity of the product) per unit of outlay.

In a similar way we derive, also as a conclusion from the law of the increasing rate of substitution, the law of increasing additional outlays (their decreasing productivity). We consider one positive unit outlay (of the factor of production) and one negative unit outlay, i.e. the return or the quantity of the commodity produced. A decrease in the unit outlay is interpreted simply as an increase in the unit return, i.e. an increase by one unit of the quantity of the product. Presenting the return as a positive quantity (denoted by x), we obtain a geometric interpretation shown in Fig. 6.

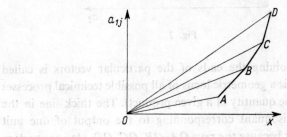

Fig. 6

7. Neo-classical theory of production

In the interpretation of quantitative relations in the process of production, presented above, it is assumed that there is a finite number (in practice rather small) of technical processes by which we can produce a given commodity. Moreover, in this interpretation we allow for available specific technical equipment and specific productive capacity for the particular processes involved. If we drop the assumption of specific technical equipment (and of a specific productive capacity) and assume that the technical processes are divisible and their number is infinite and forms a *continuum* in which the law of substitution applies to all factors of production (and, in the case of joint production, to all products), we arrive at the neo-classical theory of production.

The ends of the vectors representing the particular technical processes then form a smooth (i.e. non-angular) continuous line and, instead of the picture shown in Fig. 1 or 3, we obtain the picture shown in Fig. 7.

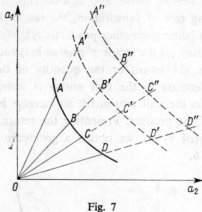

Fig. 7

The line joining the ends of the particular vectors is called *isoquant* (this is a geometric locus of all possible technical processes giving the same quantity of a given product). The thick line in the graph is the isoquant corresponding to the output of one unit of the product because the rays OA, OB, OC, OD, etc., are vectors of unit outlays. Since, according to our assumptions, there is no specific technical equipment and no specific productive capacity corresponding to the particular processes, these processes are divisible and production can be set at any level. If the quantity of the product is doubled, then the outlays of the factors of production are doubled. In place of the vectors representing unit outlays in particular technical processes, we obtain vectors of double length (OA', OB', OC', OD', etc., in the graph) which represent the outlays of the factors of production in the processes of production producing two units of the commodity. The ends of these vectors determine the isoquant presented in the graph as a broken line. This isoquant corresponds to the output of two units of the commodity. Similarly we can obtain isoquants corresponding to various quantities of commodities, i.e., as we say, to various *volumes of production*. The lengths of the vectors whose ends determine the isoquants are proportional to the quantity of commodity, i.e. to the volume of production. Thus, all the isoquants are parallel.

In consequence, we have two families of isoquants which can be shown in the case of two factors, as in Fig. 7, with the help of the equation

$$f(a_1 x, a_2 x) = x$$

and in the case of n factors used in production in the form of the equation

$$f(a_1 x, a_2 x \ldots a_n x) = x. \tag{7.1}$$

In this equation parameter x denotes the volume of production; as we can see, the outlays of the factors of production $a_1 x, a_2 x, \ldots,$ $a_n x$ are proportional to the volume of production.

Writing $v_1 = a_1 x, v_2 = a_2 x, \ldots, v_n = a_n x$ and putting the volume of production x on the left-hand side of the equation we obtain the expression

$$x = f(v_1, v_2, \ldots, v_n). \tag{7.2}$$

The volume of production x is here a function of the outlays of the factors of production $v_1, v_2, \ldots, v_n$. In the neo-classical theory this function is called *the production function*. It follows from (7.1) that it is a homogeneous function of the first degree.[4]

---

[4] The homogeneity of the production function appears as an assumption in earlier formulations of the neo-classical theory of production. It was accepted as an assumption particularly by P. H. Wicksteed, *An Essay on the Coordination of the Laws of Distribution*, London, 1894. In later formulations it was assumed that the production function is homogeneous only for a whole branch of production but not necessarily for a particular production establishment. The homogeneity of the production function for branches of production is derived from the assumption that all establishments produce an optimum quantity of a commodity. Then, the multiplication of the volume of production is accomplished by the multiplication of the number of establishments (each of which continues to produce the same optimal quantities), in consequence of which the outlays of all the factors of production are proportionately multiplied. Such a solution of the problem of homogeneity of the production function was given by K. Wicksell in *Lectures on Political Economy*, Vol. 1 (translation from Swedish), London, 1935, pp. 127–31. The question of homogeneity of the function aroused an extensive discussion described by G. J. Stigler in *Production and Distribution Theories*, New York, 1941. See also E. Schneider, *Theorie der Produktion, ed. cit.*, pp. 19–21.

The neo-classical theory assumes that the production function has first and second derivatives. The first derivatives of the production function are called the *marginal productivities* of the particular factors of production. It is assumed that

$$\frac{\partial f}{\partial v_i} > 0 \quad \text{and} \quad \frac{\partial^2 f}{\partial v_i^2} < 0 \tag{7.3}$$

for v_i exceeding a certain value $(i = 1, 2, ..., n)$. The last inequality expresses the law of diminishing returns.

Isoquants are "downwards sloping" lines (the law of substitution of outlays) and are concave to the origin of the system of co-ordinates (the law of the increasing rate of substitution of outlay). The concavity of the isoquant is expressed by the inequality

$$\frac{d^2 v_i}{dv_2^2} > 0, \tag{7.4}$$

where v_1 and v_2 are the outlays of two different factors of production (the numbering of the factors is arbitrary).

Between the law of the increasing rate of substitution of outlays expressed by the inequality (7.4) and the law of diminishing returns expressed by another inequality (7.3) there is the following relationship.

On the basis of the theorem on the derivatives of the implicit function, we have

$$\frac{dv_1}{dv_2} = -\frac{\dfrac{\partial f}{\partial v_2}}{\dfrac{\partial f}{\partial v_1}}.$$

Therefore,

$$\frac{\partial^2 v_1}{\partial v_2^2} = -\frac{\dfrac{\partial^2 f}{\partial v_2^2}\left(\dfrac{\partial f}{\partial v_1}\right)^2 - 2\dfrac{\partial^2 f}{\partial v_2 \partial v_1} \cdot \dfrac{\partial f}{\partial v_1} \cdot \dfrac{\partial f}{\partial v_2} + \dfrac{\partial^2 f}{\partial v_1^2}\left(\dfrac{\partial f}{\partial v_2}\right)^2}{\left(\dfrac{\partial f}{\partial v_1}\right)^3}. \tag{7.5}$$

The inequality (7.4) requires that this expression be positive. As a rule, this is ensured by the inequalities (7.3), the second of which expresses the law of diminishing returns.

However, in the case when

$$\frac{\partial^2 f}{\partial v_1 \partial v_2} < 0,$$

i.e. when an increase in the outlay v_2 decreases the marginal productivity of the outlay v_1, it may happen that the expression will assume the value 0 or will become negative. This happens when such a decrease in the marginal productivity is very great: the operation of the law of diminishing returns is then thwarted.

And vice versa: the inequality (7.4) can be satisfied when the second of the inequalities (7.3) does not hold (i.e. the law of diminishing returns does not operate). This may happen when

$$\frac{\partial^2 f}{\partial v_1 \partial v_2} > 0,$$

i.e. when an increase in outlay v_2 increases the marginal productivity of outlay v_1. If such an increase is very great it may make up for the fact that the law of diminishing returns does not operate.

The above-mentioned cross-operation of the influence of the outlay of one factor of production on the marginal productivity of the outlay of the other factor is limited, however, by the homogeneity of the production function. Homogeneous functions of the first degree satisfy the following relation between the second derivatives:[5]

$$\frac{\partial^2 f}{\partial v_1 \partial v_r} v_1 + \frac{\partial^2 f}{\partial v_2 \partial v_r} v_2 + \ldots + \frac{\partial^2 f}{\partial v_r^2} v_r + \ldots + \frac{\partial^2 f}{\partial v_n \partial v_r} v_n = 0$$

$$(r = 1, 2, \ldots, n).$$

[5] This relation follows from Euler's theorem for homogeneous functions. In the case of homogeneous functions of the first degree, according to this theorem, we have

$$\frac{\partial f}{\partial v_1} v_1 + \frac{\partial f}{\partial v_2} v_2 + \ldots + \frac{\partial f}{\partial v_n} v_n = f.$$

Differentiating this equality with respect to v_r, we obtain the above relation.

It follows from this relation that

$$\frac{\partial^2 f}{\partial v_r^2} = \frac{1}{v_r} \sum_{i \neq r} \frac{\partial^2 f}{\partial v_i \partial v_r} v_i \quad (i = 1, 2, \ldots, n). \quad (7.6)$$

The second of the inequalities (7.3) imposes then certain limitations on the mixed derivatives appearing on the right-hand side of (7.6).

In a special case, when the production function is a function of only two variables, the law of diminishing returns is both a sufficient and a necessary condition of the law of the increasing rate of substitution of outlays. For then (7.6) assumes the folowing form:

$$-\frac{\partial^2 f}{\partial v_2^2} = \frac{v_1}{v_2} \frac{\partial^2 f}{\partial v_1 \partial v_2}.$$

Substituting this into the expression (7.5), we obtain

$$\frac{d^2 v_1}{dv_2^2} = \frac{-\frac{\partial^2 f}{\partial v_2 \partial v_1} \frac{\partial f}{\partial v_1} \left(\frac{v_1}{v_2} \frac{\partial f}{\partial v_1} + 2 \frac{\partial f}{\partial v_2} \right) + \frac{\partial^2 f}{\partial v_1^2} \left(\frac{\partial f}{\partial v_2} \right)^2}{\left(\frac{\partial f}{\partial v_1} \right)^3}.$$

Considering that $v_1 > 0$, $v_2 > 0$, $\frac{\partial f}{\partial v_1} > 0$, $\frac{\partial f}{\partial v_2} > 0$, we find that $\frac{d^2 v_1}{dv_2^2} > 0$ when and only when $\frac{\partial^2 f}{\partial v_2^2} < 0$, i.e. when the second of the inequalities (7.3) is satisfied. This does not happen, however, in the general case when the production function is a function of more than two variables.

Joint production can be considered similarly as above by treating the products other than the reference products as factors of production whose outlays are negative, or by denoting all products by positive numbers and all outlays by negative numbers (or vice versa).[6] Treating the products as negative outlays, we

[6] The interpretation of joint production by treating outlays as negative returns was introduced by J. R. Hicks in *Value and Capital*, London, 1946, p. 319. Later this interpretation was also accepted in activity analysis, i.e. the theory of production based on considering a finite number of technical processes. See on this subject O. Lange, *Optimal Decisions*, Oxford–Warsaw, 1971, and R. D. G. Allen, *Mathematical Economics*, ed. cit., pp. 613–15.

find that inequality (7.4) expresses also the law of the decreasing rate of substitution of returns. Assuming that v_1 denotes the outlay and v_2 the quantity of the product with a minus sign, we interpret inequality (7.4) as the law of increasing additional outlays, i.e. the law of the declining productivity of additional outlays. It should be mentioned, however, that the law of decreasing productivity of additional outlays thus interpreted is of the nature of the accepted assumption and not a consequence of the law of diminishing returns interpreted as declining marginal productivity, i.e. as satisfying the second of the inequalities (7.3); for, as we know, the second inequality (7.3) and inequality (7.4) usually do not coincide.

As we can see, the neo-classical theory of production approached quantitative relations in the process of production in a highly idealized way and constituted a theoretical model far removed from the actual production process. In fact, the number of technical processes is finite (and usually small) and particular technical processes are characterized by specific technical equipment and by a specific productive capacity. Moreover, in reality, not all factors of production are subject to the law of substitution, and the law of diminishing returns, interpreted as a property of the production function, i.e. as a technological regularity, is a generalization deprived of an empirical basis.

The neo-classical theory of production should then be regarded as an attempted abortive approach to quantitative relations occurring in the process of production.[7] Historically it derives from both the theory of three parallel "factors of production"— labour, land and capital—and from attempts to justify the distribution of the social product among owners of these "factors". It is an attempt at a generalization and, at the same time, at a modernization of this theory. Its popularization was due to the fact that it lent itself to apologetic conclusions justifying the

---

[7] On the neo-classical theory of production see also O. Lange, *Optimal Decisions, ed. cit.* Interesting comments can be found in the work by H. Schultz: "Marginal Productivity and the General Pricing Process", *Journal of Political Economy*, Chicago, 1929.

distribution of social income in the capitalist mode of production as based on the principle of awarding to the owners of the factors of production the value of the marginal product of these factors. We shall have more to say about it in the next volume of this work.*

---

* The late author intended to continue his work (editor's note).

CHAPTER III

Renewal of Means of Production

Reproduction is a continuous repetition of the process of production. It necessitates, as we know, constant replacement of the used-up means of production and of the labour force. Replacement of the labour force necessitates consumption of products and utilization of services involved in the replacement of the labour force, composed of the manpower and in the replacement of generations. Since consumption and the use of certain products as a means of rendering services is also required to secure the services related to this replacement, in the final analysis, the replacement of the labour force is reduced to consumption of goods. Replacement of the labour force occurs through consumption, namely, through consumption of means necessary for the maintenance of the labour force. It takes place outside the process of production[1] and is related to production only

---

[1] In conditions of slavery, replacement of the labour force can take place directly in the process of production. This happens when the owners "breed" slaves similarly as they "breed" cattle. Such breeding is a production process and the necessary means of maintenance of the slave are means of production similarly as fodder, stables and various equipment for draught animals. As a rule, however, in societies based on a slave system of production, such breeding of slaves took place only to a limited extent. Replacement of slave labour was usually a result of spontaneous demographic processes among the slave population and primarily a result of getting new slaves (i.e. transforming free people into slaves) by wars and by capturing slaves. The acquisition of slaves by wars and slave-capturing expeditions played a great role in ancient social systems, particularly in Ancient Rome. (See N. Mashkin, *Historya drevnyego Rima* [*History of Ancient Rome*].) Mashkin states that in the second century B. C. the breeding of a slave cost more than his purchase price on the market (p. 249). Max Weber (*Agrarverhältnisse im Altertum. Gesammelte Aufsätze zur Social- und Wirtschaftsgeschichte* [*Agrarian Relations in Antiquity*], Tübin-

indirectly, so that the "product" of consumption of the necessary means of subsistence is the ability to perform work which constitutes a basis for the personal factors operative in the process of production. On the other hand, the replacement of means of production takes place in the production process itself, through the production of the necessary means required to replace those which are used up in production. For this reason we confine ourselves here to the question of quantitative relations in the replacement of means of production. The question of the replacement of the labour force is a problem in demography, hygiene, and medicine, education and care, occupational training, psychology and sociology of labour, etc.

The replacement of means of production is different for working capital means and fixed capital means. Working capital means are completely used up in the course of one period of production and they must be replaced by new ones within that period. During a calendar unit of time (e.g. one year) the amount of used-up means of production equals the amount used up during the period of production multiplied by the (whole or fractional) number of periods of production included in the unit of time under consideration. To replace the used-up means it is necessary to have a certain quantity of working capital means. Knowing the unit outlay of the particular working capital means for the technical process used in production, we can calculate this quantity; it equals the product of the unit outlay and of the quantity of the commodity produced (within a unit of time). Replacement of fixed capital means is more complicated. They wear out gradual-

---

gen, 1924 pp. 19 and 244), points out that the billeting of slaves in large estates prevented their natural reproduction. The conclusion of the period of wars and piracy brought about the transition to the colonate system. Captured slaves in Africa were a source of the formation and replenishment of the slave population in America (both on the continent, particularly in the southern states of the United States, and on the islands of the Caribbean Sea). In the years 1486–1641 about 1,400,000 slaves were shipped from the coast of Angola alone; in the years 1580–1688 about 1,000,000 slaves (i.e. about 10,000 a year) were brought to Brazil. During the 11 years from 1783 to 1793, 300,000 slaves were shipped through Liverpool. See B. Davidson, *Old Africa Rediscovered*, London, 1951.

ly and are used over several or even more periods of production, and when their usefulness ends they are withdrawn and replaced by new ones. The replacement of particular fixed capital means does not take place continuously as is the case with working capital means: the former are replaced after a long period of time, i.e. after a given means has reached the end of its life span.[2] Before the period of utilization ends a fixed capital means retains its usefulness and does not require renewal.

However, to retain their usefulness, fixed capital means require a number of outlays both of labour and of means of production. First of all, there are *maintenance outlays*. Included here are various activities, i.e. specific kinds of labour (maintenance work) and means of production, e.g. protective coating of ships, bridges and other steel equipment to prevent corrosion, plaster to cover the walls of buildings, grease for machines, fodder for draught animals, fertilizers for the soil, etc. Without maintenance outlays fixed capital means would quickly lose their usefulness, and sometimes they could become almost entirely useless. Various *repair outlays* are also necessary. Fixed capital means may be damaged in the course of their utilization and such damage must be repaired. Repairs require certain labour outlays (repair work) and a certain amount of means of production. Damage to fixed capital means is, as a rule, of a random nature, brought about by a large number of minor or more significant causes, not directly related to the course of the technical process used in production, but "external" to such process. In other words, they are disturbances in the process of production.

Damage to fixed capital means is usually the result of damage to particular parts, e.g. parts of a machine, tank, building, transportation means, etc. The repair consists in replacing the damaged part by a new one or by suitably attending to damaged parts (e.g. by mending a hole, welding a broken rod, fixing a tile that had fallen off). Frequently damage is related to the length of time over which a given means has been used. This was pointed

---

[2] The period of utilization is often also called *the period of service* of a given fixed capital means. This term is widely used in cost accounting. It was also used by Marx in *Capital*, Vol. I, *ed. cit.*, p. 185.

out by Marx: "The injuries to which individual parts of the machinery are exposed are naturally accidental, and so are therefore the necessary repairs. Nevertheless, two kinds of repairs are to be distinguished in the general mass, which have a more or less fixed character and fall within various periods of life of the fixed capital. These are diseases of childhood and the far more numerous diseases in the period following the prime of life. A machine, for instance, may be placed in the process of production in ever so perfect a condition, still the actual work will always reveal shortcomings which must be remedied by additional labour. On the other hand, the more a machine passes beyond the prime of life, when, therefore, the normal wear and tear has accumulated and has rendered its material worn and weak, the more numerous and considerable will be repairs required to keep it in order for the remainder of its average lifetime; it is the same with an old man, who needs more medical care to keep from dying than a young and strong man."[3] This is true not only of machines but also of all kinds of fixed capital means employed in production.

We should distinguish complete destruction of a fixed capital means from mere damage. Such destruction may be the consequence of a random event, such as a fire, flood, the sinking of a ship, a car, plane or train crash, etc. It differs from damage in that it affects not a particular part of a fixed capital means, but the whole means or at least such an essential part of it that it cannot be made useful again by repairs; it is necessary to replace the means entirely destroyed by new ones.

However, the border-line between renewal and repair of used up or destroyed fixed capital means is vague. Usually, a distinction is made between regular and major repairs. Regular repairs consist in repairing damage that occurs in the normal course of utilizing a given fixed capital means. They are similar to maintenance. Maintenance protects a fixed capital means against damage, while regular repairs consist in removing damage caused in the course of the production process in order to prevent major

---

[3] K. Marx, *Capital*, Vol. II, *ed. cit.*, pp. 198–9. Marx speaks here of fixed capital, but the content of the text cited applies to fixed capital means also in modes of production other than a capitalist one.

damage or complete wearing out of a given means. Means of production used up in maintenance and regular repairs are in the nature of working capital means; they are used up completely in the process of repairs and constitute, in a sense, a material which is absorbed completely by the repaired object. For instance: plaster becomes part of a building, a new screw becomes part of a machine, a new fuse part of an electrical installation, etc. Their renewal takes place directly after they are used up, forming a stock of means available for repairs, at any time, in the event of new damage.[4]

The situation is different with major repairs which consist in partial renewal of a given fixed capital means.[5] In contrast to regular repairs of ordinary damage which is caused in the course of production, in major repairs important parts of a fixed capital means, which are almost independent objects, are replaced by new ones. Thus, it means replacing specific objects which are important components of a given fixed capital means, e.g. replacing wheels or a steam-boiler of an engine, a piston of a combustion engine, a transmission shaft of a machine tool, a roof of a building, etc. These objects are replaced in the strict sense

---

[4] A certain reserve of labour power is also kept available for any new repairs that may be required. "As it is highly important to remedy any injury to a machine immediately, every large factory employs in addition to the regular factory hands a number of other staff, such as engineers, woodworkers, mechanics, smiths, etc." (*Ibid.*, p. 200.) Major production establishments, farms and transport companies have, as a rule, their own repair shops. Marx expressed certain doubts as to the nature of the means of production used up in repairs. Considering the problem under conditions of capitalist production he wrote: "This capital, invested in regular repairs, is in many respects a peculiar capital, which can be classed neither with the circulating nor the fixed capital, but still belongs with more justification to the former, since it is part of the running expenses." (*Ibid.*) Considering the problem in a broader context of a system as the one of natural (material) properties of production, it seems that the inclusion of means of production used up for regular repairs in the category of working capital means should not raise doubts.

[5] *Ibid.*, p. 201: "The repairs are further distinguished as ordinary and substantial. The last-named are partly a renewal of the fixed capital in its natural form. ..."

of this word and they have a certain independence and are not lost in a fixed capital means undergoing repairs (e.g. wheels of an engine as distinct from rivets and screws used in regular repairs). These new objects serve over a long period of time until the end of the period of utilization of the fixed capital means or until they are withdrawn and replaced by new ones in later major repairs. For this reason we include them in fixed capital means.

Major repairs may be the result of major damage to fixed capital means, or they may result from partial destruction of fixed capital means by fire, accident, etc., so that part of this means can still be used while other parts must be replaced. Not all major repairs are caused by random events. In addition to repairs of damage and partial destructions there are major repairs necessitated by the fact that individual parts of a fixed capital means do not wear out at the same pace. Some parts wear out faster than others and instead of replacing the whole fixed capital means it may suffice to replace those parts that had worn out faster, while the remaining ones may continue to be used. This is, in a sense, a "regeneration" of particular used-up parts of a given fixed capital means. This kind of replacement of a fixed capital means may often occur in stages, by consecutive major repairs. In every consecutive major repair different parts are replaced until, finally, there remains no original part of a given fixed capital means; the means has been renewed entirely.

Renewal by consecutive major repairs occurs particularly in rolling stock. Marx cites the following example: "... the supply of locomotives and cars is continually renewed; at one time new wheels are put on, at another a new frame is constructed. Those parts on which the motion is conditioned and which are most exposed to wear and tear are gradually renewed; the machines and cars may then undergo so many repairs that not a trace of the old material remains in them. ..."[6]

---

[6] K. Marx, *Capital*, Vol. II, *ed cit.*, p. 204. There we also find the following quotation: "... we maintain the locomotives forever, we renew our machines. ... You can always find a new wheel, an axle, or some other part of an old machine in usable condition, and that helps to construct cheaply a ma-

This applies in general to very durable means, i.e. the ones with a very long period of utilization, such as buildings, bridges, canals, etc. In such means parts do not wear uniformly; some of them carry a greater load when the whole means is in use (e.g. tyres of a car, a knife of a machine tool, valves of a radio set) or are more exposed to the destructive influence of the elements (e.g. the roof of a building) and must be replaced earlier than the remaining parts. It is not always possible, however, to complete renewal by consecutive major repairs. Most machines used in industrial establishments are ultimately withdrawn after a certain number of major repairs, and are replaced by new ones. This is usually necessitated by technical progress causing obsolescence of a given fixed capital means. In such cases also the example cited by Marx cannot be applied. If a steam-engine is replaced by an electric or a diesel motor, the type of replacement in stages, by consecutive major repairs, cannot be applied because a steam-engine should be completely withdrawn and replaced by an engine of some other type. The fact remains, however, that when particular parts of a given means do not wear out uniformly, some of them are replaced earlier than others and this necessitates major repairs.

The length of utilization time of a fixed capital means depends upon maintenance and repairs already performed, both regular and major ones. We assume that in the course of utilization of a fixed capital means all necessary maintenance and repair work is done, so that the means can be used as long as possible. The maximum period of utilization that can be realized under such conditions is the *period of utilization* of the fixed capital means. "The normal lifetime of fixed capital is, of course" Marx wrote, "so calculated that all the conditions are fulfilled under which it can perform its functions normally during that time, just as we assume in placing a man's average life... that he will wash himself."[7]

chine which is just as good as an entirely new one. I now produce every week one new locomotive that is to say, one that is as good as new, for its boiler, cylinder, and frame are new."

[7] *Ibid.*, p. 197.

This applies also to fixed capital means under conditions different from those obtaining in the capitalist mode of production. In consequence, every fixed capital means used in a specific technical process entails a specific period of utilization after which the means is replaced by a new one. When replacement takes place in stages by consecutive major repairs such a period does not exist for the whole capital means but only for its relevant parts. We treat these parts as independent objects of renewal, possessing a specific period of utilization.

The period of utilization may be the same for all specimens of a given fixed capital means. This requires, however, that all specimens (or objects) be completely homogeneous and used in identical conditions. As a rule, this is not so. Particular objects differ from one another, even if only slightly, by the strength of the material, the strength of construction, the weak links, etc. Also the conditions of their utilization are not identical: some bear a greater load, are exposed to greater vibrations, to a stronger impact of certain chemical processes, to different atmospheric conditions, humidity, and, finally, to different kinds of treatment by workers. In consequence, different objects, being the same specimens of the same fixed capital means of production, have different periods of utilization. From experience, however, we can determine the average period of utilization of the objects of a given type, i.e. of particular specimens of a given fixed capital means. "The lifetime of an instrument of labour, therefore", says Marx, "is spent in the repetition of a greater or lesser number of similar operations. Its life may be compared with that of a human being. Every day brings a man 24 hours nearer to his grave: but how many days he has still to travel on that road, no man can tell accurately by merely looking at him. This difficulty, however, does not prevent life insurance offices from drawing, by means of the theory of averages, very accurate and at the same time very profitable conclusions. So it is with the instruments of labour. It is known from experience how long on the average a machine of a particular kind will last."[8]

---

[8] K. Marx, *Capital*, Vol. I, *ed. cit.*, p. 186.

This suggests the treatment of renewal of fixed capital means by *actuarial methods*, i.e. methods of actuarial mathematics.[9]

[9] Actuarial science or actuarial mathematics is a branch of mathematics dealing with the calculation of risks, premiums and reserve funds in insurance. The tenor of these calculations is the frequency of occurrence of random events in a population of insured objects, events resulting in payments of insurance benefits. On this basis are determined insurance premiums required to cover the payment of benefits together with reserve funds to meet unexpected fluctuations in the frequencies of random events. Actuarial mathematics were first applied to life insurance. The numerical data needed for calculations were supplied by the records of insurance companies in which the age of the insured was given. Officials of the companies in charge of the records were called actuaries and they carried out the necessary calculations. Hence the term "actuarial science" and the use of the term "actuary" to denote a person engaged in insurance calculations. A scientific basis to insurance mathematics was given by the astronomer E. Halley, who published in 1663 the first elimination table. Before him, J. Graunt worked out an early version of the elimination table (in 1662). In the eighteenth century an elimination table was designed by J. P. Süssmilch (in 1741). Finally, P. S. Laplace (1814) applied probability calculus to studies of the death rate. This led to a mathematical approach to patterns in natural movements of population. The branch of science which deals with this problem is called *mathematical demography*. The foundations of mathematical demography were laid by G. Zeuner (1869), F. G. Knapp (1874) and W. Lexis (1875). The methods of mathematical demography were also applied to other branches of insurance, such as insurance against accidents at work, against fire, against shipping losses, etc. This finally led to a generalization of the methods of mathematical demography in the form of *the theory of replacement* which studies the properties of renewable collections, i.e. the ones from which particular elements are eliminated and to which new elements are added at the same time. Human or animal populations with which mathematical demography deals are particular cases of such renewable collections. Deaths and births are particular cases of elimination and addition of elements of a population. The theory of replacement has become a basic part of insurance mathematics because it makes possible a uniform theoretical approach to all kinds of insurance. The exposition of the theory of replacement is given by W. Saxer, *Versicherungsmathematik* (*Actuarial Mathematics*), Part 1, Berlin, 1955, Chapter 10; Part 2, Berlin, 1958, Chapter 4. In 1913, the English economist D. H. Robertson pointed out an analogy between the process of replacement of fixed capital means and the process of replacement of population. See D. H. Robertson, "Some Material for a Study of Trade Fluctuation", *Journal of the Royal Statistical Society*, 1913, and, by the same author, *A Study of Industrial Fluctuations*, London, 1915, pp. 36–45. Finally, the prominent demographer and actuary, J. Lotka,

On the basis of experience gained from statistical observations, or of records of production establishments, we can design for various types of fixed capital means distribution tables according to the duration of use of a given object.[10] Such tables are sometimes also called *survival tables* because they show the number

---

applied the mathematical theory of replacement to the replacement of fixed capital means of production in the study "Industrial Replacement", *Skandinavisk Aktuarietidskrift*, 1933. See also the work of the same author, "Contributions to the Theory of Self-renewing Aggregates with Special Reference to Industrial Replacement", *Annals of Mathematical Statistics*, 1939. This opened the way to the treatment of the problem of renewal of fixed capital means by actuarial methods. This approach has later become quite common. The result was a further development of the theory of replacement; in this connection see M. Fréchet, *Les Ensembles statistiques renouvellés et remplacement industriel*, Paris, 1949; L. Koźniewska, *Zagadnienia odnowienia* (*Problems of Renewal*), Warsaw, 1963; O. Lange, *The Theory of Reproduction and Accumulation*, Oxford–Warsaw, 1969, pp. 110–20. A Boyarski, *Matematikoekonomicheskiye ocherky* (*Studies in Mathematical Economics*), Moscow, 1962, Chapter 9. The contemporary state of the theory of replacement is presented by W. L. Smith in "Renewal Theory and Its Ramifications", *Journal of the Royal Statistical Society*, Section B, 1958, and D. R. Cox, *Renewal Theory*, London, 1962. The theory of renewal is also applied to nuclear physics for studies of the process of disintegration of nuclei. The appearance and disappearance of elementary particles in the disintegration of the nucleus is a process of renewal analogous to the demographic process of birth and death. D. R. Cox gives numerous examples in his book. One of the first to point out the importance of actuarial methods for atomic physics was the prominent statistician–economist—W. Bortkewitch. See W. Bortkewitch, *Radioactive Strahlung als Gegenstand wahrscheinlichkeits theoretischer Untersuchungen* (*Radioactive Radiations and Their Theoretical Probability Investigations*), Berlin, 1913. Another field of application of the theory of renewal are studies of renewal processes of generations in biological populations, including pathogenetic populations of bacteria in connection with studies of human populations as culture media for bacteria (epidemiology) and of mutual relationships between various biological populations (ecology). The pioneer of such studies was the prominent mathematician V. Volterra, *Leçons sur la théorie mathématique de la lutte pour la vie*, (*Lectures on the Mathematical Theory of Survival*), Paris, 1931. On this subject see also M. Bartlett, *Stochastic Population Model in Ecology and Epidemiology*, London, 1960.

[10] We are interested here in fixed capital means of production. The table of the distribution of objects according to the duration of use can be also applied to durable consumer goods, e.g. dwelling houses, passenger cars, etc.

of objects which survive a given period of utilization. They are similar to the distribution of population by age; they give the "age", i.e. the period of utilization of particular objects (speci-

TABLE 1

DISTRIBUTION OF BULBS ACCORDING TO DURATION OF USE
(Survival Table)

Age (in weeks) τ	Number of bulbs (in use) N_τ	Survival coefficient $l_\tau \dfrac{N_\tau}{N_0}$
0	100,000	—
1	100,000	1·00
2	99,000	0·99
3	98,000	0·98
4	97,000	0·97
5	96,000	0·96
6	93,000	0·93
7	87,000	0·87
8	77,000	0·77
9	63,000	0·63
10	48,000	0·48
11	32,000	0·32
12	18,000	0·18
13	10,000	0·10
14	6,000	0·06
15	3,000	0·03
16	2,000	0·02
17	1,000	0·01
18	0	0·00

mens) of a given type of fixed capital means, in the form of statistical frequency distribution. In the first column is given the length of use of a given object, i.e. its age, in the second column the corresponding number of objects. This is illustrated in Table 1, which gives the distribution of 100,000 installed bulbs according to duration of use (e.g. in weeks).[11]

[11] This example is taken from the book by C. W. Churchman, R. L. Ackoff and E. L. Arnoff, *Introduction to Operations Research*, New York, 1957, p. 493.

The distribution given in Table 1 can be presented in the form of a histogram or a diagram. This is shown in Fig. 8.

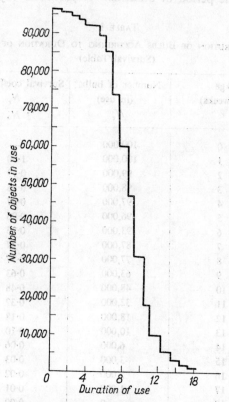

Fig. 8. Diagram of the distribution of bulbs according to the duration of use (time of survival)

The third column of Table 1 gives the ratio of the number of bulbs at a given age to the total number of bulbs in use (in our example 100,000). Generally speaking, if the number of objects originally installed is N_0, and the number of objects whose period of utilization is τ units of time (e.g. years, months, weeks) is N_τ, then the ratio is

$$I_\tau = \frac{N_\tau}{N_0}. \tag{1}$$

This ratio is called *the survival coefficient* of an object after the completion of τ units of time. It shows the percentage of objects that will survive over τ units of time.

As a rule, the number of objects used over a long period of time is smaller than the number of objects used for a short period of time. In other words, the number of old objects is smaller than the number of young ones. For, in the course of time some objects are eliminated from use. Only in exceptional cases, when all objects have the same period of utilization, do all of them decline simultaneously and all of them are eliminated from use at the same time. If, however, as is generally the case, particular objects differ by their period of utilization, some of them go out of use earlier than others. For this reason, there are fewer old objects than young ones. This is shown in Table 1 in the form of decreasing frequencies in the second column. Correspondingly also the survival coefficient declines with the increasing period of utilization τ.

In consequence, in the course of utilization, the number of objects in use declines. In the $(\tau+1)$th unit of time this decrease is $N_\tau - N_{\tau+1}$ objects; it can also be shown in the form of a frequency distribution. This is illustrated in Table 2. Table 2 gives in the first column the period of utilization, and in the second the elimination occurring during the consecutive units of the utilization period.

Such a table is called an *elimination table*.[12] It is similar to a life table used in demography. The elimination table is derived from a survival table by deducting the value in the second column of this table.

The ratio of elimination of objects within a unit of time of utilization to the number of objects originally installed is called the *elimination coefficient*. It is defined by formula (2).

---

[12] The term "elimination table" was introduced by S. Szulc in *Metody statystyczne (Statistical Methods)*, Warsaw, 1965, Chapter 14. The first collection of elimination tables for various kinds of fixed capital means of production was published by E. B. Kurtz, *Life Expectancy and Physical Property*, New York, 1930. In the theory of renewal, elimination tables are also referred to as "the order of elimination" after the fashion of the terms: "order of dying out" applied to life tables in demography.

$$p_\tau = \frac{N_\tau - N_{\tau+1}}{N_0}. \tag{2}$$

It shows the fraction of installed objects that is eliminated from use between τ and $\tau+1$ units of time of use (i.e. within the unit of time after the completion of age τ). In the third column of Table 2 are given the values of the coefficient of elimination for the population of installed bulbs. The histogram and diagram of these values are shown in Fig. 9.

It is worth mentioning here the demographic analogies for the quantities under consideration. In demography the number of deaths corresponds to elimination in a given age group. The death rate corresponds to the elimination coefficients.

TABLE 2

ELIMINATION TABLE FOR BULBS IN THE COURSE OF USE

Age (in weeks) τ	Elimination $N_\tau - N_{\tau+1}$	Elimination coefficient $p_\tau = \dfrac{N_\tau - N_{\tau+1}}{N_0}$	Intensity of elimination $m_\tau = \dfrac{N_\tau - N_{\tau+1}}{N_\tau}$
0	—	—	—
1	0	0·00	0·0000
2	1,000	0·01	0·0100
3	1,000	0·01	0·0101
4	1,000	0·01	0·0102
5	1,000	0·01	0·0103
6	3,000	0·03	0·0312
7	6,000	0·06	0·0645
8	10,000	0·10	0·1149
9	14,000	0·14	0·1818
10	15,000	0·15	0·2381
11	16,000	0·16	0·3333
12	14,000	0·14	0·4375
13	8,000	0·08	0·4444
14	4,000	0·04	0·4000
15	3,000	0·03	0·5000
16	1,000	0·01	0·3333
17	1,000	0·01	0·5000
18	1,000	0·01	1·0000

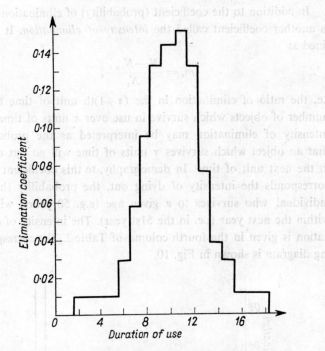

Fig. 9. Diagram of the values of the elimination coefficient

The survival coefficient and the elimination coefficient may also be interpreted as probabilities. If we draw at random[13] from a population of installed objects, then the probability that the objects drawn will survive in use over τ units of time equals the fraction of installed objects which survive τ units of time, i.e. it equals l_τ. The probability that the object drawn will be eliminated after between τ and $\tau+1$ units of time equals p_τ, i.e. the fraction of objects which in the period mentioned go out of use. Therefore, the coefficient of survival and the coefficient of elimination are also called the *probability of survival* and *the probability of elimination*.

---

[13] The drawing is random if with a large number of drawings every object is drawn with equal frequency.

In addition to the coefficient (probability) of elimination there is another coefficient called the *intensity of elimination*. It is defined as

$$m_\tau = \frac{N_\tau - N_{\tau+1}}{N_\tau}, \tag{3}$$

i.e. the ratio of elimination in the $(\tau+1)$th unit of time to the number of objects which survive in use over τ units of time. The intensity of elimination may be interpreted as the probability that an object which survives τ units of time will go out of use in the next unit of time. In demography, to this coefficient there corresponds the intensity of dying out, the probability that an individual who survives to a given age (e.g. 50 years) will die within the next year (i.e. in the 51st year). The intensity of elimination is given in the fourth column of Table 2. The corresponding diagram is shown in Fig. 10.

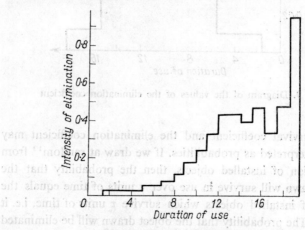

Fig. 10. Intensity of elimination of bulbs

As a rule, the intensity of elimination increases with time in the course of which the object is in use, i.e. m_τ increases with τ. The older the object, the greater the probability that it will go out of use during the next period of time. It follows from the formulae (1), (2), (3) that

$$m_\tau = \frac{p_\tau}{l_\tau}, \tag{4}$$

i.e. the intensity of elimination equals the ratio of the coefficient of elimination to the coefficient of survival. The coefficient of survival declines with an increase in the time of utilization τ because there are fewer older objects than younger ones. The only exception is a special case mentioned above when all objects have exactly the same period of utilization (then, over the whole period of utilization $l_\tau = \text{const.}$ $p_\tau = 0$ and also $m_\tau = 0$). For intensity of elimination to increase with τ it suffices then that p_τ decreases more slowly than l_τ. Usually, however, the coefficient of elimination p_τ increases, at least from a certain lower limit to a certain upper limit of the value of τ, which strengthens further the increase in m_τ. Very young objects may be eliminated in relatively greater quantities (may have a higher coefficient of elimination) because of faults in design, deficient materials, etc., which are not found in older objects which have already withstood the trial of utilization and, therefore, constitute already a properly selected population. On the other hand, very old objects may be eliminated in relatively smaller quantities because there are very few of them, and those which survive are particularly durable. Apart from this particular feature of very young and very old objects the coefficient of elimination increases with the age of the object.

Fixed capital means wear out for several reasons. The lifespan itself is related to a gradual destruction of these objects: atmospheric conditions (rain, wind, humidity, changes in temperature), changes in materials (e.g. the rusting of iron, the disintegration of construction materials) act in this direction. Fixed capital means also wear out in the process of utilization. Generally, the older the object the more it has been in use. In consequence, older objects are more likely to go out of use in the next unit of time than younger objects. Older objects are also more likely to go out of use in the next unit of time because of economic obsolescence even if they are physically homogeneous with younger objects. For, in the process of withdrawing from use because of obsolescence older objects are withdrawn in the first place because they will soon require physical renewal anyway. All this causes the intensity of elimination to increases with the length of time of utilization of the object.

Moreover, objects are also eliminated from use because of random causes: damage that cannot be repaired (or it is not profitable to repair). Such random causes usually affect objects regardless of their age. Then the intensity of elimination because of random causes may be a constant quantity, independent of the period of utilization τ. This, however, does not change the general result that the intensity of elimination, being a joint consequence of the causes mentioned here, increases with the time of utilization of the object.[14] Moreover, even if random events affect particular objects regardless of their age, the damage may depend upon the age of the object. Older objects are destroyed easier than younger ones if irreparably damaged in consequence of a given random event and, therefore, such an event necessitates more frequently their withdrawal from use.

With the help of such a table we can calculate the total number of objects withdrawn from use within a given unit of time. This number is the sum of eliminations of objects, put into use at an earlier time, which survived to a given unit of time and are withdrawn during its duration. Let us denote by t the unit of time of interest to us; for the sake of simplicity, let us call it a year (in fact it may be a year, quarter, month, week, etc.). It is an arbitrary year which for certain reasons is of interest to us; it may be the current year, the future one, the final year of the 5-year plan, or any other year. To simplify, we assume that objects last a whole number of years, e.g. 1, 2, 3, ..., years; we also assume that there is an upper limit of the life-span of the object amounting to ω

[14] A. Boyarski (*Matematiko-ekonomicheskiye ocherky, ed. cit.*, pp. 238–40) states that objects are withdrawn from use either because of random events or for reasons related to the length of time of their utilization. Therefore, the intensity of elimination can be factorized into two components $m = m'_\tau + m''_\tau$. The first component represents the effect of random events and is a constant quantity while the second increases with τ. In consequence, m_τ also increases with τ. Boyarski gives examples of particular situations in which the objects practically do not wear out and are eliminated only because of random events, e.g. pots and pans in cafeterias, shop windows, instruments of various kinds. In such cases $m''_\tau = 0$ and the intensity of elimination is determined exclusively by the probability of random events. There are, however, rather nontypical situations and they apply to a very high category of fixed capital means.

years. In year t there are available objects that were put into use a year earlier, 2 years earlier, 3 years earlier, and at the most ω years earlier, i.e. in the years $t-1$, $t-2$, $t-3$, ..., $t-\omega$. There are no older objects because they have already been withdrawn from use. Let us denote by $N_0(t-1)$ the number of objects put into use in the year $t-1$, by $N_0(t-2)$ the number of objects put into use in the year $t-2$, etc., and finally by $N_0(t-\omega)$ the number of objects put into use in the year $t-\omega$. The elimination of objects in the year t is calculated as follows. Of the objects put into use a year earlier, $N_0(t-1)$, p_1 are eliminated; of the objects put into use two years earlier, $N_0(t-2)$, p_2 are eliminated, etc. And, finally, of the objects put into use ω years earlier, $N_0(t-\omega)$, p_ω are eliminated. Here $p_1, p_2, ..., p_\omega$ denote the elimination coefficient after 1 year, 2 years, ..., ω years, in accordance with the definition given in formula (2). The total elimination in year t is then

$$N_0(t-1)p_1+N_0(t-2)p_2+ \ ... \ +N_0(t-\omega)p_\omega.$$

To maintain the stock of a given fixed capital means intact we should replace in year t the number of objects eliminated from use, i.e. the number of objects equal to the above sum. Let us denote by $N_0(t)$ the number of objects put into use in year t; this number must equal the total number of objects which are eliminated in this year, i.e.

$$N_0(t)=N_0(t-1)p_1+N_0(t-2)p_2+ \ ... \ +N_0(t-\omega)p_\omega \qquad (t\geqslant\omega). \quad (5)$$

This condition determines the number of objects which must be replaced in a given year (or within another unit of time) to offset the number of objects eliminated from use. It is called the *renewal equation*.[15] It is of a recurrent nature and enables us to determine the number of replacements consecutively in the years t, $t+1$, $t+2$, etc.[16]

---

[15] A more detailed analysis of this equation is given in the Appendix "Mathematical Analysis of the Renewal Process" at the end of this chapter.

[16] We assume that $t > \omega$, i.e. that the process of renewal is in "full course". If the first objects were introduced in year $t = 0$, then for the values $t < \omega$, the equation would appear in the "cut off" form because in year $t = 1$ the oldest objects are 1 year old, in year $t = 2$ they are 2 years old, etc. In con-

Applying the renewal equation to the data given in Table 2, i.e. the table of elimination of bulbs, we obtain the number of replacements of bulbs in consecutive units of time as in Table 3.

TABLE 3

NUMBER OF BULBS REPLACED IN CONSECUTIVE UNITS OF TIME

Unit of time t (in weeks)	Number of replacements $N_0(t)$	Unit of time t (in weeks)	Number of replacements $N_0(t)$
1	0	21	12047
2	1000	22	11706
3	1000	23	10820
4	1010	24	9697
5	1020	25	8700
6	3030	26	8288
7	6040	27	8413
8	10090	28	8862
9	14201	29	9523
10	15392	30	10100
11	16665	31	10413
12	15000	32	10503
13	9480	33	10348
14	6174	34	9999
15	6160	35	9636
16	5521	36	9079
17	7309	37	9220
18	9317	38	9271
19	10181	39	9447
20	11529	40	9669

for $t \to \infty$ we have $N_0(t) = 9709$

sequence, for the years corresponding to $t = 1, 2, ..., \omega$ the renewal equation is "cut off". It amounts to:

$$N_0(1) = N_0(0)p_1$$
$$N_0(2) = N_0(1)p_1 + N_0(0)p_2$$
$$...   ...$$
$$N_0(\omega-1) = N_0(\omega-2)p_1 + N_0(\omega-3)p_2 + ... + N_0(0)p_{\omega-1}$$

These are the initial conditions which determine the "setting in motion" of the process of renewal.

Figure 11 shows the graph of the number of replacements plotted from the data in Table 3.

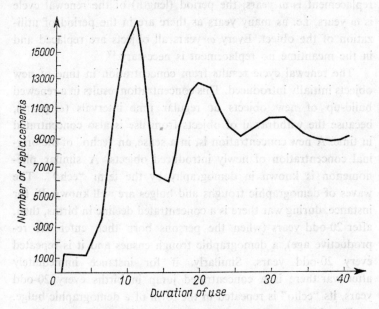

Fig. 11. Number of bulbs replaced in consecutive time units

It turns out that under certain conditions the number of replacements is subject to regular fluctuations of a cyclical nature. Such fluctuations appear clearly in Table 3 and in Fig. 11. To explain the source of these fluctuations let us consider first the case which we have described above as exceptional. It is the case when all objects have the same period of utilization. Let 100 objects be put into use in the initial year and let all objects have exactly a 5-year period of utilization. Then for 5 years there is no need for replacement, but after the end of the 5-year period we have to replace all 100 objects. Over the next 5 years there is again no need for replacement, but after 10 years have elapsed we have to replace all 100 objects again. Over the next 5 years there are no replacements, but after 15 years all objects have to be replaced, etc. There appears here a 5-year *replacement cycle* or *restitution cycle* as it is sometimes called. This cycle runs in leaps: over 5 years there are no replacements, but afterwards all objects are replaced simultaneously. Generally, if the period of replacement is ω years, the period (length) of the renewal cycle is ω years, i.e. as many years as there are in the period of utilization of the object. Every ω years all objects are replaced and in the meantime no replacement is necessary.[17]

The renewal cycle results from concentration in time of new objects initially introduced. This concentration results in a renewed build-up of new objects at regular time intervals (ω years), because the withdrawal of objects from use is also concentrated in time. A new concentration is, in a sense, an "echo" of the original concentration of newly introduced objects. A similar phenomenon is known in demography by the term "echo". The waves of demographic troughs and bulges are well known. If, for instance, during war there is a concentrated decline in births, then, after 20-odd years (when the persons born then enter the reproductive age), a demographic trough ensues and it is repeated every 20-odd years. Similarly, if for instance immediately after war there is a concentrated jump in births every 20-odd years, its "echo" is repeated in the form of a demographic bulge.

For the renewal process to have a uniform course, without cycles, it is necessary that from the very beginning the introduction of new objects be uniformly distributed over time. In our example it is necessary to start by introducing in the first year 20 objects, in the next year a further 20 objects, in the third year again 20 objects, etc. After 5 years we have 100 objects in use and every year 20 objects are eliminated and replaced. Such a uniform process of renewal is shown in Table 4.

The number of objects at various ages available in particular years appear in the middle section of the table. Diagonal lines show the shifting object at the end of each year to a higher age group, i.e. the process of ageing of the object. The last column

---

[17] In the renewal equation this means that $p_1 = p_2 = \ldots p_{\omega-1} = 0$ and $p_\omega = 1$ (because after ω years all objects are eliminated). Then the renewal equation assumes the form $N_0(t) = N_0(t-\omega)$, which is expressed by the cyclical nature of the renewal process, and the period of the cycle is ω years.

TABLE 4

UNIFORM RENEWAL PROCESS

Year	Age of objects in years					Number of replaced objects
	1	2	3	4	5	
1	20					
2	20	20				
3	20	20	20			
4	20	20	20	20		
5	20	20	20	20	20	
6	20	20	20	20	20	20
7	20	20	20	20	20	20
8	20	20	20	20	20	20
.	.	.	.	.	.	.

on the right-hand side gives the number of objects replaced in particular years. Table 4 is designed similarly as the longevity tables used in demography.[18] It can be seen from this table that it takes 5 years to initiate a uniform process of renewal. After 5 years the uniform process is "under way": the stock of objects in use is always 100 of which 20, i.e. one-fifth, are replaced annually. Generally, if the period of utilization (equal for all objects) is ω years, the initiation of a uniform renewal process requires also ω years. If the available stock of objects is N, then over ω years we

---

[18] In demography, the process of ageing and dying of the population is presented by diagonal straight lines forming, together with the co-ordinates a demographic network. See J. Holzer, *Podstawy Analizy Demograficznej* (*The Foundations of Demographic Analysis*), Warsaw, 1963, pp. 39–45. This method of graphical presentation was introduced into demography by B. Zeuner, *Abhandlungen zur mathematischen Statistik* (*Proceedings of Mathematics and Statistics*), Leipzig, 1869; G. F. Knapp, *Theorie des Bevölkerungswechsel* (*Theory of Demography*), Brunswick, 1894 and W. Lexis, *Einleitung in die Theorie des Bevölkerungsstatistik* (*Introduction to the Theory of Population Statistics*), Strasbourg, 1875; see also W. Lexis, *Abhandlungen zur Theorie der Bevölkerung- und Moralstatistik* (*Proceedings of the Theory of Demography*), Jena, 1903. Table 4 as well as Tables 6 and 7, containing similar diagonal lines, are designed according to the same principle as a demographic net.

have to put into use annually N/ω objects. In this manner the process of renewal becomes uniform: every year N/ω objects are replaced, i.e. the number of objects replaced equals the stock divided by the period of utilization of the object.[19]

Concentration in time of the renewal of objects causes a renewal cycle also in cases when the period of utilization of particular objects is different.[20] This is shown in Table 3 and Fig. 11. However, in this case, and most renewal processes encountered in practice are of this kind, fluctuations (oscillations) of the cycle decline with time, and the renewal process becomes asymptotically uniform. In the course of time, as we say, the renewal cycle fades away and its oscillations are dampened until they finally die out and *stabilization of the renewal process* sets in.

To illustrate better the process of fading away of the renewal cycle let us take the following simplified example. We assume that in the initial year 10,000 new objects are introduced simultaneously and that 10% of the objects require replacement after the first year, 30% after the second year and 60% after the third year. The longest period of utilization of the object is then $\omega = 3$ years, and the coefficient of elimination assumes the value $p_1 = 0,1, p_2 = 0\cdot3$, $p_3 = 0\cdot6$. The pattern of the renewal cycle is shown in Table 5.

The second column in Table 5 gives the numbers of new objects put into use in particular years and in the next columns the numbers of objects replaced after 1 year, 2 years and 3 years. The number of objects replaced every year is the sum of the number of objects put into use in the preceding 3 years and requiring replacement after 1 year, 2 years and 3 years. This is shown in the table by diagonal lines joining the objects that should be replaced, and were introduced 1 year, 2 years and 3 years earlier.

---

[19] The dimensions of these quantities are worth noting. The number of objects in use is their stock and its dimension (in physical units) is denoted by N. The period of utilization ω has the time dimension T. The number of objects replaced within a unit of time has then the dimension NT^{-1}, i.e. is in the nature of a flow.

[20] This problem is discussed by T. Czechowski in "Cykliczność Procesu Reprodukcji Prostych" (The Cyclical Pattern of the Process of Simple Reproduction), *Zeszyty Naukowe Szkoły Głównej Planowania i Statystyki* (*Scientific Notebooks of the Central School of Planning and Statistics*), Warsaw, 1957.

TABLE 5

FADING OF THE RENEWAL CYCLE AFTER A SINGLE INTRODUCTION OF 1000 OBJECTS

Year	Number of newly introduced objects	Number of objects replaced after		
		1 year	2 years	3 years
1	10000	1000	3000	6000
2	1000	100	300	600
3	3100	310	930	1860
4	6610	661	1983	3966
5	2191	219	657	1315
6	4062	406	1219	2437
7	5029	503	1509	3017
8	3037	304	911	1822
9	4250	425	1275	2550
10	4353	435	1306	2612
11	3532	353	1060	2119
12	4209	421	1263	2525
13	4093	409	1228	2456
14	3791	379	1137	2265
15	4132	413	1240	2479
16	4006	401	1202	2403
17	3906	391	1172	2343
18	4082	408	1225	2449
19	3983	398	1195	2390
20	3966	397	1180	2360
21	4041	404	1212	2425
22	3974	397	1192	2384
23	3969	397	1191	2281
24	4014	401	1204	2409
25	3967	397	1190	2380
↓	↓	↓	↓	↓
·	4000	400	1200	2400
·	4000	400	1200	2400
·	4000	400	1200	2400
·	4000	400	1200	2400
·	4000	400	1200	2400

For example, the number of 6610 new objects in year 4 is the sum of 310 objects introduced in the previous year already requiring replacement, of 300 objects introduced 2 years earlier and requiring replacement and 6610 objects introduced 3 years earlier and requiring replacement now. The table shows a gradual stabilization of the renewal process. The process tends to a uniform one in which 4000 objects are replaced every year. The convergence is asymptotical but beginning with the 22nd year the fluctuations in the number of replaced objects do not exceed 1 per cent of the number of objects replaced in a uniform process. We can say that beginning with the 22nd year the renewal process becomes practically uniform. Adopting as the criterion of uniformity of the renewal process the fluctuations not exceeding 1 per cent, in the example of the replacement of bulbs in Table 3, the renewal process becomes practically uniform beginning with the 36th unit of time (week).

TABLE 6

PROCESS OF AGEING AND ELIMINATION OF OBJECTS

Year	Period of utilization of (age reached by) objects in years		
	1	2	3
1	10000	—	—
2	1000	9000	—
3	3100	900	6000
4	6610	2790	600
5	2191	5949	1860
6	4062	1972	3966
7	5029	3652	1315
8	3037	4526	2437
9	4250	2733	3017
10	4353	3825	1822
.		3918	2550
.			2612
.			
.	4000	3600	2400
.	4000	3600	2400
.	4000	3600	2400
.	4000	3600	2400
.	4000	3600	2400

The process of ageing and elimination of objects corresponding to our example is shown in Table 6. Of the 10,000 objects
introduced in the first year, only 9000 are in use in the second
year and only 6000 in the third year. The diagonal lines show the
shift of the object to a higher age group at the end of each year. Table
6 is similar to Table 4 in which the process of ageing of objects
is also shown. However, in Table 6 particular objects have different periods of utilization, and, therefore, not all of them move
to the next age group (as is the case in Table 4), and some of them
are eliminated. The number of objects eliminated in transition
to the next age group equals the difference of the consecutive
items on the diagonal line. The numbers of objects eliminated
in transition to a higher age group are shown in horizontal rows
in Table 5. It is worth noting that when the renewal process is
stabilized, the numbers of objects eliminated become different in
particular years, in the same way as the numbers of objects moving
to particular age groups. In our example, 4000 objects are introduced every year. After one year 400 are eliminated and only
3600 move to the next age group; after the second year a further
1200 are eliminated and only 2400 objects move to the last age group.

The fading away of the renewal cycle is a result of unequal
periods of utilization of particular objects. In the case when all
objects have the same period of utilization the renewal cycle runs
in an undampened way and repeats itself all the time in the same
dimensions. As we have seen, the renewal cycle may be avoided
and uniformity of the renewal process can be ensured by uniformly
distributing over time the introduction of new objects (see Table
4). If particular objects have different periods of utilization, then,
in spite of the initial concentration in time of the new objects
that are being introduced, a further introduction of new objects
caused by the necessity of renewal becomes more uniform in the
course of time. The objects introduced in the initial year are not
all replaced simultaneously. In consequence, the introduction
of new objects in subsequent years is less concentrated in time
and more uniformly distributed. Unequal periods of utilization
of particular objects result in a further deconcentration in time
of the process of renewal of objects, etc. In this way, renewal is

more and more uniformly distributed over time, oscillations of the renewal cycles become smaller and smaller, until finally the renewal process becomes "asymptotically" uniform. The "echo" of the initial concentration of renewal becomes weaker and weaker, ever less noticeable, until finally it disappears.

The greater the non-uniformity of the periods of utilization of particular objects, the more strongly is the renewal cycle dampened and the more rapidly is it stabilized. It is evident that if the periods of utilization of particular objects differ only little, the replacement is strongly concentrated in time and it takes then a long period of time for the differences in the periods of utilization to diminish this build-up and to bring about a greater uniformity in the renewal time. On the other hand, if the periods of utilization of particular objects are very long, deconcentration in time of renewal ensues rapidly and the renewal cycle is then strongly dampened and dies out quickly. The periods of utilization of particular objects form, as we know, a statistical frequency distribution which is expressed in the table of elimination, giving the number of objects eliminated from use after a specific period of utilization. The inequality of the periods of utilization of particular objects may then be statistically measured by dispersion, e.g. the variance or the standard deviation. The value of the variance or of the standard deviation is determined by the degree of dampening and the speed of fading away of the renewal cycle.[21]

Since the renewal cycle is a result of the initial concentration in time of the renewal of objects, it can be avoided by a uniform distribution in time of the initial replacement of objects. Table 7 shows how, under the conditions specified in our example, renewal should be spread in time so that a renewal cycle is avoided. It turns out that 4000 objects have to be brought annually into operation during the first 3 years. After 3 years the stock of objects is 10,000. During the 3 years altogether 12,000 objects are brought in. Of this total, 400 objects are eliminated after 1 year, 1600 after 2 years, and in consequence 10,000 objects

---

[21] For a more detailed discussion see the Appendix, "Mathematical Analysis of the Renewal Process", at the end of this chapter.

TABLE 7

SETTING UP A UNIFORM RENEWAL PROCESS

Year	Number of new objects	Number of objects replaced after		
		1 year	2 years	3 years
1	4000	400	1200	2400
2	4000	400	1200	2400
3	4000	400	1200	2400
4	4000	400	1200	2400
5	4000	400	1200	2400
6	4000	400	1200	2400
.	.	.	.	.
.	.	.	.	.
.	.	.	.	.

remain in use. After 3 years, the uniform process of renewal is "under way" and every year 4000 objects are replaced.

In a uniform renewal process, each year (or during some other unit of time) the same number of objects is eliminated and replaced. In our example it is 4000 objects annually; in the example of the renewal of electric bulbs given above it is 9709 bulbs a week. This number equals the specified fraction of the existing stock of objects, namely the stock of objects divided by the *average period of utilization* of the object. In the example given in Table 5, the stock of objects is 10,000. Of these objects, 10 per cent, i.e. 0·1 are utilized over 1 year, 30 per cent or 0·3 over 2 years, and 60 per cent, or 0·6 over 3 years. The average period of utilization is $0·1 \times 1 + 0·3 \times 2 + 0·6 \times 3 = 2·5$ years. Each year $1/2·5$ portion of the available stock, i.e. 400 objects, is replaced. In the example of the renewal of electric bulbs, given in Table 3, the average period of utilization is 10·3 weeks, and so each week $1/10·3$ part of the stock of 100,000 bulbs, i.e. 9709, is replaced.

This can be explained more clearly by the following reasoning: in a uniform renewal process the number of new objects put into use each year (or during some other unit of time) is the same. The stock of available objects remains also unchanged from year to year; let us denote it by N. In any year t this stock consists of the objects put into use in years $t-1$, $t-2$, ..., $t-\omega$, which survive to year t (the objects introduced earlier had already been eliminated). The total number of these objects is $N_0(t-1)l_1 + N_0(t-2)l_2 + \dots + N_0(t-\omega)l_\omega$, where $N_0(t-1)$, $N_0(t-2)$, etc., denote the number of objects introduced before 1 year, 2 years, etc., and l_1, l_2, etc., denote the coefficients of survival of these objects over 1 year, 2 years, etc. We have then

$$N = N_0(t-1)l_1 + N_0(t-2)l_2 + \dots + N_0(t-\omega)l_\omega.$$

However, in a uniform process of renewal the number of objects put into use every year is the same, i.e.

$$N_0(t) = N_0(t-1) = N_0(t-2) = \dots = N_0(t-\omega).$$

Therefore, the above equation can be written in the form

$$N = N_0(t)(l_1 + l_2 + \dots + l_\omega),$$

and hence

$$N_0(t) = \frac{N}{l_1 + l_2 + \dots + l_\omega}. \tag{6}$$

This formula determines the number of new objects $N_0(t)$ introduced during any year t. As the right-hand side of the formula shows, this number is independent of t and is the same for all the years.

The denominator in the above formula denotes the average period of utilization of the object. Indeed, if the stock of available objects is N, then the joint time of their utilization is $Nl_1 + Nl_2 + \dots + Nl_\omega$. Dividing the joint time of utilization by the number of available objects, i.e. by N, we obtain the average period of utilization which equals $l_1 + l_2 + \dots + l_\omega$. It turns out that the number of objects replaced each year equals the stock of available objects divided by the average period of their utilization.

The average period of utilization of the object equals the average age of the objects eliminated from use, i.e. $p_1 + 2p_2 + \dots + \omega p_\omega$. It follows from the definition of the elimination coefficient (formula (2) above) that $p_\tau = l_\tau - l_{\tau+1}$, i.e. $l_\tau = p_\tau + l_{\tau+1}$. We have then $l_1 = p_1 + l_2$, $l_2 = p_2 + l_3$, $\dots$, $l_\omega = p_\omega + l_{\omega+1} = p_\omega$ (because $l_{\omega+1} = 0$, since there are no objects more than ω years old).

Substituting these relations consecutively in the expressions for $l_1, l_2, ..., l_\omega$ we obtain:

$$l_1 = p_1 + p_2 + p_3 + \cdots + p_\omega,$$
$$l_2 = p_2 + p_3 + \cdots + p_\omega,$$
$$l_3 = p_3 + \cdots + p_\omega,$$
$$\dotfill$$
$$l_\omega = p_\omega.$$

The coefficient of survival to a specific age equals then the sum of the elimination coefficients after reaching that age. This is evident because the survival of the object to a specific age is tantamount to the fact that its elimination will occur during some of the following years. Summing up the above equations, we obtain

$$l_1 + l_2 + \cdots + l_\omega = p_1 + 2p_2 + \cdots + \omega p_\omega. \qquad (7)$$

Substituting this in formula (6), we obtain:

$$N_0(t) = \frac{N}{p_1 + 2p_2 + \cdots + \omega p_\omega}, \qquad (8)$$

i.e. the number of objects replaced in any year equals the stock of available objects divided by the average age of the objects eliminated from use.

The reciprocal of the average period of utilization or, what amounts to the same thing, of the average period of the objects eliminated from use, we shall call the *average rate of wear and tear*.[22] We denote it by s, i.e.

$$s = \frac{1}{l_1 + l_2 + \cdots + l_\omega} = \frac{1}{p_1 + 2p_2 + \cdots + \omega p_\omega}. \qquad (9)$$

Therefore, formula (6) can be written in a simplified form:

$$N_0(t) = Ns. \qquad (10)$$

In a uniform renewal process, the number of objects replaced each year (for each unit of time) equals the stock of available objects multiplied by the average rate of wear and tear. In the example considered above (Table 5), the average rate of wear

---

[22] See above, Chapter I, pp. 47–48.

and tear is $s = 1/2 \cdot 5 \times 0 \cdot 4$, $N = 10{,}000$ and hence $N_0(t) = 4000$ because the renewal process becomes uniform. Similarly, in the example in Table 3, we have $s = 1/10 \cdot 3 = 0 \cdot 09709$ and $N(t) = = 0 \cdot 709$ and is a uniform process of renewal.

To set up a uniform renewal process we have to introduce in the first ω years Ns new objects annually. Then, as we have seen, after ω years, a uniform renewal process is "under way" and the stock of objects reaches level N. It requires proper planning for putting to use new objects over the period of ω years. If such planning is neglected, a renewal cycle may set in, and if the non-uniformity (dispersion) of the periods of utilization of the particular objects is small, such a cycle fades away slowly. In our example (Table 5) it takes 22 years for the renewal cycle virtually to die out (i.e. for the fluctuation to become less than 1 per cent). This happens with the average period of utilization of the objects being $2 \cdot 5$ years and $\omega = 3$ years. If it is assumed that the average period of utilization is 25 years and $\omega = 30$ years, which is fairly close to reality in developed industrial countries, then with the proportions assumed in the table it would take 220 years for the renewal cycle actually to die out. It is clear that the fluctuations of the renewal cycle lose in practical importance even much earlier because it is impossible to distinguish them from various kinds of random disturbances; for example, in Table 5, after 11 years they do not even reach 4 per cent. Nevertheless, when there is no proper planning a renewal cycle may turn out to be persistent.

Finally, renewal cycles die out and after a sufficiently long time renewal processes are stabilized.[23] The only exception is

---

[23] We assume that during the renewal process a new build-up of new objects does not take place for reasons external to the renewal process. Such build-ups appear regularly in a capitalist economy in connection with the business cycle. The business cycle causes build-ups of new objects which are being introduced in certain years (stages of the business cycle): this maintains the renewal cycle and does not let it die out. On the other hand, the renewal cycle causes oscillations in the demand for fixed capital means of production and this, in turn, strengthens the fluctuations of the business cycle. The fact that the business cycle coincides with the renewal cycle was emphasized by Marx: "One may assume that this life-cycle, in the essential

the special case mentioned above in which all objects have equal periods of utilization. In consequence, if the periods of utilization of particular objects are different, then the renewal processes, which began long ago, are uniform: in such processes the initial renewal cycle has already faded away and the renewal process has become stabilized.[24] It is a characteristic feature

branches of large-scale industry, now averages 10 years. However, it is not a question of any one definite number here. So much at least is evident that this cycle extending over a number of years, through which fixed capital is compelled to pass, furnishes a material basis for the cyclical commercial crises in which business goes through successive periods of depression, average activity, booms, and crisis. It is true that the periods of capital investment differ in time and place. But a crisis is always the starting point of large-scale new investments. Therefore, from the point of view of society it also constitutes more or less a new material basis for the next turnover cycle". (*Capital*, Vol. II, *ed. cit.*, p. 211.) In a socialist economy there are no business cycles and, therefore, there is no coincidence between the business cycle and the renewal cycle. The renewal cycle, however, may be maintained, i.e. may not die out, if during expanded reproduction there occurs excessive concentration in time of new objects that are being introduced. We have seen, however, that the renewal cycle can be avoided and so its repeated release can also be avoided by proper planning of the distribution of renewal over time. While in practice it is not always possible to avoid an original release of a renewal cycle (e.g. at the beginning of intensive industrialization which, for various reasons, cannot be implemented in "instalments"), the continuation of a renewal cycle that does not die out is in a socialist economy a manifestation of poor planning.

[24] In the theory of renewal, a renewal cycle which lasts over a long period of time and which has become uniform due to the extinction of the initial renewal cycle is called a stabilized renewal process or an equilibrium renewal process. See D. R. Cox, *Renewal Theory*, *ed. cit.*, p. 28: "Stabilized renewal process may be interpreted as a usual process of renewal, which had lasted, in a given set, for a long time before the first observation was made." It is worth noting that renewal processes appearing in nuclear physics and in certain fields of biology (such as bacteriology and epidemiology) are, as a rule, uniform. In such processes the replacement of objects occurs so quickly, in nuclear physics within a split of a second, in bacteriology and epidemiology within several hours or days, that after a short period of time the process becomes stabilized. In demographic processes, and in processes of renewal of fixed capital means of production or durable means of consumption, the length of human life or the period of utilization of many fixed capital means of production

of a uniform renewal process that its "historical cross-section" is the same as its "simultaneous cross-section." This is shown in the lower section of Table 5, which depicts a uniform process of renewal. The figures on the diagonal lines ("an historical cross-section") are the same as the figures in the horizontal rows ("a simultaneous cross-section"). The number of objects replaced every year can be calculated by adding up both the numbers on the diagonal lines (adding up according to the "historical cross-section") and the numbers in rows (adding up according to the "simultaneous cross-section"). It follows that every year the same number of objects is replaced.

The renewal equation, in the form of formula (5) given above, expresses the renewal process in "historical cross-section" by summing up the eliminated objects introduced in consecutive preceding years (units of time), namely

$$N_0(t) = N_0(t-1)p_1 + N_0(t-2)p_2 + \ldots + N_0(t-\omega)p_\omega. \qquad (5)$$

In a uniform renewal process every year the same number of objects is introduced, i.e. $N_0(t-1) = N_0(t-2) = \ldots = N_0(t-\omega) = N_0(t)$. In this case the renewal equation can be written in the following form:

$$N_0(t) = N_0(t)p_1 + N_0(t)p_2 + \ldots + N_0(t)p_\omega, \qquad (5a)$$

which corresponds to summing up according to the "simultaneous cross-section". The first form of the renewal equation corresponds to summing up along diagonal lines in Table 5, the second form corresponds to horizontal summing up along rows. It is obvious that the second form of the renewal equation can be applied only when the process is uniform.

Also the renewal coefficient in a uniform process can be calculated both on the basis of the "historical cross-section"

(such as buildings, industrial installations, some machines, ships, etc.) or durable means of consumption is so long that it takes a very long period of time (dozens of years or even more) before stabilization of the process sets in. Therefore, in demographic and economic renewal processes their periods of duration of many years do not mean that their stabilization has begun and that they are uniform: this depends upon the degree of dampening of oscillations in the renewal cycle.

and on the basis of the "simultaneous cross-section" of the renewal process. According to formula (10) this coefficient is

$$s = \frac{N_0(t)}{N},$$

and $N_0(t)$ can be obtained on the basis of both equations (5) and (5a), i.e. by "historical" or "simultaneous" summing up.

In consequence of the renewal cycle dying out the "historical" and the "simultaneous" cross-sections of the renewal process become similar in the course of time. In renewal processes which began so long ago that they had enough time to stabilize, both these cross-sections are identical and the properties of the process can be expressed by any of these cross-sections.[25]

---

[25] This is the property of the processes included in the category called ergodic processes (from the Greek words *ergos* and *hodos*, which mean the road of work). By ergodic processes we understand changes in time in a given quantity which, with the lapse of time, tend to a constant repetition of a specific value (called the state of equilibrium, the stationary state, a uniform process, etc.), independent of the initial values. The average of the successive values of a given quantity in a particular time pattern of the process (called the time average or the historical average) tends with time to the average of simultaneous values of this quantity in the collection of independent, "parallel" time patterns of this process (called the average of the stage or the average of the simultaneous cross-section). This results from the fact that after a certain time a given quantity assumes asymptotically always the same value regardless of the initial value. Under these conditions, the average of the successive values of a given quantity tends with time to the value which in the end is constantly repeated, i.e. the equilibrium value. On the other hand, particular "parallel" patterns of a given process all also tend to a constant repetition of the same value (the equilibrium value); the average value of a given quantity in "parallel" patterns of the process becomes then after a certain period of time equal to the equilibrium value. In consequence, the historical average of the particular time pattern of a given process and the average of the simultaneous cross-section in the collection of independent "parallel" time patterns of this process tend to the same value, called the equilibrium value. It follows that both these averages tend (asymptotically) to each other. The most important case of ergodic processes occurs in the field of *stochastic processes*, i.e. processes in which the value of the random variable at certain moments or units of time determines the probability distribution of this random variable at a later moment or unit of time. Stationary stochastic processes, i.e. processes in which the average value and the variance of the random variable are unchanged

The production of objects needed for replacement requires time. This is determined by the period of production corresponding to the technical process used. If this period is T years (or other units of time), the production of the objects which will be needed for replacement in year t should begin in year $t-T$. Production or replacement of the means of production, both fixed capital and working capital means (and also for the replacement of the used-up means of consumption), must begin sufficiently early. The period of production of particular objects of a given kind, however, may vary. Objects can be produced in different production establishments in which different technical processes are used and, consequently, the periods of production are also different. Even in the same production establishments the same objects may be produced by technical processes with different periods of production. In such a case, the starting up of production of a given series of objects must be so planned that at the moment old objects are withdrawn from use an appropriate number of new substitute objects are available to be put in operation.

Let us denote by $B_0(t-\tau)$ the number of objects whose production period is 0 years (units of time) and whose production began in year $t-\tau$. Let $N_0(t)$ objects be needed in year t for replacement purposes. Suppose that the productive capacities of the particular establishments and of the technical processes

---

over time, are ergodic processes. Interpreting the coefficients of elimination as probabilities, we can treat the renewal process as a stochastic one: the number of replacements $N_0(t)$ appearing on the left-hand side of the renewal equation is then the average value of the probability distribution of the number of objects eliminated in a given year. We take this distribution as invariable over time and, therefore, its average value and its variance are also invariable. The renewal process is then a stationary stochastic process and as such it is ergodic. On the ergodicity of stationary stochastic processes see J. L. Dobb, *Stochastic Processes*, New York, 1953, Chapters 10 and 11, and A. M. Yaglom, *Introduction to the Theory of Stationary Functions* (*Uspekhi matematicheskikh nauk. Vvedenye v teoriu statsionarnykh sluchaynykh funktsii*), *Progress of Mathematical Sciences*, Moscow, 1952, vol. 7. In demography the ergodicity of the renewal process manifests itself in the distribution of the population by age (a simultaneous cross-section), which tends to the probability distribution of survival (an historical age distribution of the population).

are such that not all objects needed can be produced during the same production period, but that different objects have various periods of production amounting to $1, 2, ..., T$ years. In this case, the beginning of production of the particular objects must be distributed over time so that the following equality is satisfied:

$$B_1(t-1)+B_2(t-2)+ ... +B_T(t-T) = N_0(t). \qquad (11)$$

Without proper timing of the starting up of production of objects in year t, too few or too many objects may become available for renewal requirements of objects withdrawn from use. The time of the starting up of production of objects is not co-ordinated with the time of replacement. For this reason, we shall call the above equation the *co-ordination equation* of the time of the starting up of production of objects.

By way of illustration, let us consider the following example. Suppose that the renewal process is uniform and that the number of objects replaced annually is 4000 (as in the case considered above). Each year it is necessary to have 4000 objects available to replace the ones eliminated from use. Let us suppose further that 500 objects can be produced within 1 year, 2000 within 2 years and 1500 within 3 years. Then the co-ordination of starting up production with the requisite number of objects for replacement in particular years is as shown in Table 8.

TABLE 8

CO-ORDINATED PRODUCTION OF OBJECTS FOR REPLACEMENT

Year	Number of objects whose production has begun and whose period of production is			Number of ready objects
	3 years	2 years	1 year	
1	1500	2000	500	—
2	1500	2000	500	500
3	1500	2000	500	2500
4	1500	2000	500	4000
5	1500	2000	500	4000
6	1500	2000	500	4000
.	.	.	.	.
.	.	.	.	.
.	.	.	.	.

In Table 8 the second, third, and fourth columns give the numbers of objects whose production began in particular years, and having 3-year, 2-year and 1-year periods of production respectively. The last column shows the number of objects ready in particular years. The number of ready objects is the sum of the numbers of objects began in the preceding 3 years; this is shown by diagonal lines. It can be seen from the table that after 3 years, needed for implementing the co-ordinated production process, the number of ready objects always equals the number of objects needed for replacement (in our example 4000). The production process becomes co-ordinated with the requirements of a uniform renewal process. In the general case, if the longest production period is T years, the co-ordinated production process is reached after T years of implementation.[26]

If the process of production of replacement objects is co-ordinated with a uniform process of renewal, then the process of production also becomes uniform: its "historical" and its "simultaneous" cross-sections are identical. This is shown in Table 8. Beginning with the fourth year, the figures on the diagonal lines are the same as the figures in horizontal rows of the table. Because of the uniformity of the process of production the following equation holds:

$$B_1(t-1) = B_1(t), \ B_2(t-2) = B_2(t), \ ..., \ B_T(t-T) = B_T(t),$$

i.e. the number of objects having the period of production $1, 2, ..., T$ years and begun in years $t-1, t-2, ..., t-T$ equals the number of objects with the same period of production begun in year t. Substituting this into the co-ordination equation (11) we obtain

$$B_1(t)+B_2(t)+ \ ... \ +B_T(t) = N_0(t). \qquad (11a)$$

The identity of the "historical" and "simultaneous" cross-sections in a uniform process of production means that in the production process, co-ordinated with a uniform renewal process

---

[26] This problem is discussed by H. Dunajewski, *Studia nad teorią wzrostu gospodarczego* (*Studies on the Theory of Economic Growth*), Warsaw, 1965, Chapter 1.

there is no "waiting" for a ready product. Products become available simultaneously with the demand for renewal objects to replace those eliminated from use. "Waiting" takes place only in the first T years needed for implementing a uniform production process. It appears also when the number of objects to be replaced changes because then a certain amount of time is required to achieve uniformity in the production process.

"Waiting" is then a result of the lack of uniformity in the production process caused either by the absence of co-ordination with the renewal process or by the lack of uniformity in the renewal process. It does not take place when the renewal process and the production process co-ordinated with it are simultaneous.[27]

APPENDIX TO CHAPTER III

MATHEMATICAL ANALYSIS OF THE RENEWAL PROCESS

1. Continuous renewal process

To simplify the exposition we assume that the renewal process is continuous. Let us denote by N_τ the number of objects utilized over τ units of time, i.e. at the age τ, and by N_0 the number of new objects put into use (i.e. at the age 0). The coefficient of survival to age τ is

[27] The question whether, and to what extent, a uniform production process requires "waiting" for the product was the subject of very serious controversies in the Austrian and the neo-classical schools. This was related to the question of the interpretation of return on capital as remuneration for "waiting" (particularly E. von Böhm-Bawerk and A. Marshall, against whom F. Wieser, J. B. Clark and F. H. Knight argued that in a uniform production process there is no waiting for the results of production). We shall return to this question in the next volume of this work. (The late author had intended to continue his work—editor's note.) We shall confine ourselves here to stating that this controversy shed some light on the relation between the "historical" and "simultaneous" production processes but it did not bring its participants to a full explanation of the problem because this would require a systematic application of the results of the contemporary renewal theory.

$$l(\tau) = \frac{N_\tau}{N_0}. \qquad (1.1)$$

We assume that $l(\tau)$ is a differentiable function of τ having a continuous derivative. The elimination coefficient is defined as[1]

$$f(\tau) = -l(\tau) \qquad (1.2)$$

and the intensity of elimination as

$$\mu(\tau) = \frac{f(\tau)}{l(\tau)}. \qquad (1.3)$$

The following relations hold:

$$l(\tau) \geqslant 0 \quad \text{and} \quad f(\tau) \leqslant 1 \quad \text{and} \quad \mu(\tau) \leqslant 1.$$

The survival coefficient and the elimination coefficient can be interpreted as probability density. Then $l(\tau)d\tau$ is the probability that the object will survive to the (end of) age $\tau+d\tau$ and $f(\tau)d\tau$ is the probability that the object will be eliminated from use at the age $\tau+d\tau$. The intensity of elimination is then the conditional probability density: $\mu(\tau)d\tau$ is the probability that the object utilized over time τ will be eliminated from use at the time $\tau+d\tau$.

2. Renewal equation

Let us denote by $N_0(t)$ the number of new objects introduced during time t; we assume that $N_0(t)$ is a differentiable function of t. At the moment t we eliminate $N_0(t-\tau)f\tau$ objects introduced at the moment $t-\tau$. Let ω be the longest period of utilization of the objects. Then, the joint elimination of the objects at moment t is

$$\int_0^\omega N_0(t-\tau)f(\tau)d\tau.$$

The number of objects which should be replaced at moment t (i.e. the number of new objects that must be put into use to replace the withdrawn ones) is then

---

[1] We put the minus sign on the right-hand side so that $f(\tau)$ shall not be negative. For $l(\tau)$ is a declining or at least a non-growing function (there are fewer older objects and, at any rate, not more than younger ones), and therefore $l(\tau) \leqslant 0$.

$$N_0(t) = \int_0^{\omega} N_0(t-\tau)f(\tau)\,d\tau. \tag{2.1}$$

This is *the renewal equation*.[2]

The renewal equation is an integral equation: the unknown function of this equation is the function $N_0(t)$ called the *renewal function* and function $f(\tau)$ (the function of elimination of objects) is given.

In addition to the form given in formula (2.1), there are other ways of presenting the renewal equation. Sometimes, instead of the longest period of utilization ω, it is assumed that the objects can, in principle, be utilized infinitely, i.e. that $\omega = \infty$, with the provision that the number of older objects tends asymptotically to zero with the increase in age. Then, the integral on the right-hand side of the equation (2.1) is written within the limits from 0 to ∞. Such limits of integration are at the same time a more general interpretation of the renewal equation. For, if there exists a finite longest period of utilization ω, then

$$\int_0^{\infty} N_0(t-\tau)f(\tau)\,d\tau = \int_0^{\omega} N_0(t-\tau)f(\tau)\,d\tau + \int_0^{\infty} N_0(t-\tau)f(\tau)\,d\tau$$

and the second integral on the right-hand side equals zero. The integral on the left-hand side equals then the integral appearing in the equation (2.1).

Instead of the limits of integration from 0 to ω it is often assumed that the limits are from 0 to t. The renewal equation assumes then the following form:

---

[2] The renewal equation was formulated for the first time by the Italian mathematician Vito Volterra, *Leçons sur les équations intégrales et les équations intégro-différentielles*, Paris, 1913 (these lectures were delivered in 1910). Volterra called it "the integral equation of hereditary effects", i.e. the effects that depend upon previous states of a given system and are, therefore, in a sense, an "inheritance from the past". Volterra applied this equation to the study on the development and composition of biological populations. The American demographer and actuary J. Lotka applied this to demography and then to problems of renewal of means of production.

$$N_0(t) = \int_0^t N_0(t-\tau)f(\tau)\,d\tau.$$

In this form the renewal equation takes into consideration only the objects put into use beginning with moment $t-t = 0$. For the longest period of utilization ω, when $t > \omega$, this equation is identical with equation (2.1) because the integral can be factorized into the sum of two integrals $\int_0^\omega + \int_\omega^t$, in which the second component equals 0. If $\omega = \infty$, then the renewal equation is:

$$N_0(t) = \int_0^\infty N_0(t-\tau)f(\tau)\,d\tau = \int_0^t N_0(t-\tau)f(\tau)\,dt + \int_t^\infty N_0(t-\tau)f(\tau)\,d\tau.$$

As the second integral on the right-hand side indicates, the renewal process reaches back infinitely; at moment t the objects put into use infinitely long ago are also replaced.

As a rule, however, it is assumed that the renewal process began at a finite time, let us say, at moment 0. Then, instead of the integral on the right-hand side, we take the value $N_0(0)f(t)$, i.e. the number of objects put into use at the initial moment 0; they are eliminated from use at moment t. The renewal equation looks then as follows:

$$N_0(t) = N_0(0)f(t) + \int_0^t N_0(t-\tau)f(\tau)\,d\tau.$$

Introducing the fractions

$$g(t) = \frac{N_0(t)}{N_0(0)} \quad \text{and} \quad g(t-\tau) = \frac{N_0(t-\tau)}{N_0(0)},$$

we can also write the last equation in the following form:

$$g(t) = f(t) + \int_0^t g(t-\tau)f(\tau)\,d\tau.$$

The fractions $g(t)$ and $g(t-\tau)$ are called the *renewal density*; they express the number of objects introduced at a specific moment as a fraction of the number of objects introduced at the initial moment 0, i.e. per 1 initial object.

Moreover, we can generalize the renewal equation to cover the case of expanded reproduction of fixed capital means. We add to the right-hand side of the equation in the last-mentioned form the function $\Phi(t)$, which expresses the required coefficient of increase in the number of objects (in relation to the initial moment 0) in year t.

For our purposes, the most convenient form of the renewal equation is (2.1).

3. Solution of the renewal equation

In the form (2.1) the renewal equation is a homogeneous integral equation. We assume that the solving function has the form $N_0(t) = e^{\varrho t}$ where ϱ is a parameter. By substitution into the integral equation we check if this function can be the solution of this equation. After substitution, we obtain

$$e^{\varrho t} = \int_0^\omega e^{\varrho(t-\tau)}f(\tau)\,d\tau,$$

i.e.

$$e^{\varrho t} = e^{\varrho t} \int_0^\omega e^{-\varrho\tau}f(\tau)\,d\tau. \tag{3.1}$$

Dividing both sides by $e^{\varrho t} \neq 0$, we reduce this expression to[3]

$$\int_0^\omega e^{-\varrho\tau}f(\tau)\,d\tau = 1. \tag{3.2}$$

---

[3] The left-hand side of the characteristic equation (3.2) is the Laplace transform of the coefficient of elimination $f(\tau)$ (on the limits of integration see above). This equation states that the Laplace transform of the function $f(\tau)$ equals 1. This result can be derived directly by applying the Laplace transform to the integral equation (2.1). Let us denote the Laplace transform by L. The right-hand side of equation (2.1) is a convolution of $N_0(t)$ and $f(\tau)$ (we assume that $t > \omega$ and therefore t can be taken as the upper limit of integration). We have then

$$LN_0(t) = LN_0(t)\,Lf(\tau).$$

Disregarding the trivial case $LN_0(t) = 0$ (then also $N_0(t) = 0$), this equation is satisfied if $Lf(\tau) = 1$. This is equivalent to the characteristic equation (3.1).

It turns out that function $N_0(t) = e^{-\varrho t}$ is the solution of the integral equation if parameter ϱ satisfies also equation (3.2). This is a *characteristic equation* of the integral equation (2.1). Assuming that parameter ϱ is defined on the set of complex numbers, and remembering that the function $f(t)$ is continuous, we find that the left-hand side of the characteristic equation is an analytical function over the area of the whole complex plane. We know from the theory of analytical functions that (with the exception of a trivial case when the function is a constant) the points at which the function assumes a specific finite value (in our case the value equal 1) are isolated. In a defined area the number of such points is finite and on the whole complex plane they form a denumerable set. There exists then an infinite number of values of the parameters satisfying the characteristic equation (3.2) and the set of these values is denumerable. These values form an infinite sequence $\varrho_1, \varrho_2, \ldots$. Therefore, there exists an infinite sequence of functions $e^{\varrho_1 t}, e^{\varrho_2 t}, \ldots$, which constitute the solution of the integral equation (3.2).

By substitution into the integral equation we can check that the linear combination (weighted sum) of any number of these functions is also the solution of the integral equation. The general solution of the renewal equation (2.1) has then the following form:

$$N_0(t) = \sum_{j=1}^{\infty} Q_j e^{\varrho j t}, \qquad (3.3)$$

where the coefficients Q_j are real numbers. In this general solution the parameters $\varrho_1, \varrho_2, \ldots$ are the roots of the characteristic equation and the coefficients $Q_1, Q_2, \ldots$ are free but specific values can be assigned to them by assuming that the function $N_0(t)$ has the required pattern in a defined time interval (so-called boundary conditions: in a special case when we assume that the interval begins at moment 0, we speak of initial conditions).

If the root ϱ_j is multiple and its product is r, then the functions $te^{\varrho j t}, t^2 e^{\varrho j t}, \ldots, t^{r-1} e^{\varrho j t}$ are also solutions of the integral equation (3.1).[4] Therefore, the linear combination

---

[4] Let us denote the left-hand side of the characteristic equation (3.2) by $F(\varrho)$. We say that ϱ_j is the r-fold root of the characteristic equation if

$$Q_{j0}e^{\varrho_j t}+Q_{j1}te^{\varrho_j t}+ \cdots +Q_{j,\,r-1}t^{r-1}e^{\varrho_j t}$$

is also the solution of this equation. In such a case, instead of the constant coefficient Q_j there appears the expression

$$Q_j(t) = Q_{j0}+Q_{j1}t+ \cdots +Q_{j,\,r-1}t^{r-1},$$

i.e. the multinomial of variable t of the degree by one less than the product of the root.

Considering the possible multiple of the roots of the characteristic equation, we write the general solution (3.3) in the form

$$N_0(t) = \sum_{j=1}^{\infty} Q_j(t)e^{\varrho_j t}. \tag{3.4}$$

In the case when the root ϱ_j is single the multinomial $Q_j(t)$ is reduced to the constant Q_j. In this way the case (3.3) is covered by formula (3.4) of the solution of the renewal equation.

The characteristic equation (3.2) has one and only one real root, namely $\varrho = 0$. We can check directly that $\varrho = 0$ is the root by substituting this value into the characteristic equation. We obtain then

$$\int_0^{\omega} f(\tau)d\tau = 1.$$

This equality is satisfied because of the definition of the coefficient (probability) of elimination $f(\tau)$. Within the time interval $[0, \omega]$ all objects introduced at the initial moment of this interval are eliminated and, therefore, the integral on the left-hand side of

---

$F(\varrho_j) = 1$ and $F(\varrho) = (\varrho-\varrho_j)^r\Phi(\varrho)$ where $\Phi(\varrho) \neq 0$. Therefore,

$$F'(\varrho_j) = F''(\varrho_j) = \ldots = F^{(r-1)}(\varrho_j) = 0 \text{ and } F^{(r)}(\varrho_j) \neq 0.$$

Differentiating, in turn, both sides in formula (3.1) we obtain:

$$te^{\varrho t} = te^{\varrho t}F(\varrho)+e^{\varrho t}F'(\varrho)$$

$$t^2e^{\varrho t} = t^2e^{\varrho t}F(\varrho)+2te^{\varrho t}F'(\varrho)+e^{\varrho t}F''(\varrho), \text{ etc.}$$

If ϱ_j is an r-fold root of the characteristic equation we obtain in consequence:

$$te^{\varrho_j t} = te^{\varrho_j t}F(\varrho_j), \; t^2e^{\varrho_j t} = t^2e^{\varrho_j t}F(\varrho_j), \; \ldots, \; t^{r-1}e^{\varrho_j t}F(\varrho_j).$$

Since $F(\varrho_j) = 1$, it turns out that the functions $te^{\varrho_j t}, t^2e^{\varrho_j t}, \ldots, r^{r-1}e^{\varrho_j t}$ also satisfy the integral equation (2.1).

the above expression always equals unity. Let us note also that
the left-hand side of the characteristic equation (3.2) is a continuous function of parameter ϱ and $f(\tau) \geqslant 0$. Therefore, in the
set of real values of τ this function decreases monotonically with
the increase in ϱ. Its values run from ∞ for $\varrho = -\infty$ to 0 for
$\varrho = +\infty$; therefore, there exists only one real value of ϱ for which
this function equals unity. This value is $\varrho = 0$.

There exists then one real root $\varrho = 0$ and the remaining roots
of the characteristic equation are complex. As a result, the general
solution (3.3) of the renewal equation can be written in the form[5]

$$N_0(t) = Q_1 + \sum_{j=2}^{\infty} Q_j(t)e^{\varrho_j t}, \tag{3.5}$$

where the parameters $\varrho_2, \varrho_3, \ldots$ are all complex.

4. Determination of the roots of the characteristic equation

We find the roots of the characteristic equation by the method
of consecutive approximation. To this end we develop $e^{\varrho\tau}$ into
a power series. The characteristic equation (3.2) assumes then
the following form:

$$\int_0^\omega \left(1 - \frac{\varrho\tau}{1!} + \frac{\varrho^2\tau^2}{2!} - \ldots\right)f(\tau)d\tau = 1,$$

i.e.

$$\int_0^\omega f(\tau)d\tau - \frac{\varrho}{1!}\int_0^\omega \tau f(\tau)d\tau + \frac{\varrho^2}{2!}\int_0^\omega \tau^2 f(\tau)d\tau - \ldots = 1. \tag{4.1}$$

Since $f(\tau)$ can be interpreted as the probability density, the
integrals in the above expression are *moments* of the probability
distribution of age τ at which the objects are eliminated from
use. We denote these moments by $m_0, m_1, m_2, \ldots$ and we write
the equation (4.1) in the form

$$m_0 - \frac{m_1}{1!}\varrho + \frac{m_2}{2!}\varrho^2 - \frac{m_3}{3!}\varrho^3 + \ldots = 1. \tag{4.2}$$

---

[5] The real root $\varrho = 0$ is single because $F'(0) = -\int_0^\omega \tau f(\tau)d\tau < 0$.

As we have stated earlier, the first integral on the left-hand side of the equation (4.1) equals unity, i.e. $m_0 = 1$. Therefore, we have

$$\frac{m_1}{1!}\varrho + \frac{m_2}{2!}\varrho^2 - \frac{m_3}{3!}\varrho^3 + \ldots = 0. \qquad (4.3)$$

This is an algebraic equation of an infinite degree and it has an infinite, denumerable number of roots. The coefficients of the equation are consecutive moments of the probability distribution of age of the object eliminated from use divided by the corresponding factorials.

Taking a finite number of expressions of the multinomial, appearing on the left-hand side of the equation (4.3) we find the roots of the finite multinomial. In this way, we obtain an approximation to the infinite sum (3.5) being the general solution of the renewal equation. Taking an ever-greater number of expressions of the multinomial, we can obtain any desired approximation to this solution. Since the consecutive coefficients of the multinomial decline because of the factorials appearing in their denominator, a small number of expressions suffices for obtaining a good approximation.

In equation (4.3) we can put ϱ before the bracket. It follows immediately that this equation has the real root $\varrho = 0$. As we know, this is the only real root and it is also single. For, after putting ϱ before the bracket we obtain the equation

$$-m_1 + \frac{m_2}{2!}\varrho - \frac{m_3}{3!}\varrho^2 + \ldots = 0. \qquad (4.4)$$

Here $m_1 = \int\limits_0^\omega \tau f(\tau)\, d\tau$ is the average age of the objects eliminated from use and, therefore, m_1 is greater than zero.[6] Therefore, we

---

[6] We disregard the case, without practical importance, when $m_1 = 0$, because it means that the objects are withdrawn from use at the age 0, i.e. are not put into use at all. Then we would have to have $f(\tau) = 0$ for all values of $\tau \neq 0$. If $f(\tau) > 0$ for at least one value of $\tau \neq 0$, then (considering that $\omega > 0$) all moments $m_1, m_2, \ldots$ are positive.

cannot put ϱ again before the bracket; $\varrho = 0$ is a single root of the characteristic equation (4.3).

Other roots of the characteristic equation (4.3) are at the same time the roots of equation (4.4). As we know, they are complex and, therefore, equation (4.4) can be used for determining complex roots. Since the coefficients of this equation are real, the roots appear in conjugate pairs. Thus, in approximation by a finite multinomial we should use an even degree of the multinomial (for an odd degree there would have to appear one real root).

The characteristic feature of the above method of determining the roots of the characteristic equation, and so also of the renewal function $N_0(t)$, by the method of consecutive approximations is that it is based on the moments of the probability distribution $f(\tau)$. These moments can be calculated on the basis of statistical data.

It turns out that the left-hand side of the characteristic equation is a moment generating function. We know from mathematical statistics that the (natural) logarithm of the generating function can also be developed into a power series. Applying logarithms to both sides of the characteristic equation (3.2), we obtain

$$\ln \int_0^\omega e^{-\varrho\tau}(\tau)d\tau = 0,$$

and developing the left-hand side into a power series we have

$$-\frac{k_1}{1!}\varrho + \frac{k_2}{2!}\varrho^2 - \frac{k_3}{3!}\varrho^3 + \dots = 0. \tag{4.5}$$

The coefficients $k_1, k_2, \dots$ are *semi-invariants* of the probability distribution of the age at which the objects are eliminated from use.

Taking ϱ before the bracket of the expression on the left-hand side of equation (4.5), we find that $\varrho = 0$ is a (single) real root and that

$$-k_1 + \frac{k_2}{2!}\varrho - \frac{k_3}{3!}\varrho^2 + \dots = 0. \tag{4.6}$$

Taking a finite number of expressions, giving the multinomial of an even degree, we can determine with any desired approximation the values of the complex roots of the characteristic equation.

This is an alternative way of determining the root of the characteristic equation by consecutive approximations on the basis of statistical data. It should be noted that between the semi-invariants and moments the following relationships hold:[7]

$$k_1 = m_1, \quad k_2 = m_2 - m_1^2, \quad k_3 = m_3 - 3m_2 m_1 + 2m_1^3 \quad (4.7)$$

and multinomial expressions for further semi-invariants are more complicated. Therefore, in approximating by a multinomial of the second degree we have:

$$-k_1 + \frac{k_2}{2!}\varrho - \frac{k_3}{3!}\varrho^2 = -m_1 + \frac{m_2}{2!}\varrho - \frac{m_3}{3!}\varrho^2 -$$

$$\left(\frac{m_1^2}{2!}\varrho + \frac{-3m_2 m_1 + 2m_1^3}{3!}\varrho^2\right).$$

It can be seen that the smaller the average m_1, the smaller the difference between the approximation by moments and that by semi-invariants. For large values of m_1 the difference becomes small only in approximating by multinomials of a high degree.

5. Properties of the renewal function

The general solution of the renewal equation, i.e. the renewal function, can be written in the form of formula (3.5), and the parameters $\varrho_2, \varrho_3, \ldots$ appearing under the summation sign are complex. We shall show this by writing $\varrho = \alpha_j + i\beta_j$ ($j = 2, 3, \ldots$) and by writing the equation (3.5) in the following form:

$$N_0(t) = Q_1 + \sum_{j=2}^{\infty} Q_j(t)e^{(\alpha_j + i\beta_j)t}. \quad (5.1)$$

Using Euler's theorem $e^{i\Phi} = \cos\Phi + i\sin\Phi$, we write this in the form

---

[7] See, for example, M. G. Kendall, *The Advanced Theory of Statistics*, London, 1948, Volume 1, p. 63, or M. Fisz, *Rachunek Prawdopodobieństwa i Statystyka Matematyczna* (*Probability Calculus and Mathematical Statistics*), Warsaw, 1958, p. 103.

$$N_0(t) = Q_1 + \sum_{j=2}^{\infty} Q_j(t)e^{\alpha_j t}(\cos \beta jt + i \sin \beta jt). \qquad (5.2)$$

It turns out that the renewal function $N_0(t)$ has an oscillating pattern. There is an infinite number of the denumerable oscillations which are superimposed upon one another. These superimposed oscillations form the renewal cycle. All these oscillations, and, therefore, also the renewal cycle, fluctuate around the constant value Q_1.

Substituting $\varrho = \alpha + i\beta$ into the characteristic equation (3.2) and considering Euler's theorem

$$e^{-i\Phi} = \cos \Phi - i \sin \Phi,$$

we obtain

$$\int_0^\omega e^{-\alpha \tau}(\cos \beta \tau - i \sin \beta \tau)f(\tau)d\tau = 1.$$

This equation is satisfied if the real part equals 1 and the imaginary part equals 0, i.e.

$$\int_0^\omega e^{-\alpha \tau}\cos \beta \tau d\tau = 1 \qquad (5.3a)$$

and

$$\int_0^\omega e^{-\alpha \tau}\sin \beta \tau d\tau = 0. \qquad (5.3b)$$

It follows from the first of these conditions that $\alpha_j < 0$. For $\cos \beta \tau \leqslant 1$ and $\cos \beta \tau < 1$ for almost all values of τ, and, therefore, the subintegral expression is smaller than $e^{-\alpha \tau}f(\tau)$. Hence,

$$\int_0^\omega e^{-\alpha \tau}\cos \beta \tau f(\tau)d\tau < \int_0^\omega e^{-\alpha \tau}f(\tau)d\tau.$$

As we know, the right-hand side of this inequality equals 1 if and only if $\alpha = 0$. Therefore, the left-hand side may equal 1 only for the values $\alpha_j < 0$. In consequence, $e^{\alpha_j t} \to 0$ for increasing t; the oscillations are dampened and the renewal cycle dies out.

A special case occurs if the function $f(\tau)$ is not continuous, as we have been assuming so far, but $f(\tau) = 0$ for $\tau < \omega$ and $f(\omega) = 1$.

This is the special case[8] in which all objects have the same period of utilization ω. Then, for condition (5.3a) to be satisfied it is required that $\alpha = 0$, oscillations be constant and all have the same period equal to ω. There exists then a constant non-fading renewal cycle within the period ω.

From the second of these equations it follows directly that if $\varrho_j = \alpha_j + i\beta_j$ satisfies the characteristic equation, then $\varrho_j = \alpha_j - i\beta_j$ also satisfies it. The parameters ϱ_j appear in conjugate pairs and this is also the requirement that the left-hand side of equation (5.1) or (5.2) be real.

In consequence (disregarding the special case mentioned above), the sum appearing on the right-hand side of formula (5.2) tends to 0 for $t \to \infty$. Therefore

$$\lim_{t \to \infty} N_0(t) = Q_1, \qquad (5.4)$$

i.e. the renewal function tends to a constant value.

This means that the number of objects replaced at a particular moment of time becomes closer and closer to a certain constant quantity: the renewal cycle is asymptotically transformed into a uniform renewal process. Q_1 is the number of objects replaced at each moment of time of the uniform renewal process. This makes possible the determination of its value.

In a uniform renewal process the stock of available objects is constant; let us denote it by N. At a further moment t this stock is

$$N = \int_0^\omega N_0(t-\tau)l(\tau)d\tau.$$

At each moment the same number of objects Q_1 is introduced, i.e. $N_0(t-\tau) = Q_1$ holds for every value of t and τ. Therefore

$$N = Q_1 \int_0^\omega l(\tau)d\tau,$$

---

[8] Strictly speaking, this occurs when $f(\tau) = 1$ for a certain value τ_0 and $f(\tau) = 0$ for all other values of τ. The period of utilization is then equal to τ_0, i.e. we have $\tau_0 = \omega$, which leads to the result given in the text.

i.e.

$$Q_1 = \frac{N}{\int_0^\omega l(\tau)d\tau}. \tag{5.5a}$$

The denominator of this expression is the average period of utilization of objects. The number of objects replaced at each moment of time is equal to the stock of objects divided by the average period of their utilization.

Applying the formula of integration by parts we find (for $\varepsilon > 0$)

$$\int_0^{\omega+\varepsilon} l(\tau)d\tau = [\tau l(\tau)]_0^{\omega+\varepsilon} - \int_0^{\omega+\varepsilon} \tau l'(\tau)d\tau.$$

Since ω is the upper limit of the time of utilization of the object, then $l(\omega+\varepsilon) = 0$, and we have

$$\int_0^{\omega+\varepsilon} l(\tau)d\tau = - \int_0^{\omega+\varepsilon} \tau l'(\tau)d\tau,$$

i.e. the average period of utilization equals the average age of the objects eliminated from use. Formula (5.5a) can then also be written in the following form:

$$Q = \frac{N}{m_1}. \tag{5.5b}$$

Finally, defining the renewal coefficient as

$$s = \frac{1}{\int_0^\omega l(\tau)d\tau} = \frac{1}{m_1},$$

we also have

$$Q_1 = N_s. \tag{5.6}$$

These are all equivalent ways of determining the value of Q_1.

The value of Q_1 is the marginal value of the renewal function. By an appropriate "dosage" in introducing new objects over a certain initial period of time we can achieve a uniform renewal process without the transitional renewal cycle. To this end we should introduce objects in the initial period in such quantities that the equation $N_0(t) = Q_1$ be satisfied immediately. The renewal equation (2.1) assumes then the following form:

$$Q_1 = \int_0^{\omega} N_0(t-\tau)f(\tau)d\tau. \qquad (5.7)$$

Since, as we know $\int_0^{\omega} f(\tau)d\tau = 1$, it can be seen at once that this equation is satisfied when $N(t-\tau) = Q_1$ in the interval $[t-\omega, t]$. This is, at the same time, a necessary condition; it can be checked in the following way.

Differentiating both sides with respect to t, we obtain

$$0 = \int_0^{\omega} N_0'(t-\tau)f(\tau)d\tau$$

for any values of t. It follows that $N_0'(t-\tau) = 0$, i.e. $N_0(t-\tau) =$ $=$ const. Let us denote this constant by C; substituting it into equation (5.7), we find immediately that $C = Q_1$.

During the initial period of the length ω it is necessary to put into use Q_1 objects at each moment of time. During this period, the stock of objects increases proportionately until it finally reaches $\omega Q_1 = N$ objects. After the lapse of time ω, the stock is invariably N objects of which, at each moment, $Q_1 = N_s$ objects are replaced.

6. Dampening of the renewal cycle and its duration

As we have seen, oscillations appearing in the renewal process are dampened and fade away. The degree of dampening of various oscillations [represented by the components of the sum in formula (5.2)] may be different. It is measured by $|a_j|$, i.e. the absolute value of the real part of the corresponding root of the characteristic equation. At moment t the amplitude of oscillations is $e^{\alpha_j t}$ and, therefore, during a unit of time the amplitude decreases at the ratio

$$\frac{e^{\alpha_j(t+1)}}{e^{\alpha_j t}} = e^{\alpha_j} < 1 \quad \text{for} \quad \alpha_j < 0. \qquad (6.1)$$

The quantity e^{α_j} is called the *coefficient of dampening* of oscillations. This coefficient is a constant quantity (independent of time); multiplying the amplitude of oscillations at moment t by the coefficient of dampening, we obtain the amplitude at moment $t+1$. Since $\alpha_j < 0$, the smaller the value α_j, i.e. the greater the absolute value $|a_j|$, the smaller the coefficient of dampening. Therefore, this value is used as a measure of the *degree of dampening* of oscillations.

If the values α_j of particular oscillations are different, their degree of dampening and the speed with which they die out are also different. In consequence, some oscillations fade away faster than others, and the longest lasting is the oscillation for which $|a_j|$ has the smallest value. We call it the *dominating oscillation*. We define the coefficient of dampening and the degree of dampening of the dominating oscillation as the coefficient and degree of dampening of the renewal cycle.

The degree of dampening of the renewal cycle is then determined by min $|a_j|$. We shall try to estimate this value. It is most convenient to use the development of the (natural) logarithm of the characteristic equation into a power series by means of semi-invariants, i.e. the multinomial (4.6).

First approximations by a multinomial of the second degree give the quadratic equation

$$-k_1 + \frac{k_2}{2!}\varrho - \frac{k_3}{3!}\varrho^2 = 0. \tag{6.2}$$

We know that the roots of this equation are complex and, therefore, they are conjugate and both have the same value of the real part, i.e. $\alpha_1 = \alpha_2 = \alpha$. It is known from the theory of quadratic equations that

$$\alpha = -\frac{1}{2}\left(\frac{k_2}{2!} - \frac{k_3}{3!}\right).$$

Hence we find

$$|\alpha| = \frac{3}{2}\left|\frac{k_2}{k_3}\right|. \tag{6.3}$$

From the relation (4.7), we state that the second and third semi-invariants are equal to the corresponding central moments, which we denote as follows:

$$\begin{cases} k_2 = \mu_2 = \sigma^2, \\ k_3 = \mu_3. \end{cases} \tag{6.4}$$

Here μ_2 and μ_3 denote the second and third central moments, σ^2 denotes the variance. In consequence, the estimate (6.3) can be written in the form

$$|\alpha| = \frac{3}{2} \cdot \frac{\sigma^2}{|\mu_3|} . \qquad (6.5)$$

Since $\alpha < 0$, then $\mu_3 < 0$ must hold, i.e. the probability distribution at which all objects are eliminated from use must be skewed to the left. This means that larger objects, eliminated from use, must be skewed to the left. This further means that larger objects, eliminated from use at an older age than the average age of elimination, have, *on the whole*, a greater probability of elimination than the objects eliminated at a younger age.

It turns out that the degree of dampening of the cycle, which in this case is $|\alpha|$, is proportional to σ^2, i.e. to the variance of the probability distribution of the age of elimination of the object. The greater the variance, the faster the cycle dies out; on the other hand, when $\sigma^2 \to 0$, $|\alpha| \to 0$, i.e. the cycle ceases to die out.[9]

We obtain a more accurate estimate of the degree of dampening using a multinomial of a higher degree. Let us consider the equation of the $2n$th degree

$$-k_1 + \frac{k_2}{2!} \varrho + \cdots + \frac{k_{2n}}{(2n)!} \varrho^{2n-1} \frac{k_{2n+1}}{(2n+1)!} \varrho^{2n} = 0. \qquad (6.6)$$

The roots of this equation are conjugate in pairs and, therefore the sum of all roots equals the sum of their real parts, and real parts repeat themselves twice; it suffices then to consider n of them, say $\alpha_1, \alpha_2, \ldots, \alpha_n$.

---

[9] We come then to the special case mentioned above in which all objects have the same period of utilization. In this case the probability density function $f(\tau)$ ceases to be continuous; we have then $f(\tau) = 0$ for $0 \leqslant \tau < \omega$ and $f(\tau) = 1$ for $\tau = \omega$. In consequence, the rth moment equals

$$m_r = \int_0^\omega \tau^r f(\tau) d\tau = \omega^r.$$

Considering the relation (4.7), we find in this special case

$$\sigma^2 = k_2 = 0 \quad \text{and} \quad \mu_3 = k_3 = 0.$$

Formula (6.5) becomes then indeterminate and cannot be used.

As we know, between the roots and the coefficients of equation (6.6) the following relation holds:

$$\varrho_1 + \varrho_2 + \cdots + \varrho_n = -\left(\frac{k_{2n}}{(2n)!} - \frac{k_{2n+1}}{(2n+1)!}\right). \tag{6.7}$$

Considering the fact that the roots are complex and conjugate in pairs we have

$$2(\alpha_1 + \alpha_2 + \cdots + \alpha_n) = (2n+1)\frac{k_{2n}}{k_{2n+1}},$$

and hence

$$|\alpha_1 + \alpha_2 + \cdots + \alpha_n| = \frac{2n+1}{2}\left|\frac{k_{2n}}{k_{2n+1}}\right|. \tag{6.8}$$

Denoting the arithmetic mean on the left-hand side of this expression by $\bar{\alpha}$ (i.e. $n\bar{\alpha} = |\alpha_1 + \alpha_2 + \cdots + \alpha_n|$), we obtain

$$\bar{\alpha} = \frac{2n+1}{2n}\left|\frac{k_{2n}}{k_{2n+1}}\right| \cong \left|\frac{k_{2n}}{k_{2n+1}}\right|. \tag{6.9}$$

Since all α_j have the same sign (are negative), then $\min_j |\alpha_j| \leqslant \bar{\alpha}$.
It follows that:

$$\min_j |\alpha_j| \leqslant \frac{2n+1}{2n}\left|\frac{k_{2n}}{k_{2n+1}}\right|. \tag{6.10}$$

This estimate determines the upper limit of the degree of dampening of the renewal cycle.

Using the multinomial (4.6) we can also obtain an approximate estimate of the coefficients β_j appearing with the imaginary part of the roots of the characteristic equation (let us remember that $\varrho_j = \alpha_j + i\beta_j$). Taking the quadratic equation (6.2) and considering that both its complex roots are conjugate, we find

$$(\alpha + \beta i)(\alpha - i\beta) = \alpha^2 + \beta^2 = -\frac{3! k_1}{k_3}. \tag{6.11}$$

Therefore

$$\beta = \sqrt{-\frac{\sigma k_1}{k_3} - \alpha^2}.$$

Considering the above-mentioned relation between the semi-invariant and moments we obtain:

$$\beta = \sqrt{-\frac{\sigma m_1}{\mu_3} - \alpha^2},$$ (6.12)

where $\alpha^2 = \frac{9}{4}\left(\frac{\sigma^2}{\mu_3}\right)^2$ because of (6.5). As we know, $\mu_3 < 0$ and $m_1 > 0$, and, therefore, the expression under the root is positive.[10]

Let us denote by T the period of the renewal cycle. We have therefore $\beta T = 2\pi$. Hence

$$T = \frac{2\pi}{\beta};$$

hence, we find

$$T = \frac{2\pi}{\sqrt{-\dfrac{\sigma m_1}{\mu_3} - \alpha^2}}.$$ (6.13)

This is the estimated period of the renewal cycle on the basis of a multinomial of the second degree.

It can be seen that the greater the degree of dampening of the cycle $|\alpha|$, the greater T. With the remaining conditions given, cycles dampened more strongly are longer than cycles dampened less strongly or, in other words, cycles dampened weakly have a greater frequency than cycles dampened strongly.[11] On the other hand, with the remaining conditions given, the smaller m_1, i.e. the average age of the objects eliminated from use, the greater T.[12] The longer the "life" of objects, the shorter the renewal cycle. We can say roughly that the length (period) of the renewal cycle is in the inverse relation to the square root of the average age of the objects eliminated from use. This is explained by the fact that the longer the "life" of objects, the more room there is for fluctuations in the number of objects replaced during a given period of time. The higher the frequency of fluctuations,

---

[10] Since $\mu_3 = k_3 < 0$, we introduce the minus sign into the right-hand side of formula (6.11).

[11] We define frequency as the reciprocal of the period of oscillation, for the renewal cycle frequency is then $1/T$.

[12] Let us note that the expression $-\dfrac{\sigma m_1}{\mu_3}$ appearing in formula (6.13) is positive.

the shorter the renewal cycle. Finally, there is an increase in the absolute skewness of the probability distribution of age for withdrawal of objects from use, i.e. the increase $|\mu_3|$ acts in the same way as a decrease in the average length of "life" of the object m_1, i.e. it leads to the lengthening of the period of the renewal cycle.

7. Discrete renewal process

The right-hand side of the renewal equation (2.1) can also be expressed in the form of the Stieltjes integral. We write $f(\tau)d\tau = = -dl(\tau)$ The renewal equation assumes then the following form:

$$N_0(t) = - \int_0^\omega N_0(t-\tau)dl(\tau). \tag{7.1}$$

In this form the renewal equation can be interpreted in a more general way, comprising both the continuous and the discrete renewal processes.

If the renewal process is continuous, there exists the probability density $f(\tau)$, and for the discrete process the variable τ assumes only a sequence of discrete values. For the sake of simplicity, we assume that the intervals between these values are equal, and, therefore, τ assumes integer values $1, 2, 3, \ldots$. In this case $dl(\tau)$ also changes in a discrete way, assuming the values $dl(1)$, $dl(2)$, ..., $dl(\omega)$, and $dl(s) = l(s+1)-l(s)$ for $s = 1, 2, \ldots, \omega$.

Writing $p_s = -dl(s)$, we can present equation (7.1) in the form

$$N_0(t) = \sum_{s=1}^\omega N_0(t-s)p_s. \tag{7.2}$$

This is a discrete renewal equation.

This equation is a linear difference equation (of the order ω) and its solution has the following form:

$$N_0(t) = \sum_{j=1}^\omega Q_j(t)\lambda_j^t, \tag{7.3}$$

where λ_j are the roots of the characteristic equation and $Q_j(t)$ are multinomials ωt of the degree by one less than the product of the root. Because of the discrete nature of the process, variable t also assumes only integer values.

The characteristic equation has the form:

$$\lambda - p_1 \lambda^{\omega-1} - \ldots - p_\omega = 0. \tag{7.4}$$

Since $\sum\limits_{s=1}^{\omega} p_s = 1$ (the sum of the coefficients of the probability of elimination), this equation has, among others, the root $\lambda = 1$, which is single. Therefore the (discrete) renewal function [the solution of equation (7.1)], can be written in the following form:

$$N_0(t) = Q_1 + \sum_{j=2}^{\omega} Q_j(t)\lambda_j^t. \tag{7.5}$$

In contrast to the continuous renewal function (3.4), the sum on the right-hand side comprises a finite number of components.[13]

It can be shown that the remaining roots of the characteristic equation (7.4), namely λ_2, λ_3, ..., are all negative and that their absolute value is less than unity (with the exception of the special case in which all objects have the same period of utilization, and then $|\lambda_j| = 1$). Therefore, the components under the summation sign in formula (7.5) are of an oscillating nature.

This result can be obtained directly from formulae (3.2) and (3.5) by interpretation of these formulae. Similarly as in (7.1), we substitute the Stieltjes integrals for the integrals appearing in these formulae. Then these formulae correspond to the discrete renewal process now considered. In these formulae, we write $e^{\varrho j} = \lambda_j$, and hence we obtain immediately from formula (3.4) the discrete renewal function (7.5). To the real root $\varrho = 0$ of the characteristic equation (3.2) there corresponds the root $\lambda = 1$ of equation (7.4). In the case of complex roots we write $e^{\alpha_j} = |\lambda_j|$, where α_j is a real part of the root ϱ_j. We assume, moreover, that λ_j has the same sign as α_j, i.e. sign $\lambda_j = $ sign α_j. Disregarding any special case in which all objects have the same period of renewal, $\alpha_j < 0$, and thus $e^{\alpha_j} < 1$, i.e. $\lambda_j < 0$ and $|\lambda_j| < 1$. In consequence, the components under the summation sign on the right-hand side of formula (7.5) represent dampened oscillations.

---

[13] This is related to the fact that there is a finite upper limit of the age of the objects ω. If $\omega = \infty$, then equation (7.4) becomes an equation of an infinite degree and the number of components under the summation sign becomes infinite.

CHAPTER IV

Equilibrium Conditions of Reproduction

The process of reproduction requires that certain commodities be constantly produced. Means of production must be renewed by replacing the worn-out fixed means and used-up working capital means. Renewal of labour power requires the production of means of consumption, called means of maintenance. Requirements of reproduction determine the production of specific quantities of commodities and their material form. Moreover, with the exception of very primitive societies there are, as a rule, certain surplus commodities produced; they are called the *surplus product*.

The surplus product may consist of various kinds of means of consumption and their quantity and quality may exceed the means of maintenance. How these additional means of consumption are used depends upon the peculiarities of the social system within which the process of reproduction takes place. In social systems based on antagonistic modes of production, additional means of consumption are usually consumed by the class (or classes) of owners of means of production and by the social strata connected with it, as well as by workers rendering various services to them. In special situations, owners of means of production may be forced to give up a certain share of the additional means of consumption in favour of the workers employed in the production process. In systems based on non-antagonistic modes of production, the additional means of consumption employed in the process of production are consumed by the producers themselves, and by the workers rendering services to them.

Besides, the surplus product may also contain means of production. They constitute a surplus over and above the quantities

172

(and possibly also the material qualities) of means of production needed for renewal. In consequence, the stock of means of production increases, and we have expanded reproduction (in contrast to simple reproduction in which the surplus product does not include means of production). Increases in the stock of the means of production taking place in the process of expanded reproduction are called *accumulation*.[1] Accumulation of means of production usually entails increased employment of labour to operate the additional means of production. Therefore, in expanded reproduction, part of the additional means of consumption must be used as a necessary means of maintenance of the additional labour force. In the process of expanded reproduction part of the surplus product assumes the form of means of production and of means of maintenance.

Production must be adapted to renewal requirements, and in expanded reproduction also to accumulation requirements in means of production. This adaptation means that it is necessary to produce means of production in the material form and in the quantities required to replace used-up means of production and possibly also for accumulation. All used-up means of production— be they fixed capital or working capital means—must be replaced by newly produced means of production. All means of production added to the existing stock of such means must also be produced. It is also necessary to produce the requisite means of maintenance for the labour power employed and possibly also for the additional labour power employed in consequence of accumulation. Thus, reproduction requirements determine the commodities that must be produced, their quantities and their material form; they also determine the quantitative relations (proportions) in the production of particular commodities. In other words, re-

---

[1] By accumulation we understand the cumulation of products for future use. We can accumulate both the means of production (fixed capital and working capital means) and means of consumption (durables, such as houses or domestic appliances, and perishables, such as foodstuffs). Expanded reproduction is based on the accumulation of means of production; accumulation of means of consumption is related to the structure of consumption and of its distribution over time.

quirements of reproduction determine the material and quantitative structure of the process of production.

If production is adapted to requirements of reproduction in the way described above we say that the process of reproduction is *in equilibrium*. The kind of commodities produced and their quantities are exactly those required for the process of reproduction. If there is no such equilibrium, the process is *disturbed*, and too little or too much of certain commodities is produced. If some means of production are produced in insufficient quantities, planned accumulation or even renewal of such means of production becomes impossible; expanded or even simple reproduction is also no longer possible. If too little of the required means of maintenance is produced, it may be impossible to employ additional labour power and even replacement of existing labour power may be hampered; this makes expanded or simple reproduction impossible. In such cases we say that there are *bottlenecks*[2] in the process of reproduction and they disturb its course.

If, on the other hand, too much of certain commodities is produced in relation to requirements of the process of reproduction, we say that there is *excess production*. The course of reproduction is disturbed because in future the excess production of certain commodities cannot be continued. Quite frequently production of certain commodities in excess is accompanied by insufficient production of other commodities, i.e. by the appearance of bottlenecks. We speak then of *disproportions* in the process of reproduction. Bottlenecks, excess production and, more generally, disproportions, constitute disturbances in the process of reproduction. Equilibrium of the process of reproduction is needed if its pattern is to be *smooth*, without disturbances.

As we can see, equilibrium of the process of reproduction requires that a number of equalities between production of commodities and their replacement and accumulation requirements be satisfied. In order to determine these equalities let us recall that in the process of production the human and material factors of production, i.e. labour and means of production, are welded together. For a given technical process which we consider here

---

[2] In Russian, *uzkiye myesta*; in German, *Engpasse*.

as determined there obtains a defined quantitative relation between the quantity of commodities produced and the outlay of particular means of production and various specific kinds of labour. We represent this relation in the form of the following scheme:[3]

$$\begin{bmatrix} Q_1 \\ Q_2 \\ \vdots \\ Q_r \\ L_1 \\ L_2 \\ \vdots \\ L_s \end{bmatrix} \rightarrow \mathbf{P}.$$

In this case $Q_1, Q_2, ..., Q_r$ determine the outlays of particular means of production (fixed and working capital means) and L_1, $L_2, ..., L_s$ denote outlays of various kinds of labour (direct labour); $\mathbf{P}$ denotes the quantity of commodities produced (return).

Let the number of commodities produced be n, of which r are means of production and $n-r$ are means of consumption. We denote the quantities of means of production produced by $P_1, P_2, ..., P_r$, and the quantities of means of consumption produced by $P_{r+1}, P_{r+2}, ..., P_n$. Let us denote by Q_{ij} the outlay of the ith means of production, and by L_{kj} the outlay of the kth kind of labour in producing the jth commodity, assuming that there are s various kinds of labour. The outlays and the products are measured in physical units and are flows. We write, therefore, the quantitative relations between outlays and returns, introducing the jth commodity in the following form:

$$\begin{bmatrix} Q_{1j} \\ Q_{2j} \\ \vdots \\ Q_{rj} \\ L_{1j} \\ L_{2j} \\ \vdots \\ L_{sj} \end{bmatrix} \rightarrow \mathbf{P}_j \ (j = 1, 2, ..., n).$$

[3] See above, Chapter II.

With simultaneous production of the commodity (including r means of production and $n-r$ means of consumption), the quantitative relations mentioned above can be presented in the form of a table (Table 9). This table is called the *balance-sheet of inputs and outputs*. The columns in the four sections of the

TABLE 9

INPUT–OUTPUT BALANCE-SHEET (IN PHYSICAL UNITS)

	Means of production inputs	Means of consumption inputs	Inputs earmarked for accumulation of means of production	Total inputs
Demand for means of production	$Q_{11}, Q_{12}, ..., Q_{1r}$ $Q_{21}, Q_{22}, ..., Q_{2r}$ .... $Q_{r1}, Q_{r2}, ..., Q_{rr}$	$Q_{1,r+1} ... Q_{1a}$ $Q_{2,r+1} ... Q_{2a}$ .... $Q_{r,r+1} ... Q_{rn}$	Q_{1a} Q_{2a} ... Q_{ra}	Q_1 Q_2 ... Q_r
Demand for means of labour	$L_{11}, L_{12}, ..., L_{1r}$ $L_{21}, L_{22}, ..., L_{2r}$ .... $L_{s1}, L_{s2}, ..., L_{sr}$	$L_{1,r+1} ... L_{1a}$ $L_{2,r+1} ... L_{2a}$ .... $L_{s,r+1} ... L_{sn}$	L_{1a} L_{2a} ... L_{sa}	L_1 L_2 ... L_s
Quantities of commodities produced	$\downarrow$ $\downarrow$ ... $\downarrow$ $P_1, P_2, ..., P_r$	$\downarrow$ ... $\downarrow$ $P_{r+1} ... P_n$		

table show the input required for the production of quantities $P_1, P_2, ..., P_n$ of particular commodities. These products are divided into means of production and means of consumption, and the former are denoted by the indicators $1, 2, ..., r$, while the latter are denoted by $r+1 ... n$. The quantities of commodities produced are given at the bottom under the arrows from the columns (the arrows denote the process of production), the rows in the table give the demand for particular means of production and inputs of labour. The parts of the row located in the sections specify the demand for a given means of production or a given kind of labour for producing particular commodities (which are divided into means of production and means of consumption). This is the requirement for producing a given quantity of commodities, i.e. for maintaining production at a given level: it is the requirement for replaced or used-up means of production and for maintaining constant the specific labour input, i.e. the requirements of simple reproduction. Moreover, in every row (to the right of the labour section) are given the requirements for a given means of production or the input of labour for the purpose of accumulation of means of production (i.e. expanded reproduction). These requirements we denote respectively by

$$Q_{1a}, Q_{2a}, ..., Q_{ra} \quad \text{and} \quad L_{1a}, L_{2a}, ..., L_{sa}.$$

The quantities to the right of the double vertical line denote the sum of all preceding terms of a given row, and so represent joint requirements for particular means of production or inputs of labour, e.g.

$$Q_1 = Q_{11} + Q_{12} + \cdots + Q_{1r} + Q_{1, r+1} + \cdots + Q_{1n} + Q_{1a}$$

or, similarly,

$$L_1 = L_{11} + L_{12} + \cdots + L_{1r} + L_{1, r+1} + \cdots + L_{1n} + L_{1a}.$$

All the terms in Table 9 are measured in physical units, and are flows, i.e. they represent quantities per unit of time, e.g. year.

The expressions in the rows of the table (with the exception of those below the double horizontal line) can be added together, because the particular expressions in each row pertain to the same commodity or kind of labour and are measured in the same physical units. We cannot add up, however, the expressions in the columns because every column comprises expressions measured in different physical units, namely, inputs of different means of production and of different kinds of labour. Quantities $P_1, P_2, ..., ..., P_n$, at the bottom of the table, are not sums but *products* of inputs shown in the corresponding column; we symbolize this by arrows. It should also be noted that the particular expressions in the table (with the exception of those to the right of the double vertical line and those below the double horizontal line) may equal 0. So, if $Q_{ij} = 0$ or $L_{kj} = 0$, this means that the ith means of production or the kth kind of labour is not used in producing the *j*th commodity. For instance, to produce steel we do not use cotton or tailoring labour. If particular expressions in the columns of inputs earmarked for accumulation equal 0, this means that the corresponding means of production or labour is not involved in the accumulation of means of production. If all the expressions in a given column equal 0, there is no accumulation of means of production and we have simple reproduction.

From Table 9, we can set up a number of equations (and inequalities) giving the equilibrium requirements of the process of reproduction. We call these equations (or inequalities) *balance conditions*. For means of production we obtain *r* balance equations, stating that the production of each means must be equal to the demand, e.g.

$$P_1 = Q_1,$$
$$P_2 = Q_2,$$
$$...$$
$$P_r = Q_r.$$

Since $Q_1, Q_2, ..., Q_r$ equal the sum of the expressions of the corresponding row to the left of the double vertical line (Table 9), we have

$$P_1 = Q_{11} + Q_{12} + ... + Q_{1r} + Q_{1, r+1} + ... + Q_{1n} + Q_{1a},$$
$$P_2 = Q_{21} + Q_{22} + ... + Q_{2r} + Q_{2, r+1} + ... + Q_{2n} + Q_{2a},$$
$$... \quad (1)$$
$$P_r = Q_{r1} + Q_{r2} + ... + Q_{rr} + Q_{r, r+1} + ... + Q_{rn} + Q_{ra}.$$

They are *the balance equations of means of production*. A set of these equations we call briefly *the balance of means of production*. This balance states that part of the last row (below the double horizontal line) in Table 9, expressing the production of means of production, equals the part of the last column (to the right of the double vertical line) expressing the demand for means of production. If this equality holds, we say that the balance of means of production is satisfied.

In a similar way we obtain *the balance of labour power*. For any kind of labour, demand cannot exceed the joint capacity of performing the work involved, i.e. the labour power of a given kind. Let us denote by $L_1^{(0)}$, $L_2^{(0)}$, ..., $L_s^{(0)}$ the quantity of a particular kind of labour power, then the balance of the labour power is expressed in the form of *s balance inequalities*:

$$L_1^{(0)} \geqslant L_1,$$
$$L_2^{(0)} \geqslant L_2,$$
$$\ldots\ldots\ldots$$
$$L_s^{(0)} \geqslant L_n.$$

Considering that $L_1, L_2, ..., L_s$ equal the sum of the terms of the corresponding row to the left of the double vertical line, we have:

$$L_1^{(0)} \geqslant L_{11}+L_{12}+ ... +L_{1r}+L_{1,r+1}+ ... +L_{1n}+L_{1a},$$
$$L_2^{(0)} \geqslant L_{21}+L_{22}+ ... +L_{2r}+L_{2r,+1}+ ... +L_{2n}+L_{2a}, \quad (2)$$
$$\ldots\ldots\ldots\ldots\ldots\ldots\ldots\ldots\ldots\ldots\ldots\ldots\ldots\ldots\ldots\ldots\ldots\ldots\ldots\ldots\ldots\ldots$$
$$L_s^{(0)} \geqslant L_{s1}+L_{s2}+ ... +L_{sr}+L_{s,r+1}+ ... +L_{sn}+L_{sa}.$$

These are non-sharp inequalities and, if any of them are an equality, then the amount of available labour power of a given kind is fully exhausted. If, however, a given inequality is sharp, i.e. we have $>$, then there remains a surplus of labour which does not find employment in the process of production (it may find employment in non-productive jobs or may remain unemployed).

Denoting such surpluses of labour power by $R_1, R_2, ..., R_s$, we can transform the balance inequalities (2) into equations. Namely,

$$L_1^{(0)} = L_{11}+L_{12}+ ... +L_{1r}+L_{1,r+1}+ ... +L_{1n}+L_{1a}+R_1,$$
$$L_2^{(0)} = L_{21}+L_{22}+ ... +L_{2r}+L_{2,r+1}+ ... +L_{2n}+L_{2a}+R_2,$$
$$\ldots\ldots\ldots\ldots\ldots\ldots\ldots\ldots\ldots\ldots\ldots\ldots\ldots\ldots\ldots\ldots\ldots\ldots\ldots\ldots \quad (3)$$
$$L_s^{(0)} = L_{s1}+L_{s2}+ ... +L_{sr}+L_{s,r+1}+ ... +L_{sn}+L_{sa}+R_s.$$

In this way, instead of inequalities we obtain *balance equations of the labour power*. In the case when, for instance, the ith kind of labour does not show a surplus in relation to demand, we have $R_i = 0$. Unfortunately, these equations cannot be presented in the form of equality of the corresponding part of the last row and the last column in Table 9, as is the case for means of production.

The balance of means of production and the balance of labour power can be presented in an abbreviated form as vectors. The columns in the system of equations (1) and (3) can be interpreted as vectors and denoted respectively by $P_1, Q_1, Q_2, ..., Q_n, Q_a$ in equations (1) and by $L^{(0)}, L_1, L_2 ..., L_n, L_a, R$ in equations (3). Remembering that two vectors are equal when and only when their corresponding components[4] are equal (4), these equations can be written in abbreviated forms

$$P = Q_1 + Q_2 + ... + Q_r + Q_{r+1} + ... + Q_n + Q_a \qquad (1a)$$

and

$$L^{(0)} = L_1 + L_2 + ... + L_r + L_{r+1} + ... + L_n + L_a + R. \qquad (3a)$$

In this way the balance of means of production is presented by one equation only (a vector equation); similarly, the balance of labour power is represented by one equation.

The balance of means of production requires one more supplement. The balance equations (1) or the vector equations (1a) determine the production of particular means of production needed to satisfy the requirements of reproduction. For such production to be possible, however, an appropriate productive capacity must be available. The balance of means of production should be supplemented by the corresponding *balance of productive capacity*. Let us denote the productive capacities in the branches producing means of production by $\hat{P}_1, \hat{P}_2, ..., \hat{P}_r$,[5] then the following inequalities must be satisfied:

$$\hat{P}_1 \geqslant P_1,$$
$$\hat{P}_2 \geqslant P_2, \qquad (4)$$
$$.........$$
$$\hat{P}_r \geqslant P_r.$$

---

[4] See above, Chapter II.

[5] See Appendix, "Mathematical Note" to Chapter II where the definition of the productive capacity is given in formula (3.2). Let us remember that productive capacity depends upon technical equipment and upon the maximum time of its utilization during a given period of time.

Denoting the unutilized productive capacities by $\hat{R}_1$, $\hat{R}_2$, ..., $\hat{R}_r$ (some or all of them may equal 0), we can transform these in-equalities into balance equations. Namely:

$$\hat{P}_1 = P_1 + \hat{R}_1,$$

$$\hat{P}_2 = P_2 + \hat{R}_2,$$ (5)

$$\ldots\ldots\ldots\ldots\ldots$$

$$\hat{P}_r = P_r + \hat{R}_r.$$

This can be written in the form of one vector equation:

$$\hat{\mathbf{P}} = \mathbf{P} + \hat{\mathbf{R}}.$$ (5a)

We could introduce productive capacities and their unutilized part into Table 9, e.g. in the form of additional rows at the bottom of the table. Then the balance of productive capacities would be expressed in the table. We do not do this in order to avoid com-plicating the table further, but we understand that the balance of means of production resulting from the table can be satisfied only if the balance of productive capacities is satisfied.

Table 9 and the balance of means of production (together with the balance of productive capacities), as well as the labour power balance based on it, do not show, however, any complete con-nection between the production of means of production, the input of direct labour and the production of means of consumption. The second section of the table shows the quantities of means of production used up in producing means of consumption, but the production of the means of consumption itself is not subject here to any balance conditions. Such conditions appear, however, if we consider that for performing the particular kinds and amounts of work mentioned in the third and fourth sections of the table (or in the balance of the labour power), it is required to have cer-tain quantities of means of consumption which constitute the necessary means of subsistence for the required labour power.

We denote by $Q_{r+1,i}$, $Q_{r+2,i}$, ..., Q_{ni} the quantities of partic-ular means of consumption, necessary for the subsistence of the labour power, performing L_{1i}, L_{2i}, ..., L_{si}, i.e. the labour power employed in the production of quantity P_i of the ith commodity. Between the means of subsistence mentioned above and the inputs of labour there is correspondence which we write in the following form:

$$
\begin{bmatrix} Q_{r+1,i} \\ Q_{r+2,i} \\ \vdots \\ Q_{ni} \end{bmatrix} \sim \begin{bmatrix} L_{1i} \\ L_{2i} \\ \vdots \\ L_{si} \end{bmatrix}, \tag{6}
$$

i.e. in the form of correspondence of two vectors: the vector of the necessary means of maintenance and the vector of labour inputs.[6] It is obvious that some components of these vectors may equal 0, namely, in the case when certain means of consumption do not form part of the necessary means of maintenance in the production of the ith product or when certain kinds of labour are not used.

Substituting these correspondences into Table 9, we obtain Table 10 in which, instead of inputs of labour, there appear inputs of the necessary means of subsistence.[7]

---

[6] This correspondence is not an equality; the components of both vectors are measured in different physical units and the number of components is different. Correspondence holds between two vectors as a whole and not between their particular components. More precisely, this correspondence can be presented in the following way. Let us denote by $Q_{r+1,ji}, Q_{r+2,ji}, ..., Q_{n,ji}$, the set (vector) of necessary means of maintenance of the labour power performing work L_{ji}, i.e. the jth input of labour in the production of the ith commodity. Then we can write the following correspondences:

$$L_{1i} \sim (q_{r+1,1i}, q_{r+2,1i}, ..., q_{n1i}),$$
$$L_{2i} \sim (q_{r+1,2i}, q_{r+2,2i}, ..., q_{n2i}),$$
$$...$$
$$L_{si} \sim (q_{r+1,si}, q_{r+2,si}, ..., q_{n,si}),$$
$$(Q_{r+1,i}, Q_{r+2,i}, ..., Q_{ni}).$$

The terms in the columns on the right-hand side can be added because they pertain to the same means of consumption and are expressed in the same physical units. Denoting the sums of the terms of the columns by $Q_{r+1,i}$, $Q_{r+2,i}, ..., Q_{ni}$ (they are written below the horizontal line), we obtain the correspondence (6) given in the text.

[7] A similar table is given by B. Kłapkowski and A. Nykliński in: *Zagadnienie obliczania wartości środków produkcji i środków konsumpcji (The*

TABLE 10
BALANCE OF COMMODITIES PRODUCTION AND THEIR DEMAND

	Means of production inputs	Means of consumption inputs	Means of production inputs earmarked for accumulation	Sum of inputs	Means of consumption other than maintenance necessities
Demand for means of production	Q_{11} Q_{12} $\cdots$ Q_{1r} Q_{21} Q_{22} $\cdots$ Q_{2r} $\cdots\cdots\cdots\cdots$ Q_{r1} Q_{r2} $\cdots$ Q_{rr}	$Q_{1,r+1}$ $\cdots$ Q_{1n} $Q_{2,r+1}$ $\cdots$ Q_{2n} $\cdots\cdots\cdots\cdots$ $Q_{r,r+1}$ $\cdots$ Q_{rn}	I Q_{1a} II Q_{1a} I Q_{2a} II Q_{2a} $\cdots\cdots\cdots$ I Q_{ra} II Q_{ra}	Q_1 Q_2 $\vdots$ Q_r	
Demand for means of consumption	$Q_{r+1,1}$ $Q_{r+1,2}$ $\cdots$ $Q_{r+1,n}$ $\cdots\cdots\cdots\cdots$ Q_{n1} Q_{n2} $\cdots$ Q_{nr}	$Q_{r+1,r+1}$ $\cdots$ $Q_{r+1,n}$ $\cdots\cdots\cdots\cdots$ $Q_{n,r+1}$ $\cdots$ Q_{nn}	I $Q_{r+1,a}$ II $Q_{r+1,a}$ $\cdots\cdots\cdots$ I Q_{na} II Q_{na}	Q_{r+1} $\vdots$ Q_n	M_{r+1} $\vdots$ M_n
Quantities of commodities produced	$\rightarrow$ P_1 P_2 $\cdots$ P_r	$\rightarrow$ P_{r+1} $\cdots$ P_n			
Non-utilized productive capacities	$\hat{R}_1$ $\hat{R}_2$ $\cdots$ $\hat{R}_r$	$\hat{R}_{r+1}$ $\cdots$ $\hat{R}_n$			
Productive capacities	$\hat{P}_1$ $\hat{P}_2$ $\cdots$ $\hat{P}_r$	$\hat{P}_{r+1}$ $\cdots$ $\hat{P}_n$			

Table 10 is called *the balance of commodities production and of their demand*. This table differs from Table 9 in that there appear in it inputs of necessary means of maintenance instead of labour inputs (the third and fourth sections and the terms to their right). Moreover, the inputs (both of means of production and of necessary means of maintenance) earmarked for accumulation of means of production are divided into two parts: inputs for increasing the stock of means of production in the division of means of production and inputs for increasing the stock of means of production in the division of means of consumption. The former are denoted by symbol I and the latter by symbol II, placed at the top. We shall need this distinction in the future. Finally, at the bottom of Table 10 we have the unutilized productive capacities $\hat{R}_i$ and the total available productive capacities $\hat{P}_i$. This will also turn out to be useful.

From Table 10 we determine *the balance of means of production* and the balance of means of consumption. These balances are in the form of *r equations* for the means of production:

$$P_1 = Q_1,$$
$$P_2 = Q_2, \tag{7}$$
$$\ldots\ldots\ldots$$
$$P_r = Q_r$$

and *n−r inequalities* for means of consumption:

$$P_{r+1} \geqslant Q_{r+1},$$
$$P_{r+2} \geqslant Q_{r+2}, \tag{8}$$
$$\ldots\ldots\ldots\ldots$$
$$P_n \geqslant Q_n.$$

The quantities on the right-hand side of these equations and the inequalities represent the total demand for means of consumption and for necessary means of maintenance (the sums appearing on the right-hand side of the double vertical line in

Problem of Calculating the Value of Means of Production and of Means of Consumption), Scientific Series, Academy of Mining and Metallurgy, Cracow, No. 40/1961, p. 90.

Table 10). The necessary means of maintenance do not exhaust (as a rule), however, the total production of means of consumption and, therefore, the means of consumption balance is in the nature of an inequality. We denote the excess production of particular means of maintenance by $M_{r+1}, M_{r+2}, ..., M_n$. Then the balance of means of consumption can be written in the form of equations (instead of inequalities):

$$P_{r+1} = Q_{r+1} + M_{r+1},$$
$$P_{r+2} = Q_{r+2} + M_{r+2}, \qquad (8a)$$
$$................................$$
$$P_n = Q_n + M_n.$$

In this form there appear clearly in the balance of means of consumption (on the right-hand side) the necessary means of maintenance and other means of maintenance.[8]

Writing quantities $M_{r+1}, M_{r+2}, ..., M_n$ on the right-hand side of Table 10, we can show in table that the balance conditions both for means of consumption and for means of production are satisfied and that the row below the first double horizontal line, containing the quantities of production $P_1, P_2, ..., P_r$, equals

---

[8] Marx used the term "articles of luxury" to denote means of consumption which are not necessary means of maintenance. (See *Capital*, Vol. II, *ed. cit.*, p. 467.) In conditions prevailing today, this term may cause some misunderstandings. The necessary means of maintenance in a developed industrial society (socialist or capitalist) include the things which in earlier stages of economic development were regarded as luxuries and sometimes are considered as such today in everyday language. For instance, automobiles, books, TV sets., etc. are for many types of workers' necessary means of maintenance needed to commute to work or to maintain or improve occupational qualifications. Moreover, Marx (in the place cited) argues that part of the necessary means of maintenance is acquired by capitalists, and so he makes a division into the necessary means of maintenance and luxuries according to the natural properties of commodities and not to their functions in the process of reproduction. Such a division obscures the problem of renewal of labour power. Our definition of the necessary means of maintenance is purely functional and comprises all the means of consumption needed for the renewal of labour power, and no other means. Their natural form is a matter of indifference.

the sum of the last two columns of the table (to the right of the double vertical line). In this way both the means of consumption and the means of production are covered by the balance.

It is obvious that the balances of means of consumption can be satisfied only if the requisite productive capacities are available. We have to add then *the balance of productive capacities,* which now comprises not only the production of means of production but also the production of means of consumption. Denoting, as before, the productive capacities by P_i and the unutilized part of the productive capacities by R_i, this balance can be presented in the form of n equations:

$$\hat{P}_1 = P_1 + \hat{R}_1,$$
$$\hat{P}_2 = P_2 + \hat{R}_2, \qquad\qquad (9)$$
$$\dots\dots\dots\dots\dots$$
$$\hat{P}_n = P_n + \hat{R}_n.$$

These equations include means of production and means of consumption.

The balance of productive capacities is shown at the bottom of Table 10. The row at the bottom (under the second double horizontal line) must equal the sum of the two rows directly above it (i.e. between the two double horizontal lines). In this way, Table 10 shows all balance conditions appearing in the reproduction process of means of production and of means of consumption.

It turns out that all balance conditions of the process of reproduction expressed by equations (7), (8a) and (9) are shown in Table 10 in the form of equalities of the corresponding rows and columns (or sums of rows or columns). Interpreting these rows and columns as vectors, we can express the totality of balance conditions in the form of two vector equations, namely:

$$\mathbf{P} = \mathbf{Q} + \mathbf{M} \qquad\qquad (7a, 8a)$$

(where means of production $\mathbf{M} = 0$) and

$$\hat{\mathbf{P}} = \mathbf{P} + \hat{\mathbf{R}}. \qquad\qquad (9a)$$

The first of these equations expresses the joint balance of means of production and of means of consumption, i.e. the balance of commodities production and of their demand [equations (7) and (8a)]; the second equation expresses the balance of productive capacities [equation (9)].

In consequence, Table 10 gives the picture of the whole process of reproduction. The joint set of commodities, produced during a given period of time (e.g. one year) is the *total social product*. It is shown in the table in the row below the first double horizontal line and it comprises the quantities of all commodities produced, $P_1, P_2, ..., P_n$, i.e. vectors **P**. The table gives the structure of the total social product. Quantities Q_{ij}, contained in the four sections, represent the part of the social product earmarked for replacement of means of production and of the labour force. This is the part of the total social product needed to ensure simple reproduction. This part is divided appropriately into means of production and necessary means of maintenance. Moreover, the table shows the allocation of means of production for replacement and of necessary means of maintenance for the production processes of means of production and of means of consumption. To the right of the four sections of the table we find the surplus products. It comprises columns Q_{1a} and Q_{1a} and the last column M_n.

$$\begin{array}{cc} \text{I} & \text{II} \end{array}$$

It can be seen that the surplus product can be presented in the form of the sum of vectors

$$\begin{array}{cc} \text{I} & \text{II} \end{array}$$
$$Q_a + Q_a + M.$$

The first two components of this sum represent the portion of the social product earmarked for the accumulation of means of production, i.e. for ensuring expanded reproduction; the first component is earmarked for expanding the production of means of production, and the second for expanding the production of necessary means of consumption. Table 10 gives the internal division of each of these components into means of production and means of consumption (necessary means of maintenance). The last component represents means of consumption other than necessary means of maintenance. These means are not involved in the process of reproduction; they constitute a pure surplus of this process (over and above the requirements of expanded re-production). If consumption of necessary means of maintenance is defined as *reproduction consumption*, consumption of the above-mentioned surplus can be defined as *pure consumption*.

Table 10 shows the process of reproduction in its *structural* aspect and it splits the particular quantities appearing in the process of reproduction into component parts: the component of the sums (in the rows of the table) or the components of the vectors (in the columns of the table). However, in the process of reproduction products are constantly used up and replaced and, moreover, production is expanded owing to accumulation.[9] The process of reproduction is then a process of "perpetual motion" in which one quantity is constantly being transformed into another. The particular material objects change their economic function. From end-product of the process of reproduction they are transformed into means of production or into necessary means of maintenance; from the sphere of means of consumption they move into the sphere of means of production (as necessary means of maintenance in the production of means of production) from the sphere of means of production they move to the sphere of means of consumption (as means of production in the production of means of consumption); from component parts of surplus product they are transformed into means of production and into necessary means of maintenance (in the accumulation of means of production), etc.

To grasp this "motion"—the transformation of the economic function, performed by various material objects—it is necessary to divide the social economy into a number of divisions and possibly also branches and sub-branches which correspond to the particular economic functions performed by a given material object in the process of reproduction. Then, we can interpret the transformation of the function performed by a material object

---

[9] We disregard here the case of contracted reproduction as rather exceptional. Formally, such a case can be treated as a special kind of expanded reproduction in which the accumulation of means of production is a negative quantity.

as a transfer or *flow*, as we usually say, from one industry to another (or from one branch to another).[10]

---

[10] The first to analyse the process of reproduction in the form of "motion" in which material objects move from one branch of the socialist economy to another was the founder of the physiocrats, F. Quesnay. He published in 1758 the work *Tableau économique avec explication* (*The Economic Table and Its Interpretation*). In this work he presented the "circulation" of products between particular social classes, each of which performs a specific function in the process of reproduction. He presented this process in the form of a table which he called *tableau économique* (the economic table). On the subject of Quesnay see K. Marx, *Theories of Surplus Value*, London, 1951; J. Zagórski, *Ekonomia Franciszka Quesnaya* (*F. Quesnay's Economics*), Warsaw, 1963, Chapters 1, 11 and 14; and V. S. Nemchinov, *Ekonomiko-matematischeskiye metody i modeli* (Economic-mathematical Methods and Models), Moscow, 1956. In the third chapter of the second volume of *Capital*, Marx made an extensive analysis of the process of reproduction, based on the "transfer" of products from the department producing means of production to the department producing means of consumption, and vice versa. In his analysis, Marx was the first to formulate the equilibrium conditions of the process of reproduction and he presented them in the form of numerical and algebraic schemes. From this Marx formulated the whole theory of reproduction. Although this theory is, in principle, based on the study of reproduction in the capitalist system it has, as Marx has pointed out himself, a wider application and its part is applicable to the process of reproduction in all social systems (see *Capital*, Vol. II, *ed. cit.*, pp. 493 and 545–7). Extensive comments on the theory of reproduction were also made by Marx in *The Theory of Surplus Value*, *ed. cit.* See also Marx's letter to Engels, dated 6 July 1863, in which he outlines, for the first time, the principles of his theory of reproduction and gives a table modelled after Quesnay's *tableau économique* with which he compares his own table (see also K. Marx and F. Engels, *Letters on "Capital"*). The Marxian theory of reproduction remained unknown for a long time because the second volume of *Capital* was published only in 1885 (by Engels 2 years after Marx's death). But even after its publication, the Marxian theory of reproduction was little noticed. It was "discovered" as late as the end of the nineteenth century. Two facts contributed to this. The first was controversy between Marxists and "narodniks" in Russia on the subject of the possibility of creating a market economy that would promote the development in Russia of a capitalist mode of production. In this discussion Lenin came out with an analysis based on the Marxian scheme of reproduction, published in 1893 in the dissertation: "W związku z tak zwaną kwestią rynku" in *Dzieła, ed. cit.*, Vol. I (On the So-called Market Question in *Works, ed. cit.*, Vol. I). In this dissertation Lenin developed further the Marxian schemes: see on this subject V. S. Nemchinov, *op. cit.*, pp. 197–211. The second fact was the contention by

In this connection we divide the social economy into two basic departments—production of means of production and production of means of consumption. These departments we denote, after Marx, by I and II. "In each of these two departments" says Marx, "all the various lines of production belonging to them form one single great line of production, the first of means of production, the second of articles of consumption."[11] In the process of reproduction the products flow from one department to the other, or, as Marx defined it, products are exchanged between departments.[12]

To present this exchange, we write the balance equations for means of production and means of consumption, (7) and (8a), in the developed form, i.e. on the right-hand side of these equations we enter, instead of Q_1, the corresponding sums derived from the rows of Table 10. After changing somewhat the order of the components we obtain the system of equations (10).

---

the Russian economist M. Toughan-Baranovsky that capitalism as an economic system has unlimited possibilities of development (*Studia o Teorii i Istorii Torgowykh Kryzisof w Anglii* [*Studies on the Theory and History of the Trade Crises in England*], Petersburg, 1894). Toughan-Baranovsky supported his thesis by the Marxian schemes of reproduction. This gave rise to extensive discussion in which the Marxian theory of reproduction (particularly its schemes) has become a basic tool in arguments. Of the more important papers on this subject worth noting are: R. Hilferding, *Das Finanzkapital* (*Finance Capital*), Berlin, 1947; R. Luksemburg, *Die Akkumulation des Kapital* (*Capital Accumulation*), Berlin, 1913; O. Bauer, "Die Akkumulation des Kapital", *Die Neue Zeit*, 1913; H. Grossman, *Das Akkumulation—und Zusammenbruchsgesetz des kapitalistischen Systems* (*Accumulation and the Law of the Collapse of the Capitalist System*), Leipzig, 1929. On the subject of the Marxian schemata of reproduction see also O. Lange, *Theory of Reproduction and Accumulation*, Oxford–Warsaw, 1969, Chapters 1 and 2. The Marxian theory constitutes a basis for all contemporary analyses of the process of reproduction. Its main principles have been adapted (and sometimes "rediscovered") by many economists dealing with this problem, including those who otherwise are far removed from the Marxian approach to political economy. In this connection see also O. Lange's article "Ekonomia Polityczna" (Political Economy) in *Wielka Encyklopedia Powszechna* (*Great Universal Encyclopaedia*), PWN, Warsaw, 1964, Vol. 3, p. 332.

[11] K. Marx, *Capital*, Vol. II, *ed. cit.*, p. 457.
[12] See *ibid.*, p. 460.

$$(10)$$

$$
\begin{aligned}
P_1 &= Q_{11}+Q_{12}+\cdots+Q_{1r}+Q_{1a}+Q_{1,r+1}+\cdots+Q_{1n}+Q_{1a},\\[2pt]
P_2 &= Q_{21}+Q_{22}+\cdots+Q_{2r}+Q_{2a}+Q_{2,r+1}+\cdots+Q_{2n}+Q_{2a},\\[2pt]
&\ \ \vdots\\[2pt]
P_r &= Q_{r1}+Q_{r2}+\cdots+Q_{rr}+Q_{ra}+Q_{r,r+1}+\cdots+Q_{rn}+Q_{ra},\\[2pt]
P_{r+1} &= Q_{r+1,1}+Q_{r+1,2}+\cdots+Q_{r+1,r}+Q_{r+1,a}+Q_{r+1,r+1}+\cdots+Q_{r+1,n}+Q_{r+1,a}+M_{r+1},\\[2pt]
P_{r+2} &= Q_{r+2,1}+Q_{r+2,2}+\cdots+Q_{r+2,r}+Q_{r+2,a}+Q_{r+2,r+1}+\cdots+Q_{r+2,n}+Q_{r+2,a}+M_{r+2},\\[2pt]
&\ \ \vdots\\[2pt]
P_n &= Q_{n1}+Q_{n2}+\cdots+Q_{nr}+Q_{na}+Q_{n,r+1}+\cdots+Q_{nn}+Q_{na}+M_n.
\end{aligned}
$$

Exchange between the two departments is shown in the system of equations (10). Department I passes on to Department II means of production shown in the rectangle at the top to the right, and receives from Department II means of consumption (the necessary means of maintenance) shown in the rectangle at the bottom to the left. In this way each of these departments can continue production at its volume so far: Department I obtains the requisite means of maintenance for the labour force employed by it and Department II obtains the necessary means of production for the replacement of the used-up means. It can be seen that this exchange is an essential condition of continuation of the process of production, i.e. of reproduction. Without it, Department I would not have the necessary means of maintenance for its labour force, and Department II would be deprived of the means of production.

Schematically we present this exchange in the following way:

$$
\text{I} \qquad\qquad\qquad \text{II}
$$

$$
\begin{bmatrix} Q_{1,r+1}Q_{1,r+2}\cdots Q_{1n}Q_{1a} \\ Q_{2,r+1}Q_{2,r+2}\cdots Q_{2n}Q_{2a} \\ \cdots\cdots\cdots\cdots \\ Q_{r,r+1}Q_{r,r+2}\cdots Q_{rn}Q_{ra} \end{bmatrix} \leftrightarrow \begin{bmatrix} Q_{r+1,1}Q_{r+2,2}\cdots Q_{r+1,r}Q_{r+1,a} \\ Q_{r+2,1}Q_{r+2,2}\cdots Q_{r+2,r}Q_{r+2,a} \\ \cdots\cdots\cdots\cdots\cdots \\ Q_{n1}\quad Q_{n2}\quad\cdots Q_{nr}\quad Q_{na} \end{bmatrix}.(11)
$$

This formula presents *the equilibrium condition of inter-branch flows*. If the conditions are not satisfied, production cannot be carried on at its present level because there is either a shortage of means of production in Department II or a shortage of necessary means of maintenance in Department I.[13] In the form given here,

---

[13] The sign of arrows pointing in opposite directions "↔" denotes here exchange. We cannot put the equality sign because the rectangles contain different products measured in different physical units and even the number of products in both rectangles is, as a rule, different. Marx uses the sign of equality because the quantities are measured in units of value. Therefore, all sets of different products (vectors and matrices) are transformed into scalar quantities which, without limitations, can be added and compared with respect to their magnitudes; in the exchange between Department I and Department II values are also exchanged. In our consideration, however, we are concerned exclusively with products in their material form, measured in physical units; we shall deal in Chapter 5 (see editor's note on p. 151,

the formula expresses the equilibrium conditions of inter-branch flows in expanded reproduction; if the last column on both sides consists of zeros (then we may not write it), the formula expresses equilibrium conditions of flows in simple reproduction.

Equilibrium conditions of inter-branch flows can be written in an abbreviated form as follows. Denoting the content of the rectangles (matrices) in (10) by $Q_{\mathrm{I,II}}$ and $Q_{\mathrm{II,III}}$ and the sets of quantities Q_{ij} outside the rectangles by $Q_{\mathrm{I,I}}$ and $Q_{\mathrm{II,II}}$, we write equations (10) in the form:

$$\text{Department I: } \mathbf{P}_{\mathrm{I}} = Q_{\mathrm{I,I}} + \boxed{Q_{\mathrm{I,II}}}$$
$$\text{Department II: } \mathbf{P}_{\mathrm{I}} = \boxed{Q_{\mathrm{II,I}}} + Q_{\mathrm{II,II}} + \mathbf{M}. \tag{10a}$$

$\mathbf{P}_{\mathrm{I}}$ and $\mathbf{P}_{\mathrm{II}}$ denote the sets (vectors) of products, being the means of production, $\mathbf{Q}_{\mathrm{I,II}}$ means of production transferred from Department I to Department II; $Q_{\mathrm{II,I}}$ means of consumption (necessary means of maintenance) transferred by Department I to Department II. The means of production kept in Department I, for its own needs, are presented by $\mathbf{Q}_{\mathrm{I,I}}$ and the means of consumption kept in Department II are denoted by $\mathbf{Q}_{\mathrm{II,II}}$. Finally, $\mathbf{M}$ represents the means of consumption other than necessary means of maintenance, which, as we know, are not involved in the process of reproduction. In consequence, we obtain, instead of (11), an abbreviated form of equilibrium conditions of inter-branch flows:[14]

$$Q_{\mathrm{I,II}} \leftrightarrow Q_{\mathrm{II,I}}. \tag{11a}$$

ft. 27) with the theory of reproduction under conditions of commodity production when the value category operates.

[14] The exchange of commodities between Department I and Department II, necessary for the equilibrium of the process of reproduction, comprises only $\mathbf{Q}_{\mathrm{I,II}}$ and $\mathbf{Q}_{\mathrm{II,I}}$. What happens to $\mathbf{M}$ is a matter of indifference, because this quantity is not involved in the process of reproduction; it may all be consumed by the persons connected with Department II, it may all be transferred to persons connected with Department I, or, it may be divided arbitrarily between these two groups; it is of no consequence to the course of the reproduction process. This is so if, as we are doing now, we approach the process of reproduction in a material (natural) form, i.e. as a process of *reproduction of commodities*. Marx studies reproduction, in principle, as a process of *reproduction of value*. This process comprises as its component part the process of repro-

Inter-branch and intra-branch flows in the process of reproduction can be illustrated by Fig. 12.

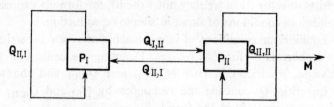

Fig. 12. Block diagram of the process of reproduction

In Fig. 12 the blocks represent the production of means of
production and of means of consumption respectively (vectors
P_I and P_{II}). The arrows pointing from one block to the other
indicate the flows from one department to the other ($Q_{I,II}$ and
$Q_{II,I}$), and the arrows returning to the same block from which
they started indicate the product kept in a given department for
its own needs ($Q_{II,I}$ and $Q_{II,II}$). The one-way arrow on the right-
hand side, starting with the second block and not returning,
represents means of consumption which do not constitute necessary
means of subsistence **M**. It can be seen that these means are not
involved in the process of reproduction. The remaining quantities

---

duction of commodities (in a natural form), but does not stop at that. In the
Marxian Department I not only commodities are produced, but also values,
including surplus value. In consequence, the flow from Department II to
Department I comprises also a part of **M**, namely that part which corresponds
to the surplus value produced in Department I and not earmarked for accumulation (under conditions prevailing in capitalism the part of the surplus value
consumed by the capitalists in Department I). Under these conditions the
scheme (10a) has the following form:

Department I: $P_I = Q_{I,I} + \boxed{Q_{I,II} + M_{II,I}}$

Department II: $P_{II} = \boxed{Q_{II,I}} + Q_{II,II} + M_{II,II}$.

Here $M_{II,I}$ is the part of means of consumption which does not constitute the
necessary means of subsistence transferred by Department II to Department I
while $M_{II,II}$ is the part of these means of consumption kept in Department II.
    Then, formula (11a) assumes the following form:

$$Q_{I,II} + M_{II,I} = Q_{II,I}.$$

This corresponds to the formulae appearing in Marx's writings. We shall
return to this question in further chapters (see editor's note on p. 151, ft. 27).

which are involved in the process of reproduction are shown by the arrows starting from and returning to a block (the same or another).

Figure 12 shows that the process of reproduction is a system of coupled operations[15] whose operating elements are particular production processes. The operations of the particular elements are coupled with one another and there appear a number of *feedbacks*. They appear in each of the two departments in the form of a quantity of products of the relevant department retained as inputs in its own process of production. This is symbolized by arrows returning to the same blocks from which they originated; they represent closed loops.[16] Feedback occurs also between the two departments; it consists in the exchange of commodities. The arrows joining both blocks go in opposite directions and, therefore, also represent a closed loop. These feedbacks occurring in the process of reproduction suggest that this process should be analysed by *cybernetic methods*. Such an analysis is given in the Annex (Appendix to Chapter IV "Equilibrium Conditions of Reproduction").

The division of products into means of production and means of consumption is based on the economic function which these products perform; it is not uniquely determined by the material nature (natural form) of the products. In the case of specialized tools of labour, such as instruments and machinery, they belong, indeed, by their material form, to the row of means of production because they are not suitable for any other use. The situation is different with means which in the process of production play an auxiliary role. Many such implements can be used as means of consumption. This is so primarily with buildings which can be used both as workshops and for housing (or both); air conditioning, ventilation or lighting equipment can be means of production when installed in a home. Means of transportation (a horse with a wagon or a car) can be used as means of production and means of consumption. Most objects of labour, and particularly raw

---

[15] See above, Chapter I.

[16] The term "closed loop" is used in literature on cybernetics and automation.

materials, can also be used for consumption; for example, coal used for heating an apartment, electric power used in an apartment for lighting and for various household purposes, petrol used for a passenger car, various chemical products which in everyday classification are treated as means of consumption can be used as means of production, particularly in agriculture. Grain can be used also for sowing, potatoes as feed for pigs, and sometimes even bread is used for feeding domestic animals. Many products which perform, as a rule, the function of durable consumer goods in a household can be used as means of production, i.e. refrigerators, TV sets, tables, chairs, etc.

The division of means of consumption into necessary means of subsistence and means which do not perform this function in the process of reproduction is even less related to the material form of the products. Undoubtedly, it is possible to single out certain means of subsistence which because of their material nature customarily do not constitute the necessary means of subsistence of the labour force, e.g. luxury foodstuffs, such as caviar, luxury clothing, luxury housing, even though also here there may be differences depending upon geographic conditions (owing to differences in the sources of nutrition) and cultural conditions. Usually, however, the products in the same material form (e.g. bread, meat, clothing, motor-cars, books) serve both as necessary means of subsistence and as means of pure consumption, i.e. consumption not related to the replacement of the labour force. This depends upon the quantities in which given means of consumption are consumed and upon the persons who consume them, i.e. whether these persons are, or are not, employed in the process of production or in activities necessary for the replacement of the labour force (e.g. health care, training in different skills, etc.). The division is here exclusively functional.

It can be seen that the relationship between the economic function of the products in the process of reproduction and their material form is fairly loose. Therefore, the reproduction equilibrium conditions given in the form of a separate balance of means of production and of means of consumption, singling out additionally in the latter means of maintenance of the labour force, do not find direct expression in the material nature of the process of production. Neither are they directly reflected in economic statistics in which the products are classified according to their material nature. The most important point, however, is that the functional division is not related to the technical conditions of the process of production, which depend exclusively upon the material nature of the products and not upon their economic function. In order to tie up the conditions of the process of reproduction with the technical conditions of production it is necessary to consider the products in their material form.

To this end we consider the national economy as consisting of various *branches of production*, each of which produces a given product (or products) of a specific material nature (of a specific natural form), e.g. coal, steel, various types of machines, means of transportation, textile products, buildings, grain, meat, various chemical products, paper, etc. Let the number of singled-out branches be n: let us denote by X_i the quantity of the commodity (in physical units per unit of time, e.g. year) produced in the ith branch. This quantity we call the *total product* of a given branch. Part of the product of a given branch is used as means of production for the replacement of means of production used up during a given period (e.g. year). It can be partly retained in a given branch for its own needs (e.g. grain for sowing, coal as a source of power in coal mines), and partly transferred to other branches, which is the rule to meet their needs in these products as means of production (e.g. coal transferred to steel plants, to thermo-electric power plants or to railways). Let us denote by X_{ij} the quantity of products of the ith branch transferred to the jth branch (covering also the case when $j = i$) to be used as a means of consumption. We call quantity X_{ij} the *reproduction input*. The rest of the products not used up as reproduction input are called the *end-product* (or *final product*) of a given branch; we denote it by Y_i. It can be seen that quantities X_i, X_{ij} and Y_i are flows.

Using the same division for all branches of production we obtain an *input–output flow table* (Table 11).

The left-hand side of the table shows both the quantities of products transferred by each branch of production to other

TABLE 11
INTER-BRANCH FLOW BALANCE (IN PHYSICAL UNITS)

Reproduction inputs	End-products	Global product
$X_{11}, X_{12}, ..., X_{1n}$	Y_1	X_1
$X_{21}, X_{22}, ..., X_{2n}$	Y_2	X_2
....	......	.
		.
		.
$X_{n1}, X_{n2}, ..., X_{nn}$	Y_n	X_n

branches for reproduction purposes and the quantities of products retained for this purpose by particular branches (quantities X_{11}, $X_{22}, ..., X_{nn}$ on the diagonal of the first section of the table). This portion of the table is usually called the *inter-branch flow matrix* and the whole table is called the *inter-branch flow balance*.[17]

[17] Inter-branch flow balances were designed in connection with planning of the national economy in the Soviet Union and subsequently in other socialist countries. At first, they were applied to raw materials and other production materials in the form of material balances. In the course of preparations for the first five-year plan in the Soviet Union (for the years 1928–32), the idea of broader input–output balances of production was conceived. A general theory of such balances, and especially its mathematical interpretation, relating the balances to technical conditions of production, was developed by the American economist Vassily Leontief and presented by him in 1941 in the book *The Structure of American Economy, 1919–1930*, New York, 1953. Already prior to this he had published in 1937 a paper on this subject in the *Review of Economic Statistics*. It is worth noting that the first paper containing the basic concepts of inter-branch flows was published by Leontief in 1925 in the Soviet periodical *Planovoye Khoziaystvo* (*Economic Planning*), No. 12 under the title: "Balans Narodnovo Khoziaystva SSSR" (Balance of the National Economy of the U.S.S.R.). Leontief lived then in the Soviet Union but he developed his theory later in the United States. The inter-branch flows method was called by Leontief *input–output analysis*. This term, in its English formulation, is used extensively in various countries. Later, the terms *inter-branch flow analysis*, *inter-branch balances*, etc., also came into use. This method is today used extensively in both capitalist and socialist countries. In the latter it is more and more related to the practice of planning of the national economy. On the historical background from which the inter-branch flows method grew and on its popularization and importance in various social

The products of particular branches are determined according
to their material form and in principle can be used both as means
of production and as means of consumption. If the product of the
ith branch is not used in the jth branch as a means of production,
then $X_{ij} = 0$; if the product is not used at all as a means of production, i.e. serves exclusively for consumption purposes, then the
whole corresponding row in the inter-branch flow matrix consists
of zeros and the whole total product is an end-product. The
end-product Y_n can be used either for consumption or for production or for both these purposes. If the end-product or part
of it is used for production, accumulation of means of production
occurs, because the replacement requirements in means of production are already satisfied by the reproduction input X_{ij}. When
a given product is used exclusively as a means of production, the
whole end-product constitutes accumulation of means of production.

It can be seen that Table 11 covers also cases when products
perform exclusively the economic function of means of production or of means of consumption, but it is not confined to
these cases alone. Dividing the total product which can be used
as means of production and means of consumption into a part
constituting means of production and a part constituting means
of consumption, we can transform Table 11 into the upper part
of Table 9 (i.e. the part of the table which does not contain labour

systems see O. Lange, *Political Economy*, Vol. I, *ed. cit.*, pp. 182–6. An introduction into the theory of inter-branch flows is given by O. Lange in *Introduction to Econometrics*, Oxford–Warsaw, 1966, Chapter 3; and in *The Theory
of Reproduction and Accumulation, ed. cit.*, Chapter 3; P. Sulmicki, *Przepływy
międzygałęziowe (Inter-branch Flows)*, Warsaw, 1959. See also R. Dorfman,
P. A. Samuelson and R. M. Solow, *Linear Programming and Economic Analysis*, New York, 1958, Chapters 9 and 10; W. B. Chenery and P. S. Clark,
Inter-industry Economics, New York, 1959; I. Yamada, *Theory and Application
of Inter-industry Analysis*, Tokyo, 1961; V. S. Nemchinov, *Ekonomiko-mate-
maticheskiye metody i modeli* (Economic-mathematical Methods and Models),
ed. cit., Chapter 8, and T. Czechowski, *Wstep matematyczny do analizy prze-
pływów międzygałęziowych (Mathematical Introduction to the Analysis of
Inter-branch Flows)*, Warsaw, 1958.

inputs). We switch then the classification of products according to their economic function.

The columns of the matrix of inter-branch flows represent inputs of particular means of production for producing a given commodity. However, the terms in the columns of Table 11 cannot be added together, because they represent quantities expressed in different physical units. But the terms in particular rows (up to the double vertical line) can be added and their sums give the end-products of the particular branches (shown to the right of the double vertical line). Such summing up produces the equations:

$$X_1 = X_{11} + X_{12} + \cdots + X_{1n} + Y_1,$$
$$X_2 = X_{21} + X_{22} + \cdots + X_{2n} + Y_2, \quad (12)$$
$$\cdots\cdots\cdots\cdots\cdots\cdots\cdots\cdots\cdots$$
$$X_n = X_{n1} + X_{n2} + \cdots + X_{nn} + Y_n.$$

These equations are called the *balance of production by branches*. They express equilibrium conditions of the reproduction process by branches.

Equation (12) can also be written in vector form. Let us denote by X the vector (i.e. the set) of aggregate products, by Y the vector of end-products and by X_{ij} the vector of reproduction inputs.[18]

These vectors represent the *aggregate social product*, the *social end-product* and the *social reproduction input*, respectively, all by branches. We write equation (12) in the form of one equation:

$$X = X_{ij} + Y. \quad (12a)$$

The process of reproduction, expressed by equation (12a), can also be presented by a block diagram (Fig. 13). The block

---

[18] These vectors have the following form:

$$X = \begin{bmatrix} X_1 \\ X_2 \\ \vdots \\ X_n \end{bmatrix}, \quad Y = \begin{bmatrix} Y_1 \\ Y_2 \\ \vdots \\ Y_n \end{bmatrix}, \quad X_{ij} = \begin{bmatrix} X_{11} + X_{12} + \cdots + X_{1n} \\ X_{21} + X_{22} + \cdots + X_{2n} \\ \vdots \\ X_{n1} + X_{n2} + \cdots + X_{nn} \end{bmatrix}.$$

represents the total social product divided into two parts: one is the social end-product which no longer returns to the block,[19]

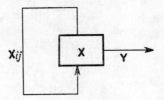

Fig. 13. Block diagram of reproduction by branches

and the other is the social reproduction input which does return to the block. It can be seen that there is feedback (closed loop) in the process of reproduction; it manifests itself in that part of the social product which returns to the process of production as a reproduction input. This process can be dealt with by the method of cybernetic analysis.[20]

---

[19] We assume here simple reproduction. In expanded reproduction a part of the social end-product Y is turned into accumulation of means of production and returns to the block. We shall consider this problem in the next chapter (see editor's note on p. 151, ft. 27).

[20] See Appendix to this chapter "Equilibrium Conditions of Reproduction".

represents the total social product divided into two parts: one is the social end product which no longer returns to the black."

Fig. 12. Block diagram of reproduction as ... branches

and the other is the social reproduction input which does return to the black. It can be seen that there is feedback (closed loop) in the process of reproduction; it manifests itself in that part of the social product which returns to the process of production as a reproduction input. This process can be dealt with by the method of cybernetic analysis.

Annex

INTRODUCTION TO THE BOOK
*MAN AND PRODUCTION TECHNIQUES**

Production is the basis of all economic activities by men. By production men produce material goods which are then distributed and consumed. The products of the processes of production become objects of a complex network of inter-human relations brought about by the economy of a modern society. In production there develop specific patterns which must be taken into consideration in managing socio-economic processes. These patterns are of two kinds. One is in the nature of material relations between particular products, the other is the result of value accounting used in economic processes.

The first kind of pattern is the result of the technical features of the process of production as a process in which man transforms nature, adapting it to his needs and ends. Thus, for instance, to produce a specific quantity of steel it is necessary to have (under given technological conditions) specific quantities of iron ore, coal, electric power, various kinds of skilled and unskilled labour. This necessitates proper proportions in producing various products as well as training staff in various skills. Means of production are used up (at once or gradually) and must be replaced in order to continue the process of production. Various technical processes used in production are characterized by different efficiencies, different ratios between inputs of means and outputs in the form of resulting products. All such material relations must be considered in managing the process of production.

The second kind of pattern is the result of social relations which arise between men and the process of production. In a commodity type of economy these relations manifest themselves in the value of products, and become a basis for the evaluation of particular aspects of the production process. Usually these

* Published in the Omega series, PWN, Warsaw, 1965.

evaluations take the form of monetary accounting.

Material and value relations appear in production both in a socialist and in a capitalist economy. However, in a socialist economy material relations appear more clearly and more directly than in a capitalist economy.

In a capitalist economy material relations arising in the process of production are completely covered by value relations. The aim of capitalist production is surplus value. Value–monetary accounting or the calculation of profit and loss is of decisive importance for the quantities of commodities produced and the technical processes used. This accounting, in turn, depends upon the pattern of market processes which influence the profitability of particular decisions taken in the process of production. Material relations in the process of production are not directly visible. They can be felt, however, when their requirements are not taken into account. And this happens frequently, because the mechanism of a capitalist economy leads to contradictions between the results of value–monetary accounting of profitability of the enterprise and the material requirements of the process of production in a socialist economy. These contradictions manifest themselves in the form of crises and other disturbances. The material requirements of the process of production become visible only when these disturbances occur.

In socialism, on the other hand, the material requirements of the process of production are directly apparent. Plans for the national economy determine, in a material form, the production targets of particular branches of the national economy, of integrated and individual enterprises. They balance the production of particular commodities and strive to ensure proportions consistent with the material requirements of the production process. Value–monetary accounting plays in a socialist economy an auxiliary role. It is the yardstick of social efficiency of production activities as well as the basis for operating economic incentives necessary for the efficient functioning of the economy. In this way a study of material relations appearing in the process of production assumes in socialism special importance and forms directly a consistent part of the practice of economic planning.

APPENDIX TO CHAPTER IV

EQUILIBRIUM CONDITIONS OF REPRODUCTION

CYBERNETIC SCHEMES OF THE THEORY OF REPRODUCTION*

1. Scheme of simple reproduction

In this chapter we discuss a cybernetic analysis and interpretation of the Marxian schemes of reproduction. Initially we consider this problem jointly for the whole national economy, and we then take into account the division of the economy into two parts. Finally, we consider the problem in its general form, assuming that the national economy is divided into n branches.

The total product X, expressed in value units, may be defined as the sum of three components:

$$X = c + (v+m). \tag{2.1}$$

The first component c denotes the volume of outlays of means of production needed to produce quantity X and the sum $(v+m)$ is the outlay of direct labour.[1]

Let us now introduce into our considerations the *coefficient of outlays* of means of production and of direct labour defined respectively by the formulae

$$a_c = \frac{c}{X} \quad \text{and} \quad a_{v+m} = \frac{v+m}{X} \tag{2.2}$$

(where $a_c + a_{v+m} = 1$).

Then, formula (2.1) can be presented in the following form:

$$X = a_c X + (v+m)$$

or

$$(1-a_c)X = v+m.$$

---

* Fragments of Chapter 2 of Oskar Lange's *Introduction to Economic Cybernetics*, Oxford–Warsaw, 1970, pp. 49–60. Numeration of formulae according to the edition cited. Numeration of figures runs on throughout this volume.

[1] The division of direct labour outlays into two components v and m is irrelevant in this context.

Hence

$$X = \frac{1}{1-a_c}(v+m).$$ (2.3)

It is evident from the form of formula (2.3), which represents the process of generation of value, that there exists some feedback relationship in this process. Indeed, the process of the formation of value may be presented in the form of a cybernetic block diagram shown below (Fig. 14).

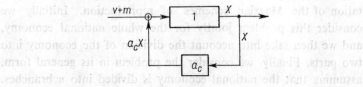

Fig. 14

It follows from Fig. 14 that direct labour $v+m$ is transformed into product X and this identity transformation is denoted by symbol 1. In some sense, the regulated system includes a governor with a proportionality operator a_c whose existence is due to the fact that part of product X must be used to replace the used-up means of production. Transformation that takes place in this kind of regulated system is defined by formula (2.3).

Let us now assume that the national economy is divided into two divisions: Division 1 producing means of production, and Division 2 producing means of consumption. We write the formulae, defining the aggregate products of particular divisions of the national economy in the following form:

$$\begin{cases} X_1 = c_1+(v_1+m_1) = a_{1c}X_1+(v_1+m_1) \\ X_2 = c_2+(v_2+m_2) = c_2+a_{2(v+m)}X_2. \end{cases}$$ (2.4)

In formulae (2.4) a_{1c} denotes the coefficient of outlays of means of production in Division 1 and $a_{2(v+m)}$ denotes the coefficient of outlays of direct labour in Division 2. The well-known condition of equilibrium of the process of simple reproduction is:

$$c_2 = v_1+m_1.$$ (2.5)

This condition means that the value of the means of production which Division 2 acquires from Division 1, i.e. $v_1 + m_1$, must be equal to the value of the means of consumption transferred from Division 2 to Division 1, i.e. c_2.[2]

From formulae (2.4) we obtain the transformed formulae for the total quantities of means of production and of means of consumption produced:

$$\left.\begin{aligned} X_1 &= \frac{1}{1 - a_{1c}}(v_1 + m_1), \\[2mm] X_2 &= \frac{1}{1 - a_{2(v+m)}}c_2, \end{aligned}\right\} \qquad (2.6)$$

which agrees with the transformation presented in the form of block diagrams for Division 1 in Fig. 15, and for Division 2 in Fig. 16.

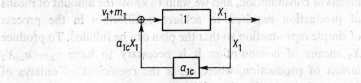

Fig. 15

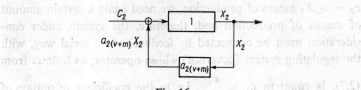

Fig. 16

From formulae (2.6) we calculate the ratio of values of aggregate products in both divisions. Considering equilibrium conditions (2.5), and taking into account that

$$a_{2c} + a_{2(v+m)} = \frac{c_2}{X_2} + \frac{v_2 + m_2}{X_2} = 1,$$

---

[2] A detailed analysis of this subject can be found in the book by O. Lange, *The Theory of Reproduction and Accumulation*, Oxford–Warsaw, 1969.

we obtain

$$\frac{X_1}{X_2} = \frac{1-a_{2(v+m)}}{1-a_{1c}} = \frac{a_{2c}}{1-a_{1c}}.$$

Hence

$$X_1 = \frac{a_{2c}}{1-a_{1c}} \cdot X_2. \qquad (2.7)$$

Transformation (2.7) may also be presented in the form of the block diagram shown in Fig. 17. From the point of view of economics this diagram may be interpreted as follows.

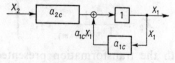

Fig. 17

Let us assume that we intend producing the amount X_2 of means of consumption, and we want to know the amount of means of production required to achieve equilibrium in the process of simple reproduction so that the plan can be fulfilled. To produce X_2 means of consumption it is necessary to have $c_2 = a_{2c}X_2$ means of production, where a_{2c} is the coefficient of outlays of means of production in Division 2. This transformation takes place in a system with the operator a_{2c}. However, to produce $c_2 = a_{2c}X_2$ means of production, we need again a certain amount of means of production and, therefore, the system under consideration must be connected by feedback, in a serial way, with the regulating system (governor) whose operator, as follows from (2.7), is equal to $a_{1c} = \dfrac{c_1}{X_1}$, i.e. to the coefficient of outlays of means of production in Division 1.

In a similar way as before, we can obtain the ratio of the total product in Division 2 to the total product in Division 1:

$$\frac{X_2}{X_1} = \frac{a_{1(v+m)}}{1-a_{2(v+m)}},$$

and hence

$$X_2 = \frac{a_{1(v+m)}}{1-a_{2(v+m)}} X_1. \qquad (2.8)$$

The block diagram corresponding to transformation (2.8) is shown in Fig. 18.

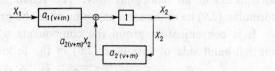

Fig. 18

Formula (2.8) and the block diagram shown in Fig. 18 have the following economic meaning. Let us assume that we are planning to produce X_1 means of production and we want to determine the amount of means of consumption needed to realize this plan. To produce X_1 means of production it is necessary to have means of consumption in the amount $v_1+m_1 = a_{1(v+m)}X_1$. But, in turn, to produce these means of consumption it is necessary to have an additional amount of means of consumption. Therefore, in a regulated system there appears a regulating system working on a feedback relationship; its operator equals $a_{2(v+m)} = \dfrac{v_2+m_2}{X_2}$, i.e. the coefficient of outlays of direct labour in Division 2.

2. Scheme of expanded reproduction

We shall now discuss the cybernetic analysis of the scheme of expanded reproduction, assuming, similarly as in the preceding section, that the national economy is divided into two divisions. The Marxian schemes in the case of expanded reproduction can be written as follows:

$$c_1+v_1+m_{1c}+m_{1v}+m_{10} = X_1, \\ c_2+v_2+m_{2c}+m_{2v}+m_{20} = X_2. \quad (2.9)$$

In the first of these formulae m_{1c} and m_{1v} denote the parts of the value of the surplus product[3] in Division 1 earmarked for increasing the stock of means of production and for employing additional labour in production, while m_{10} denotes the part of

[3] The use of the term "the value of the surplus product" enables us to interpret formula (2.9) and the following ones as valid for both a socialist and a capitalist economy.

the value of the surplus product in Division 1 which is not productively consumed. The quantities m_{2c}, m_{2v} and m_{20} should be interpreted in an analogous way. The remaining quantities in formulae (2.9) have the same meaning as in the preceding section.

It is convenient to group the components which appear on the left-hand side of formulae (2.9) in the following order:

$$c_1+m_{1c}+\boxed{v_1+m_{1v}+m_{10}} = X_1,$$
$$\boxed{c_2+m_{2c}}+v_2+m_{2v}+m_{20} = X_2. \tag{2.9a}$$

In the first of these formulae the sum c_1+m_{1c} denotes the total requirements of Division 1 in means of production, and the sum $v_1+m_{1v}+m_{10}$ denotes the total requirements of Division 1 in means of consumption. From the form of formulae (2.9a) we can also derive the known equilibrium condition for the process of expanded reproduction:

$$c_2+m_{2c} = v_1+m_{1v}+m_{10}. \tag{2.10}$$

It means that the requirement of Division 2 in means of production c_2+m_{2c} equals the requirements of Division 1 in means of consumption for workers already employed and for increasing employment v_1+m_{1v} as well as for the non-productive consumption m_{10} of part of the value of the surplus product.

Introducing the coefficient of outlays of means of production in Division 1: $a_{1c} = \dfrac{c_1}{X_1}$, the coefficient of accumulation of means of production in Division 1: $\alpha_{1c} = \dfrac{m_{1c}}{X_1}$, the coefficient of direct labour outlays in Division 2: $a_{2v} = \dfrac{v_2}{X_2}$, the coefficient of accumulation of variable capital (i.e. means of consumption for expanding employment) in Division 2: $\alpha_{2v} = \dfrac{m_{2v}}{X_2}$, and the rate of non-productive consumption of part of the value of the surplus product in Division 2: $\alpha_{20} = \dfrac{m_{20}}{X_2}$ formulae (2.9a) can also be presented in a different way:

$$a_{1c}X_1 + \alpha_{1c}X_1 + v_1 + m_{1v} + m_{10} = X_1, \\ c_2 + m_{2c} + a_{2v}X_2 + \alpha_{2v}X_2 + \alpha_{20}X_2 = X_2. \Big\} \quad (2.9b)$$

hence, we obtain

$$X_1 = \frac{1}{1-(a_{1c}+\alpha_{1c})}(v_1 + m_{1v} + m_{10}), \\ X_2 = \frac{1}{1-(a_{2v}+\alpha_{2v}+\alpha_{20})}(c_2 + m_{2c}). \Bigg\} \quad (2.11)$$

From formulae (2.11) it is possible to show the process of formation of the value of products in Divisions 1 and 2 by block diagrams as in Figs. 19 and 20 respectively.

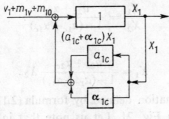

Fig. 19

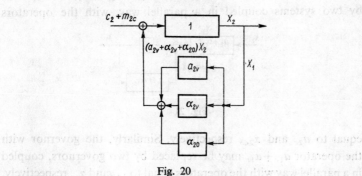

Fig. 20

It follows from Fig. 19 that the sum $v_1 + m_{1v} + m_{10}$ is transformed identically into the product of Division 1. Part of this product is retained in the given division and, as follows from the first formula (2.11), there takes place here a transformation which corresponds to the feedback relationship between two regulating systems, connected in a parallel way, and whose pro-portional operators equal a_{1c} and α_{1c}.

In a similar way, we can explain the operation of the regulating system presented in Fig. 20, provided that three regulating systems are present here connected in a parallel way, with the operators: a_{2v}, α_{2v}, α_{20}.

From formulae (2.11) we can calculate the ratio of the aggregate product in Division 1 to the aggregate product in Division 2. Considering the equilibrium conditions (2.10) of the process of expanded reproduction and taking into account that

$$1-(a_{2v}+\alpha_{2v}+\alpha_{20}) = a_{2c}+\alpha_{2c},$$

we obtain

$$\frac{X_1}{X_2} = \frac{a_{2c}+\alpha_{2c}}{1-(a_{1c}+\alpha_{1c})}.$$

Hence

$$X_1 = \frac{a_{2c}+\alpha_{2c}}{1-(a_{1c}+\alpha_{1c})} X_2. \tag{2.12}$$

The transformation defined by formula (2.12) is shown in the block diagram in Fig. 21. Let us note that in this diagram the regulated system with the operator $a_{2c}+\alpha_{2c}$ may be replaced by two systems coupled in a parallel way, with the operators

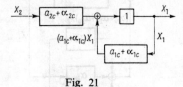

Fig. 21

equal to a_{2c} and α_{2c}, respectively. Similarly, the governor with the operator $a_{1c}+\alpha_{1c}$ may be replaced by two governors, coupled in a parallel way with the operators equal to a_{1c} and α_{1c} respectively.

It is easy to calculate in an analogous way that

$$X_2 = \frac{a_{1v}+\alpha_{1v}+\alpha_{10}}{1-(a_{2v}+\alpha_{2v}+\alpha_{20})} X_1 \tag{2.13}$$

and to present this transformation in a corresponding block dia-gram. An economic interpretation of formulae (2.12) and (2.13) and of their corresponding block diagrams is similar to the interpretation of formulae (2.7) and (2.8) in the preceding section.

Let us note finally that formulae (2.7) and (2.8), representing simple reproduction, are special cases of formulae (2.12) and (2.13) for expanded reproduction. To ascertain that this is so it is enough to assume that in formulae (2.12) and (2.13) the coefficients of accumulation equal zero.

We have shown in this way that the schemes of simple and expanded reproduction can be explained by the basic formula of the theory of control. This is not surprising because in these schemes there appear feedbacks characteristic of the regulating processes. We can see then that not only the Keynesian theory of the formation of national income in the sense of expenditures in the national economy, but also the Marxian schemes of reproduction, may be interpreted and analysed on the basis of the general theory of control.

3. Multi-branch scheme of reproduction

We shall now discuss the cybernetic analysis of the process of reproduction in the case when the national economy is divided into n branches.

The input–output table corresponding to such a situation, is shown below.

X_1	$c_{11}, c_{12}, ..., c_{1n}$		Y_1
X_2	$c_{21}, c_{22}, ..., c_{2n}$		Y_2
...	....		...
X_n	$c_{n1}, c_{n2}, ..., c_{nn}$		Y_n
V	$v_1, v_2, ..., v_n$		
M	$m_1, m_2, ..., m_n$		
	$X_1, X_2, ..., X_n$		

In this table $X_1, X_2, ..., X_n$ denote the values of aggregate products in particular branches; c_{ij} $(i, j = 1, 2, ..., n)$ denotes the values of inter-branch flows of means of production from branch i to branch j; $Y_1, Y_2, ..., Y_n$ are the final products in the particular branches; $v_1, v_2, ..., v_n$ are outlays of labour; m_1, $m_2, ..., m_n$ are values of the surplus product obtained in particular branches of the national economy.

On the basis of inter-branch flow tables it is easy to write (by adding up the rows in the table) the following *balance equations of product allocation*:

$$X_i = c_{i1} + c_{i2} + ... + c_{in} + Y_i \quad (i = 1, 2, ..., n) \qquad (2.14)$$

and (by adding up the columns of the table) *the balance equations of production outlays*:

$$X_i = c_{1i} + c_{2i} + ... + c_{ni} + v_i + m_i \quad (i = 1, 2, ..., n). \qquad (2.15)$$

Denoting the sum $c_{1i} + c_{2i} + ... + c_{ni}$ in the last equation by c_i, we obtain the following equation:

$$X_i = c_i + v_i + m_i \quad (i = 1, 2, ..., n), \qquad (2.15a)$$

which is of the same type as the equations appearing in the Marxian schemes.

By equating the right-hand sides of equations (2.14) and (2.15) we obtain the *equilibrium equations of inter-branch flows*, which are equivalent to the equilibrium equations of the process of reproduction given by Marx.[4]

To simplify further considerations, we can introduce the *outlay coefficients of means of production* defined by the formulae

$$a_{ij} = \frac{c_{ij}}{X_i} \quad (i, j = 1, 2, ..., n).$$

The balance equations of production outlays can be written as follows:

$$X_i = a_{1i}X_i + a_{2i}X_i + ... + a_{ni}X_i + v_i + m_i \quad (i = 1, 2, ..., n). \qquad (2.16)$$

Hence we obtain

$$X_i = \frac{1}{1 - (a_{1i} + a_{2i} + ... + a_{ni})} (v_i + m_i) \quad (i = 1, 2, ..., n). \qquad (2.17)$$

[4] A detailed development of the theory of inter-branch flows and multi-branch schemes of reproduction can be found in the book by O. Lange, *Introduction to Econometrics*, Oxford–Warsaw, 1967, and in his *Theory of Reproduction and Accumulation*, Oxford–Warsaw, 1969.

If the sum $a_{1i}+a_{2i}+\ldots+a_{ni}$ is denoted by a_i, then formulae (2.17) can be transformed into

$$X_i = \frac{1}{1-a_i}\,(v_i+m_i) \quad (i = 1, 2, \ldots, n).\qquad (2.18)$$

These formulae are analogous to formula (2.6) corresponding to the transformation obtained from the Marxian scheme of simple reproduction.

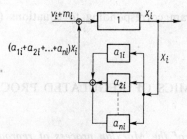

Fig. 22

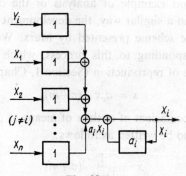

Fig. 23

Transformations defined by formulae (2.17) may be presented in the form of the block diagram shown in Fig. 22. In drawing this block diagram we use the theorem on the sum of operators which can be interpreted as a parallel coupling of elementary systems (Section 6, Chapter 1).

Let us now deal with the balance equations of product allocation which assume the following form after outlay coefficients are introduced in them:

$$X_i = a_{i1}X_1 + a_{i2}X_2 + \ldots + a_{ii}X_i + \ldots + a_{in}X_n + Y_i$$
$$(i = 1, 2, \ldots, n) \qquad (2.19)$$

or

$$X_i(1-a_{ii}) = \sum_{j \neq 1} a_{ij}X_j + Y_i \quad (i = 1, 2, \ldots, n),$$

hence

$$X_i = \frac{1}{1-a_{ii}} \left(\sum a_{ij}X_j + Y_i \right) \quad (i = 1, 2, \ldots, n). \qquad (2.20)$$

The block diagram corresponding to equations (2.20) is shown in Fig. 23.

DYNAMICS OF REGULATED PROCESSES

5. *Dynamics of the Marxian process of reproduction**

As the second example of analysis of the dynamic process we shall study, in a similar way, the development of the economy according to the scheme presented by Marx. We start with the equation, corresponding to this process, which appears in the Marxian scheme of reproduction (Section 1, Chapter 2):

$$x = a_c x + (v+m), \qquad (3.22)$$

where a_c is the coefficient of outlays of means of production. This equation can also be written as follows:

$$x = \frac{1}{1-a_c}(v+m). \qquad (3.22a)$$

The quantities x, v and m are expressed in units of value or prices.

Studying the dynamics of the process of reproduction we must introduce the element of time in the equation under consideration (3.22), i.e. we must "date" the quantities. We introduce indicator t denoting the period of time, which, to simplify, we shall

* Fragment of Chapter 3 of Oskar Lange's *Introduction to Economic Cybernetics*, ed. cit., pp. 77–80. Numeration of formulae according to the edition cited. Numeration of figures runs on throughout this volume.

take as 1 year. We assume that the outlay of the means of production in the given year $a_c x_{t-1}$ is proportional to production in the preceding year. The equation then assumes the form

$$x_t = a_c x_{t-1} + (v_t + m_t). \qquad (3.23)$$

This means that production in the year $t-1$ determines the quantity of means of production used up in the year t. In other words, the quantity of means of production used up in a given year (i.e. the value of the means of production transferred to the product) is a certain constant fraction of production of the preceding year $(0 < a_c < 1)$.

We solve the difference equation (3.23), as usual, by the recurrent method. If, to simplify, we assume that the annual direct labour outlay $v_t + m_t$ is constant, and the same as in the initial year, namely $v_0 + m_0$, and that in the initial year there were no means of production, we obtain the following system of equations which express the value of production in consecutive years:

$$x_0 = v_0 + m_0,$$
$$x_1 = a_c x_0 + (v_0 + m_0) = (v_0 + m_0) \cdot (1 + a_c),$$
$$x_2 = a_c x_1 + (v_0 + m_0) = (v_0 + m_0) \cdot (1 + a_c + a_c^2).$$
$$\dots\dots\dots\dots\dots\dots\dots\dots\dots\dots\dots\dots\dots\dots$$

Generally

$$x_t = a_c x_{t-1} + (v_0 + m_0) = (v_0 + m_0) \cdot (1 + a_c + a_c^2 + \dots + a_c^t). \qquad (3.24)$$

It follows from the general solution (3.24) that the process studied tends to equilibrium if $|a_c| < 1$, which is the case here because $0 < a_c < 1$. Then

$$\lim_{t \to \infty} x_t = (v_0 + m_0) \cdot \frac{1}{1 - a_c}. \qquad (3.25)$$

In this way, we have obtained a picture of the pattern of the Marxian process of reproduction in time. The feedback operator $\frac{1}{1 - a_c}$, which appears in formula (3.25), is the ratio of the value of the product to direct labour outlay. Since $0 < a_c < 1$, then

$\dfrac{1}{1-a_c} > 1$. This operator is then an amplifier which expresses an increase in the value of the product (in relation to direct labour outlay) in consequence of using up the means of production.

Let us note that similarly as in the first example, the study of the dynamics of this process can be simplified. We can assume that there is a value of production $\hat{x}_t = \dfrac{v_0+m_0}{1-a_c}$ which corresponds to the state of equilibrium:

$$\bar{x}_t = x_t - \hat{x}_t = x_t - \frac{v_0+m_0}{1-a_c}. \qquad (3.26)$$

After transformation, similarly as before, we obtain the following difference equation in the reduced (homogeneous) form

$$\bar{x}_t = a_c \bar{x}_{t-1}. \qquad (3.27)$$

The solution of this equation is

$$\bar{x}_t = a_c^r x_0. \qquad (3.28)$$

It follows from solution (3.28) that the deviations from the state of equilibrium eliminate themselves if the process is stable because $0 < a_c < 1$. The Marxian process of reproduction can be illustrated graphically in a similar manner as the process of formation of the national income on the basis of the Keynesian multiplier.

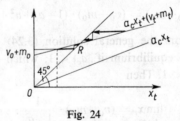

Fig. 24

The assumption, accepted by us, on the stability of direct labour outlays v_0+m_0 is not necessary. It can be shown, even by a graphical method, that the basic results of the analysis do not change when direct labour outlays change from year to year. In the corresponding graph the line representing production $x_t =$

$= a_c x_{t-1} + (v_t + m_t)$ will then not be parallel to the straight line representing the outlays of means of production $a_c x_{t-1}$, even though $0 < a_c < 1$ and the process will tend to equilibrium as shown in Fig. 24. The line corresponding to production in year t need not be a straight line but it should intersect the straight line which goes through the origin of the system of co-ordinates, and its slope to the positive direction of the x-axis is 45°.

TABLE OF CONTENTS TO THE WHOLE WORK AND TO
VOLUME 2

Photostat of the first draft version of the Table of Contents of the whole work (pp. 222–223)

Contents of the First Draft of the Table of Contents of the Whole Work

OSKAR LANGE
Outline of Political Economy

Part I: General Assumptions

Chapter I. Political Economy as a Science

1. Subject Matter of Political Economy. Introductory Concepts
2. Mode of Production and Social Systems, Materialistic Interpretation of History
3. Economic Laws
4. Methods of Political Economy
5. Principles of Rational Management
6. Diverse Approaches to the Subject Matter and Methods of Political Economy
7. Social Conditioning and Social Function of Political Economy as a Science

Chapter II. General Laws of Social Reproduction

1. General Features of the Production Process
2. Reproduction Process—Simple and Expanded Reproduction
3. Social Product and Net Incomes
4. Renewal of Means of Production and Accumulation. Investments and Their Effectiveness
5. Equilibrium Laws of Simple and Expanded Reproduction
6. Efficiency of Labour, Economic Incentives and Development of Productive Forces

Chapter III. Natural Production and Commodity Production

1. Co-operation and Division of Labour
2. Scope of the Productive Society. Exchange and the Commodity
3. Commodity Production. The Market
4. Indirect Exchange and Money

Part II: Political Economy of Capitalism
A. Pre-Capitalistic Social Systems and the Origin of the Capitalistic Mode of Production
B. *Laissez-faire* Capitalism
C. Monopoly Capitalism
D. Historical Boundaries of the Capitalistic Mode of Production

Part III: Political Economy of Socialism
A. Historical Tasks for the Period of Socialism Construction
B. Economic Laws of the Transition Period Shaping of Socialistic Economic Laws
C. The Laws of Non-uniform Growth of a Socialist Economy
D. Mutual Influences of Socialist and Capitalist Economies in the Transition Period
E. Political Economy of a Socialist Society

Photostat of the second draft version of the Table of Contents of the whole work (pp. 227–229)

II

6. Prawo wartości jako regulator produkcji towarowej oraz jako wyraz towarowych stosunków produkcji. Fetyszyzacja stosunków produkcji.

7. Sposoby działania prawa wartości. Konkurencja i monopol

8. Ogólne prawa obiegu pieniężnego. Wartość i siła nabywcza pieniądza

9. Wymienność produkcji towarowo-pieniężnej. Przekształcenie przychodów w dochody. Racjonalizacja działania gospodarczego

10. Społeczna reprodukcja wartościowo-pieniężna. Dochód społeczny. Amortyzacja i akumulacja.

11. ¼ Inwestycje a dochód narodowy.

Rozdział IV   **Ekonomiczna teoria formacji społecznych**

1. Ogólne prawa ekonomiczne i prawa ekonomiczne specyficzne dla formacji społecznej. Podstawowe prawo ekonomiczne formacji społecznej

2. Stosunki produkcji i stosunki dystrybucji. Rola produkcji towarowej i prawa wartości w rozmaitych formacjach społecznych

3. Praca produkcyjna i nieprodukcyjna. Dochody pierwotne i pochodne. Praca dodatkowa i produkt dodatkowy

4. Klasy społeczne i warstwy społeczne. Rozmaite źródła przywileju społecznego. Rozmaite formy wyzysku

5. Przymus pozaekonomiczny w rozmaitych formacjach społecznych. Rola ekonomiczna państwa

6. Formacje społeczne a bodźce ekonomiczne

Dodatek 1.   Ogólny schemat reprodukcji w gospodarce naturalnej i towarowej

Dodatek 2.   Teoria popytu i podaży

Dodatek 3.   Teoria kształtowania się cen w warunkach konkurencji i monopolu

Dodatek 4.   Ekonometryczne badania procesów rynkowych

II.   **Część druga : Ekonomia polityczna kapitalizmu**

A. Przedkapitalistyczne formacje społeczne i powstanie kapitalistycznego sposobu produkcji

B. Kapitalizm wolnokonkurencyjny

C. Kapitalizm monopolistyczny

D. Historyczne granice kapitalistycznego sposobu produkcji

III

III. Część trzecia : Ekonomia polityczna socjalizmu

A. Historyczna geneza okresu budowy socjalizmu oraz jej zadania

B. Prawa ekonomiczne okresu przejściowego. Kształtowanie się socjalistycznych praw ekonomicznych

C. Prawo nierównomiernego wzrostu gospodarki socjalistycznej

D. Wzajemne oddziaływanie na siebie gospodarki socjalistycznej i gospodarki kapitalistycznej w okresie przejściowym

E. Ekonomia polityczna socjalistycznego społeczeństwa

Contents of the Second Draft of the Table of Contents of the Whole Work

OSKAR LANGE

Outline of Political Economy

Part I: General Assumptions

Chapter I: Political Economy as a Science

1. Subject Matter of Political Economy. Introductory Concepts
2. Mode of Production and Social Systems. Materialistic Interpretation of History
3. Economic Laws
4. Methods of Political Economy
5. Principles of Rational Management
6. Diverse Approaches to the Subject Matter and Methods of Political Economy
7. Political Economy and Praxeology
8. Social Conditioning and Social Function of Economic Knowledge Versus Objectivity of Political Economy as a Science

Chapter II: Social Process of Production and Reproduction

1. General Features of the Production Process
2. Reproduction Process—Simple and Expanded Reproduction
3. Social Product and Net Income
4. Renewal of Means of Production and Accumulation. Investments and Their Effectiveness
5. Equilibrium Laws of Simple and Expanded Reproduction
6. Efficiency of Labour, Economic Incentives and Development of Productive Forces

Chapter III: Commodity Production and the Law of Value

1. Co-operation and Division of Labour
2. Scope of the Productive Society. Exchange and the Commodity

Appendix 3: Theory of Price Formation Under Conditions of Competition and Monopoly

Appendix 4: Econometric Study of Market Processes

Part II: Political Economy of Capitalism

A. Pre-capitalistic Social Systems and the Origin of the Capitalistic Mode of Production

B. *Laissez-faire* Capitalism

C. Monopoly Capitalism

D. Historical Boundaries of Capitalistic Modes of Production

Part III: Political Economy of Socialism

A. Historical Tasks for the Period of Socialist Construction and Their Dependence upon Historical Conditions of Decay of Capitalism in Particular Countries

B. Economic Laws of the Transition Period. Shaping of Socialistic Economic Laws

C. The Laws of Non-uniform Growth of a Socialist Economy

D. Mutual Influences of Socialist and Capitalist Economies in the Transition Period

E. Political Economy of a Socialist Society

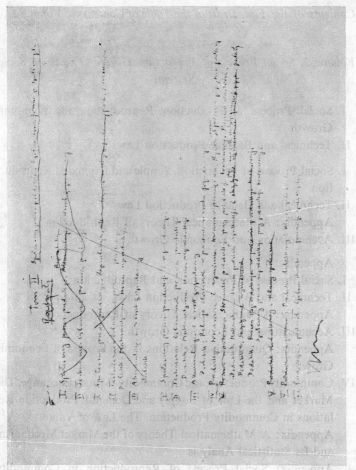

Photostat of the first draft version of the Table of Contents of Volume 2

234 *Political Economy*

Contents of the First Draft of the Table of Contents of Volume 2

Volume 2. Social Process of Production. General Theory of Social Systems

Photostat of the second draft version of Summary Contents of Volume 2
(pp. 235–236)

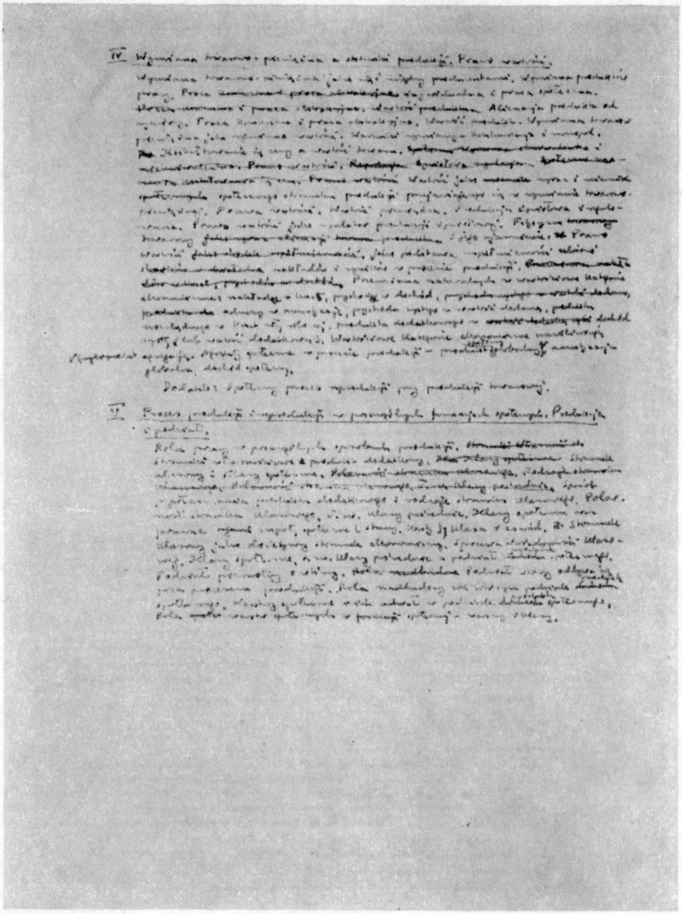

ment Period and Its Influence on the Effectiveness of Investments. Accumulation and Growth in Employment, Labour–Output Ratio of Investments and Production. Accumulation, Investments and Changes in the Efficiency of Social Labour.

Appendix: Quantitative Relations in the Process of Economic Growth.

Chapter III. Commodity Production and Commodity–Money Exchange

Private Production under Conditions of Social Division of Labour. Transformation of the Product into Commodity. Exchange of Commodities. Use Value and Exchange Value. Money and Its Role in Exchange. The Market and the Price Structure. Process of Commodity Circulation. Equilibrium Conditions of the Circulation Process. Role of Money in Circulation—Money Circulation. Disturbances in the Circulation Process. Circulation Crises.

Appendix: Econometric Analysis of Market Mechanisms.

Chapter IV. Commodity–Money Exchange and Production Relations. The Law of Value

Commodity–Money Exchange as a Bond between Producers. Exchange of the Product of Labour. Individual Labour and Social Labour. Alienation of the Product from the Producer. Concrete Labour and Abstract Labour. Value of the Product. Commodity–Money Exchange as Exchange of Value. Conditions of Exchange—Competition and Monopoly. Price Formation and Commodity Value. Value as the Expression and Measure of Social Relations of Production Apparent in Commodity–Money Exchange. The Law of Value. The Value of Money. Spontaneous and Regulated Production. The Law of Value as a Regulator of Spontaneous Production. Commodity—Fetishism and Its Manifestations. The Law of Value as a Basis for the Commensurability of Inputs and Outputs in the Production Process. Transformation of Natural into Economic Value Categories: of Outlay into Cost, of Revenue into Income, of Renewal into Depreciation, of Net Income into Value Added, of the Necessary Product into the Cost of Labour, of the Surplus Product into Net Income (or Surplus Value). Economic Value Categories Make Possible Aggregation. Social Aggregates in the Production Process—the Social Total Product, Total Depreciation, Social Income.

Appendix: Social Production Process in Commodity Production.

Chapter V. Production and Reproduction Processes in Particular Social Systems. Production and Distribution

Role of Labour in Particular Modes of Production. Ownership Relations and Surplus Product. Class Relations and Social Classes. Appropriation of the Surplus Product and the Kind of Class Relations. Polarity of Class

Relations. So-called Intermediate Classes. Social Classes and Legal Social Groups. Estates, Castes, Class and Occupation. Class Relations as Objective Economic Relations. The Question of Class Consciousness. Social Classes, So-called Intermediate Classes and Distribution of the Social Product. Primary and Secondary Distribution. Secondary Distribution Outside the Production Process. Role of the Superstructure in Secondary Distribution of the Social Product. Social Strata and Their Share in the Distribution of the Social Product. Role of Social Strata in a Social System—Strata and Classes.

Index of Names

241

Weber, M.   31–32, 113
West, E.   78
Wicksell, K.   78, 107
Wicksteed, P. H.   60, 78, 107
Wiener, N.   17, 18, 24–26
Wieser, F.   151

Yaglom, A. M.   148
Yamada, I.   199

Zagórski, J.   189
Zeuner, G.   121, 135
Zeuthen, F.   89

Index of Terms

— process of 48, 172
— — balance conditions of 186
— — block diagram of 194, 201
— — cybernetic analysis of 211
207
— — disproportions in 174
— — disturbed 174
— — dynamics of 218–20
— — equilibrium of 174
— — smooth 174
— — structural aspects of 188
— simple 52, 173, 217
— — scheme of 207–11, 217
— social process of 48
— theory of, cybernetic schemes of
207–8
Return 59
Returns 175
— as flows of physical units in time
59
— substitution, the law of 71, 80
— — decreasing, the law of 71, 108

Scalars 62
Scale, economies of 90
— increasing returns of 90
Semi-invariants 160
Semi-products 7
Servo-mechanism 17, 20, 23
Social systems, economic theory of
viii
Specialization 37
Stochastic processes 147
Stocks 59
Subsistence, means of 51, 114, 182
— — necessary 114
Substitution 84, 99
— law of 84
— rate of 72–73, 104
— — constant 77
— — decreasing 77
— — increasing 77
— — properties of 102–5

Surplus product 51, 172, 187, 212
Survival coefficient 125, 152
— probability of 127
— tables 122

Technical process, alternative, selection from among 79
— — effective 69–71, 84
— — — choice of 92
— — inefficient 69–71
— — — elimination of 83
— — joining of 88
— — linear (divisible) 69, 74
— — mixed 68, 100–2
— — multiplication of 88
— — praxeological principle of eliminating 90
— — productive capacity of 85, 98
— — pure 68
— — selection of 92

Units, physical (units of measurement) 59
Use, duration of 123
Use-value 10
Utilization, period of 46, 80–81,
125–30, 139
— — as a unit of time 47
— — average 141–3
— — methods of measurements of
47

Value, process of formation of 208
— — — cybernetic diagram of 208
— reproduction of 193
Vectors 61, 95

Watt's governor 18
Wear and tear, average rate of 143
— — moral 46
— — physical 45
Working period of objects 43